Education and the C...

AUSTRALIA
The Law Book Company
Brisbane • Sydney • Melbourne • Perth

CANADA
Carswell
Ottawa • Toronto • Calgary • Montreal • Vancouver

Agents
Steimatzky's Agency Ltd., Tel Aviv;
N.M. Tripathi (Private) Ltd., Bombay;
Eastern Law House (Private) Ltd., Calcutta;
M.P.P. House, Bangalore;
Universal Book Traders, Delhi;
Aditya Books, Delhi;
Macmillan Shuppan KK, Tokyo;
Pakistan Law House, Karachi, Lahore.

Education and the Constitution

Michael Farry

B.C.L., Dip. Ed. Admin., M.Litt., Ph.D

Barrister-at-Law
Lecturer in Law, Carlow Regional Technical College

DUBLIN
ROUND HALL SWEET & MAXWELL
1996

Published in 1996 by
Round Hall Sweet & Maxwell
Brehon House, 4 Upper Ormond Quay,
Dublin 7.

Typeset by
Gough Typesetting Services,
Dublin.

Printed by Colourbooks,
Dublin.

ISBN 1-899738-35-5

A catalogue record for this book
is available from the British Library

*All rights reserved. No part of this publication may
be reproduced or transmitted in any form or by any means,
including photocopying and recording, without the written
permission of the publisher and the individual contributors.
Such written permission must also be obtained before any
part of this publication is stored in a retrieval system
of any nature.*

The material contained in this book is not published or presented as legal advice and the author and publishers do not accept responsibility for loss or damage howsoever caused to any person acting or refraining from acting as a result of the material in this publication.

©

Michael J. Farry
1996

This book is dedicated to my father Michael Senior
and in memory of my mother.

FOREWORD

The late Professor John M. Kelly in writing the foreword to his own *Fundamental Rights in the Irish Law and the Constitution* noted modestly: "This study is intended to fill, however imperfectly, one of the many gaps in the literature of modern Irish Law". That was written in 1961. The intervening years have seen an expanding case load of constitutional law cases in the courts and a corresponding growth in legal literature on the subject. Dr Farry's book is, so far as I am aware, the first to deal exclusively with education and the Constitution.

Family law and domestic relations have changed dramatically since the Constitution came into effect. The present age is one in which blame for almost every social ill is cast upon the State, the Church or the school. It is salutary to note that the provisions of the Constitution expressly recognise the inalienable right and duty for education is that of parents. The supportive role of the State, Church and schools in this vital task of parents is lucidly and comprehensively set out by the author. He not only presents the very interesting historical background to the constitutional provisions and the several Acts of the Oireachtas relative thereto, but deals with case law in a manner with which lawyers and law students are familiar yet can be readily understood by teachers and others who may be engaged in the field of education. The text is enlivened by informed criticism of judgments. The provocation to thought is the hallmark of a good textbook: this may cause reflection by leaders of Church and State and stimulate debate in the legal and teaching professions.

The resourcefulness and resilience of the courts to be astute to protect not only the enumerated but more particularly the unenumerated rights is now taken for granted by legal practitioners and public alike. A mere 35 years ago judicial activism in this area of law was a noted novelty. Society is now at a cross-roads 'twixt pluralism and secularism. The courts meet this challenge by rigorous analysis of the terms of the Constitution. Decisions such as that of Costello P. in *Campaign to Separate Church and State v. Minister for Education* may signify the road ahead.

I have no doubt this book is timely and that it represents a welcome and worthwhile contribution to Irish jurisprudence and will establish Dr Farry as an authority in the field of education law.

T.C. Smyth

The High Court
October 1996

PREFACE

This book grew out of a number of lectures given to teachers studying educational administration. Recent developments in Irish education have highlighted the Constitution as never before with varying groups now citing the Constitution as the basis of their rights and claims.

With new education legislation in prospect the time may be opportune to examine some of the available material on education and the Constitution and the present writer has ventured a first tenuous step into the minefield that is Irish education law.

One difficulty in any aspect of education law is that many cases take place in the lower courts and are thus not reported in the official law reports. In addition many comments and opinions are only available in articles, some of which are extremely difficult to trace. It seems likely however that in future documentation of education legal cases will receive greater attention as parents and students become more assertive of their rights.

I am conscious of a degree of overlap and repetition particularly in relation to citation of Articles of the Constitution. I ask the readers indulgence bearing in mind that the book seeks to be intelligible to different types of reader. The shortcomings and errors in the book are entirely my own. Extracts from the Report of the Constitution Review Group published in May 1996 are reproduced with the permission of the Controller, Stationary Office.

I particularly express my gratitude to the Hon. Mr Justice T.C. Smyth for providing an insightful foreword.

My sincere thanks to Gerry Whyte, B.L., Fellow of Trinity College, Dublin; Dr Damien Ó Muirí, St. Patrick's College Maynooth; Mrs Bríd Uí Mhuirí, M.A., B.L.; Seamus Puirseil, NCEA, NCVA; Margaret Byrne, Librarian and Mary Gaynor, Assistant Librarian, the Law Society of Ireland. My thanks also to my friends and colleagues Martin Nevin, Austin Kinsella, Frank Quinn, the Director and Governing Body of Carlow RTC and Farry Reynolds Whelan, Solicitors, Dublin.

Michael J. Farry

Feast of Ignatious Loyola, 1996

INTRODUCTION

The present Constitution, Bunreacht na hÉireann was adopted by the people in a plebiscite on July 1, 1937.[1] It is more extensive that its 1922 predecessor, the Constitution of the Irish Free State which was enacted by Dáil Éireann by means of legislation. The Constitution is divided into a preamble and twenty five sections with each section containing the Article or Articles which are relevant to the topic indicated by the section.

The section headed "The President" contains Articles 12, 13 and 14 dealing with the office of President. The section headed "The National Parliament" contains Articles 15 to 27 and deals with The National Parliament, Constitution and Powers, Dáil Éireann, Seanad Éireann and Legislation. Other sections deal with the Government, the Courts, the Trial of Offences and Fundamental Rights.

Among the matters dealt with in the fundamental rights section of the Constitution are Personal Rights, The Family, Education, Private Property and Religion. The Articles in the fundamental rights section guarantee a number of basic fundamental human rights and these enjoy a specially protected position, being unalterable except by the wish of the people expressed in a referendum. The rights of the citizen expressly enumerated in the document are not the totality of such rights; many more rights are implied and not expressly stated. The rights which are expressly stated in the Constitution are sometimes referred to as enumerated rights, those which are not expressly stated but which are implied are sometimes referred to as unenumerated rights. Chapter 1 seeks to explain this development.

There is an inevitable degree of overlap among the Articles within the fundamental rights section because it was not possible to divide the subject matter into watertight compartments. For example Article 41 deals with the Family while Article 42 deals with Education but the first paragraph of Article 42 is the acknowledgement by the State that the Family is the natural educator of the child. Similarly Article 44 deals with Religion yet paragraph 4 of that Article deals with legislation providing state aid for schools under the management of different religious denominations. Article 43 deals with Private Property yet paragraph 6 of Article 44 on Religion deals with the property of a religious denomination. Indeed a harmonious interpretation requires that one provision be interpreted in harmony with other provisions.

In *McGrath v. The Trustees of Maynooth College*[2] where a professor and a lecturer claimed they had been dismissed on grounds of religious status under a college statute, Article 44.2.3° was construed by the Supreme Court in

---

1. For details see Foley and Lalor (eds.), *Annotated Constitution of Ireland* (1995), p. 19.
2. Unreported, Supreme Court, November 1, 1979.

conjunction with Article 44.2.5°. Henchy J. with Kenny J. and Parke J. in agreement stated: "The Constitutional provision invoked here must be construed in terms of its purpose." The classification and arrangement of the rights of the citizen in the words of the late Professor John Kelly are "unmethodical and in other ways unsatisfactory."[3]

The validity of all domestic legislation is dependant on compliance with the Constitution. In 1972 by virtue of the Third Amendment of the Constitution Act 1972 Article 29 was amended to enable the State to join the European Community and it provides that: "No provision of the Constitution invalidates laws enacted, acts done or measures adopted by the State . . . or prevents laws enacted, acts done or measures adopted by the Communities, or institutions thereof, from having the force of law in the State." If a law, act or measure does not fall within this category then it is still subject to the Constitution for its validity and is invalid or unconstitutional in so far as it is in conflict with the provisions of the Constitution. Although Article 42 is entitled "Education", the major aspect of education dealt with in this Article relates to primary education.

This book is an attempt to draw together the material and to set the provisions relating to education in a legal context. Chapter 1 contains a review of the development of unenumerated constitutional rights and Chapter 2 deals with primary education and constitutional rights, as a preliminary to the recognition of the constitutional right to free primary education in Chapter 3.

The extent of the State's obligation in relation to primary education in the wake of the *Crowley* case (see facts in Chapter 3) is examined in Chapter 4 in addition to state aid, and aid to private and corporate educational initiatives. Chapter 5 looks at the meaning of education as decided by the courts and Chapter 6 at the quality of primary education which a child must receive. The pre-eminent role of the family and parents in education, and control of education under the constitution and the comparatively subservient role of the State is explored in Chapters 7 and 8.

The question of control of schools and the Minister's desire to democratise management structures has dominated the educational agenda since 1992. Chapter 8 deals with control and parents. Chapters 9 and 10 deal with the topic of control of education by religious denominations and by state interference with education in two senses, *viz.* the right of the State to regulate it and unlawful interference with primary education which infringes the constitutional right to it. Chapter 12 outlines the remedies which might be available should such an infringement take place.

The interaction between religion and education in Ireland is examined in Chapter 13 while some idea of the influence of the Papal Encyclical, *Divini Illius Magistri* (the English title is: *On the Christian Education of Youth*, 1929) on the educational provisions of the Constitution may be gathered from the Appendix.

---

3. Kelly, *Fundamental Rights in the Irish Law and Constitution* (2nd ed., 1967) p. 37.

TABLE OF CONTENTS

Foreword	vii
Preface	ix
Introduction	xi
Table of Cases	xix
Table of Constitutional Provisions	xxiv
Table of Statutes	xxvi

Chapter 1	**Unenumerated/Implied Constitutional Rights**	1
	Unenumerated/Implied Rights	1
	Ryan v. Attorney General and after	5
	The Role of the Courts	6
	The Constitution and Education	7
	The Constitution Review Group	7

Chapter 2	**Primary Education and Constitutional Rights**	9
	Drafting Decision	9
	Criticism of Article 10 of 1922 Constitution	10
	1922 Constitution	10
	1937 Drafts	11
	Compulsory School Attendance	11
	The Constitution Review Group	12

Chapter 3	**The Constitutional Right to Free Primary Education**	13
	Crowley v. Ireland	13
	The High Court Judgment	14
	The Supreme Court Judgment	14
	Constitutional Intereptation	16
	1937 Drafts	16
	The Judges	17
	Existence of Right Acknowledged	17
	De Valera Papers	18
	The INTO	19
	The Role of the Courts	19
	The Constitution Review Group	21

Chapter 4	**The Extent of the State's Obligation**	23
	Irish Version	24
	State Subsidy	24
	Judicial Opinions	25
	Comments	26
	Rules for National Schools	28
	The Kenny Judgment	30
	The Contra-Kenny Interpretation	30
	Is the State's duty an absolute one?	32
	Compulsory School Attendance	37
	The Constitution Review Group	37
Chapter 5	**The Meaning of Education**	38
	The Irish Version	38
	Landers v. Attorney General	39
	O'Donoghue v. Minister for Health	40
	The State (C.) v. Frawley	41
	The Constitution Review Group	42
Chapter 6	**The Quality of Primary Education**	44
	Factors which influence Quality	44
	Children with Special Needs	44
	O'Donoghue v. Minister for Health	45
	Article 42.5	47
	Article 42.3.2°	48
	Resources Required	53
	The Constitution Review Group	54
Chapter 7	**Rights and Duties of the Family and Parents**	56
	Article 42.1	56
	Article 42.2	64
	Article 42.3.1°	64
	Article 42.3.2°	65
	Article 42.4	68
	Article 42.5	69
	Parents and Syllabi	73
	The Constitution Review Group	73
Chapter 8	**Control of Education and Parents**	75
	Private Schools	75
	Primary Education	76
	Model Schools	77
	Parents	77
	Admission Tests	79

Table of Contents xv

Chapter 8 (contd.)
        Teacher Selection   80
        Control of Syllabi   81
        Representation of Parents   82
        Convention on Human Rights   84
        Article 44.4   84
        The Constitution Review Group   85

Chapter 9   **Control of Education and Religious Denominations**   86
        Stanley's Letter   87
        The Managerial System   87
        The Constitution   88
        Boards of Management   89
        Management by a Religious Denomination   90
        Religious Denomination   93
        State Funding   94
        Limitations on the State   95
        State Powers   96
        Criticism of Present Methods   97
        Staff and Ethos   97
        The *Crizzle* Case   98
        Control and Ownership of School Premises   99
        The Constitution Review Group   100

Chapter 10   **Control of Education and the State**   102
        The Department of Education   102
        Rules for National Schools   104
        Recognition by the Department   105
        Post Primary Schools   105
        Private Secondary Schools   105
        Vocational Schools and Community Colleges   106
        Comprehensive Schools   107
        Community Schools   107
        Community Colleges   109
        Rules for Secondary Schools   109
        State Right to Regulate   110

Chapter 11   **Interference with Education**   111
        Landers v. Attorney General   111
        Inhibiting education   112
        The Conspiracy in *Crowley v. Ireland*   113
        The Primary Purpose   113
        Other Conspiracies   114

Chapter 12 Remedies 116
- Special Category of Claim — 116
- General Damages — 117
- Exemplary Damages — 118
- Reasons for Exemplary Damages — 119
- Other Remedies — 120
- Mandamus — 121
- Injunction — 122
- A Declaratory Order — 123
- Criminalisation — 123
- Assessment of Damages — 124
- Assessment of Exemplary Damages — 125
- The Obligation on the State — 125
- Statute of Limitations — 126

Chapter 13 Religion and Education 127
- Article 44.2.2° — 127
- Chaplains — 128
- Primary Education — 129
- School Closures — 130
- UN Report — 130
- Religious Instruction — 131
- Drafting the Constitution — 131
- Northern Ireland — 133
- *McGrath and O'Ruairc v. Trustees of Maynooth College* — 133
- Integrated Curriculum and Endowment of Religion — 134
- Article 44.2.3° — 134
- State Aid — 135
- Article 44.2.6° — 136
- Article 44.2.1° — 138
- The Constitution Review Group — 138

Chapter 14 The White Paper and the Constitution 141
- Consitutional Interpretation — 141
- Harmonious Interpretation — 141
- Express Limitation of Constitutional Rights — 142
- Limitation of Constitution Rights Generally — 144
- The Preamble — 146
- School Governance and Property Rights — 147
- Consitutional Proportionality — 148
- Criteria for Proportionality — 149
- Application of Proportionality — 150
- The Constituion Review Group — 151

Table of Contents xvii

Chapter 15 New Education Legislation 152
    Estoppel and Legitimate Expectation 152
    Relevance of Legal Principles 155
    Minister fettering his/her discretion 157
    The power of the State to legislate 157
    Government Contracts and Executive Power 158
    Legislation and School Governance 159
    State Control through Legislation 159
    Agreement on School Governance 159
    Limits on State Intervention 160
    Indications in the White Paper 161
    Equality and Article 40.1 161
    Equality and Legislation 164
    "The Common Good 165

Appendix 167

Index 171

TABLE OF CASES

Abrahamson v. Law Society of Ireland, unreported, High Court,
    McCracken J., July 15, 1996 154
Article 26 and the Adoption (No. 2) Bill 1987, Re [1989]
    I.R. 656; [1989] I.L.R.M. 266 (Sup. Ct.) 19, 31, 47, 60, 70, 71
Article 26 and the School Attendance Bill 1942,
    Re [1943] I.R. 334; 77 I.L.T.R. 96 .... 48, 49, 65, 70, 110
Article 26 and the Regulation of Information (Termination of
    Pregnancies) Bill 1995, Re [1995] 1 I.R. 1 2
Association of General Practitioners v. Minister for Health
    [1995] 2 I.L.R.M. 481 153
Attorney General (S.P.U.C.) v. Open Door Counselling [1988] I.R. 593;
    [1987] I.L.R.M. 477; [1989] I.L.R.M. 19 123
Attorney General v. S.I.T. Ltd (1960) 94 I.L.T.R. 161 .... 19, 146
Attorney General v. X [1992] 1 I.R. 1 .... 3, 69, 141, 142, 144
Attorney General (New South Wales) v. Quinn (1990)
    170 C.L.R. 1 154

Beesley v. Halwood Estates Ltd [1960] 1 W.L.R. 549; [1960]
    2 All E.R. 314 158
Berrisford v. Woodard Schools (Midland Division) Ltd, *The Times*,
    March 14, 1991 98
Bevan v. Shears [1911] 2 K.B. 936 67
Blake (decd.), Re [1955] I.R. 89 58
Board of Governors of St. Matthias (C of E) School v. Crizzle [1993]
    I.C.R. 401; [1993] I.R.L.R. 472 98
Boland v. An Taoiseach [1974] I.R. 338 46
Bourke v. Attorney General [1972] I.R. 36 19
Bradford v. Roberts 1175 U.S. 291 (1899) 134
Borwick, Re [1917] 2 Ch. 126 58
Buckley v. Attorney General [1950] I.R. 67 35
Burke v. Burke [1951] I.R. 216 58
Byrne v. Ireland [1972] I.R. 241 120

Caldwell and Stuart, Re (1985) 15 D.L.R. (4th) 1 97
Campaign to Separate Church & State Ltd v. Minister for Education,
    unreported, High Court, Costello P., January 17, 1996 ... 69, 85, 128, 132
Campbell and Cosans v. United Kingdom (1981)
    3 E.H.R.R. 531 .... 37, 42, 63, 65, 82 *et seq.*
Carmody v. Meehan and Cullen, unreported, High Court,
    September 14, 1993 66
Chaplin v. Hicks [1911] 2 K.B. 786 124
Combe v. Combe [1951] 2 K.B. 215 153

Conway v. INTO, unreported, High Court, Barron J.,
    December 7, 1988 115
Conway v. INTO [1991] 2 I.R. 305; [1991] I.L.R.M. 497
    (Sup. Ct.) 19, 118, 125
County Council of Derry v. McGlade [1929] N.I. 47 133
Cosgrave v. Ireland [1982] I.L.R.M. 48 117
Cox v. Ireland [1992] 2 I.R. 503 .... 126, 143
Crichton v. Land Commission and Gault (1950) 84 I.L.T.R. 87 137
Crofter Hand Woven Harris Tweed Co. Ltd v. Veitch [1942]
    A.C. 435 114
Crowley v. Ireland [1980] I.R. 102 .... 7, 12, 13 *et seq.*, 23 *et seq.*,
                                                        89, 113, 117, 125
Crowley v. Ireland, unreported, High Court, McWilliam J.,
    December 1, 1977 .... 24, 43, 104, 121
CSSU v. Minister for the Civil Service [1985] A.C. 374 153

D.D. (a minor) v. Eastern Health Board, unreported, High Court,
    Costello J., May 3, 1995 .... 36, 47
D.T. v. Eastern Health Board, unreported, High Court, Geoghegan J.,
    March 24, 1995 48
Daly v. Revenue Commissioners [1995] 3 I.R. 1 .... 144, 150
de Burca and Anderson v. Attorney General [1976] I.R. 38 .... 163, 165
Devitt v. Minister for Education [1989] I.L.R.M. 639 .... 154, 157
Dillane v. Ireland [1980] I.L.R.M. 167 .... 162, 164
Doyle, An Infant, Re: State (Doyle) v. Minister for Education
    [1989] I.L.R.M. 277 (Sup. Ct.) .... 63 *et seq.*
Duggan v. An Taoiseach [1989] I.L.R.M. 710 153

East Donegal Co-Op. v. Attorney General [1970] I.R. 317 .... 50, 162
Educational Company of Ireland v. Fitzpatrick [1961] I.R. 345 .... 4, 12, 31
Edwards v. Hall 25 L.J. Ch 82 128

Fajujonu v. Minister for Justice [1990] 2 I.R. 151; [1990]
    I.L.R.M. 224 .... 146, 165
F.N. v. Minister for Education, unreported, High Court,
    Geoghegan J., March 24, 1995 .... 36, 41, 47
Fielding v. Harrison [1908] 7 C.L.R. 393 128
Flynn v. Power [1985] I.R. 648 97

G. v. An Bord Úchtála [1980] I.R 32 .... 6, 47, 60
G.L. v. Minister for Justice, unreported, High Court, Geoghegan J.,
    March 24, 1995 47
Gilheaney v. The Revenue Commissioners, unreported, High Court,
    Costello J., October 4, 1995 157
Greendale Building Co. Ltd, Re [1977] I.R. 256 158
Griffitt v. Evans (1882) 46 L.T. 417 158

Hand v. Dublin Corporation [1989] I.R. 26 148

Table of Cases

Hanrahan v. Merck Sharps and Dohme [1988] I.L.R.M. 629 31
Haughey, Re [1971] I.R 217 5
Hawkins v. Rogers [1951] I.R.48 124
Hayes v. Ireland [1987] I.L.R.M. 651 .... 19, 28, 32, 115, 117
Heaney v. Ireland [1994] 3 I.R. 593; [1994] 2 I.L.R.M. 420 .... 149, 150
Hempenstall v. Minister for the Environment
    [1993] I.L.R.M. 318 155
Hickey & Co. v. Roches Stores (Dublin) Ltd, unreported, High Court,
    July 14, 1976 124
Hinchley v. Rankin [1961] 1 W.L.R. 421; 7 L&B 186 66
Hopgood v. Brown [1955] 1 All E.R. 550 153
Hosford v. John Murphy and Sons Ltd [1987] I.R. 621;
    [1988] I.L.R.M. 300 70
Hynds v. Spillers French Baking [1974] I.T.R. 261 65

J., Re [1966] I.R. 295 60

Kearney v. Ireland, unreported, High Court, Costello J.,
    March 13, 1986 117
Keegan v. Ireland (1994) E.H.R.R. 342 61
Kennedy v. Ireland [1987] I.R. 587 .... 2, 31, 119
Kjeldsen, ECHR, D 75277/76 (UK) 5.7.77,11/147 36

Lachford & Sons Ltd v. Minister for Industry & Commerce [1950] I.R.
    33 104
Landers v. Attorney General (1975) 109 I.L.T.R. 1 .... 39, 111
"La Lavia", Re [1996] 1 I.L.R.M. 194 154
Leydon v. Attorney General [1926] I.R. 334 (Sup. Ct.) 77, 88, 102
Lonrho v. Fayed [1991] 3 W.L.R. 188; [1991] 3 All E.R. 303 115
Lovett v. Gogan [1995] 1 I.L.R.M. 12 122

M.F. v. Superintendent Ballymun Garda Station [1991] 1 I.R. 189 47
Macauley v. Min. for Posts & Telegraphs [1966] I.R. 345 5
Matrimonial Home Bill 1993, Re [1994] I.L.R.M. 241 150
McDonnell v. Ireland, unreported, High Court, Carroll J.,
    January 19, 1996 126
McEneaney v. Minister for Education [1941] I.R. 430
    (Sup. Ct.) 28, 88, 104
McGee v. Attorney General [1974] I.R. 284 .... 1, 2, 3, 5, 7, 145, 147
McGrath and Ó Ruairc v. Trustees of Maynooth
    [1979] I.L.R.M. 166 .... 94, 133, 135
Meade v. Harringay LBC. [1979] 2 All E.R. 1016 .... 114, 121
Meskell v. C.I.E. [1973] I.R. 21 .... 5, 113, 116, 117, 123
Molloy v. Minister for Education [1975] I.R. 88 135
Moynihan v. Greensmyth [1977] I.R. 55 143
Murphy v. Attorney General [1982] I.R. 241 164
Murphy v. Ireland, unreported, High Court, Carroll J.,
    February 21, 1996 .... 116, 126

Murphy v. Stewart [1973] I.R. 97 113
Murray v. Ireland [1985] I.R. 532 (High Ct.) 61, 141, 144, 145, 147
Murray v. Ireland [1991] I.L.R.M. 463 (Sup. Ct.) 145
Murtagh Properties v. Cleary [1972] I.R. 330 5

Newell v. Gillingham Corporation [1941] 1 All E.R. 552 65
Newell v. Starkie [1917] 2 I.R. 73 76
Norris v. Attorney General [1984] I.R. 36 .... 2, 124, 147
Northampton County Council v. A.B.F. & M.B.F. [1982] I.L.R.M. 164 ... 161

O'B. v. S. [1984] I.R. 316 164
O'Brien v. Keogh [1972] I.R. 144 .... 163, 165
O'Callaghan v. Minister for Education, unreported, Supreme Court,
    March 31, 1955; unreported, High Court, November 31, 1955 29
O'Donoghue v. Minister for Health, unreported, High Court,
    O'Hanlon J., May 27, 1993 .... 39 et seq., 45 et seq., 59, 121, 123
O'Donovan v. Attorney General [1962] I.R. 114 .... 68, 143

Parsons v. Kavanagh [1990] I.L.R.M. 560 122
People v. Madden [1977] I.R. 336 21
People v. Shaw [1982] I.R.1 30
Phelan v. Co. Laoise VEC & Parsons, unreported, High Court,
    McWilliam J, February 28, 1977 31
Pickard v. Sears (1837) 6 Ad. & El 469; 45 R.R. 538 153
Public Trustee v. Bryant [1936] 2 All E.R. 878 58

Queen v. Bernardo [1891] Q.B. 194 .... 57, 62 et seq.
Quick Bear v. Leupp 210 U.S. 50 (1908) 134
Quinn v. Leatham [1901] A.C. 495 124
Quinn's Supermarket v. Attorney General [1972] I.R. 1 161

R. v. Clarke 7 L.& B. 186; R.R. 110 .... 57, 70
R. v. Edwards Books and Arts Ltd [1986] 35 D.L.R (4th) 1 149
R. v. ILEA, *ex p*. Ali, *The Times*, February 21, 1990 26
R. v. London Borough of Bexley, *ex p*. Jones [1994] Crown Office
    Digest 393 157
R. v. Secretary of State for Education, *ex p*. London Borough of
    Southwark [1994] Crown Office Digest 298 154
Rederiaktie Amphotrite v. The King [1921] 3 K.B. 500 158
Rookes v. Barnard [1964] A.C. 1129 119
Ryan v. Attorney General [1965] I.R. 294 .... 1, 5, 6, 12, 17, 38, 44,
                                                    46, 60, 81, 112, 164

S., Re, *The Times*, March 30, 1993 116
Sandbrook, Re [1912] 2 Ch. 471 58
Shaw v. Director of Public Prosecutions [1961] 1 W.L.R. 911;
    [1962] A.C. 237, C.A 124
Sorrell v. Smith [1925] A.C. 700 114

State (Bouzagou) v. Station Sergeant, Fitzgibbon St. [1985] I.R. 426 161
State (C.) v. Frawley [1976] I.R. 365 .... 41, 44, 46, 47
State (Ennis) v. Farrell [1966] I.R. 107 16
State (Healy) v. Donoghue [1976] I.R. 325 .... 3, 6, 145, 147
State (K.M.) v. Minister for Foreign Affairs [1979] I.R. 73 (High Ct.) 2, 6
State (Nicolaou) v. An Bord Úchtála [1966] I.R. 567 .... 60, 62, 162, 163
State (Quinn) v. Ryan [1965] I.R. 70 116
Staunton v. St. Laurence's Hospital Board, unreported, High Court,
    February 21, 1986 104
Sweeney v. Duggan [1991] 2 I.R. 274 31

Tara Prospecting Ltd v. Minister for Energy [1993] I.L.R.M. 771 155
Tormey v. Attorney General and Ireland [1985] I.R. 289; [1985]
    I.L.R.M. 375 91

Ward of Court, Re A [1995] 2 I.L.R.M. 401 73
Wavin Pipes Ltd v. Hepworth Iron Co. Ltd, unreported, High Court,
    Costello J., May 8, 1981 19
Webb v. Ireland [1988] I.R 353 .... 153, 154, 155
Westby Minors (No.2), Re [1937] I.R. 311 58

Youman v. The Commonwealth 189 Ky 152 21

TABLE OF CONSTITUTIONAL PROVISIONS

Constitution of the Irish Free State 1922

Art. 8	132, 137
Art. 10	9, 10, 28, 120

Constitution of Ireland 1937

Preamble	144, 146, 147, 165
Art. 16.2.3°	143
Art. 25.5.4°	16, 17, 142
Art. 26	136, 159
Art. 34.3.1°	91
Art. 34.3.4°	91
Art. 34.3.2°	20
Art. 38	150
Art. 38.1	150
Art. 40	5, 7, 31, 35, 72, 111, 123, 125, 143, 144, 147, 161, 163
Art. 40.1	161, 162, 163, 164, 165
Art. 40.3	31, 72, 142, 163
Art. 40.3.1°	5, 6, 7, 8, 30, 125, 150
Art. 40.3.2°	5, 7, 8, 11, 50, 142, 143, 144, 150
Art. 40.3.3°	69
Art. 40.4.2°	44
Art. 40.6	142
Art. 40.6.1°	4
Art. 40.6.1°iii	5
Art. 41	5, 6, 7, 60, 61, 70, 71, 73, 74, 145, 150, 161
Art. 41.1	72
Art. 41.2.2°	34
Art. 41.3.1°	60
Art. 42	5, 6, 7, 10, 31, 32, 40, 56, 58, 59, 60, 61, 70, 71, 73, 74, 79, 89, 91, 104, 111, 112, 123, 129, 148, 167
Art. 42.1	15, 38, 41, 53, 56, 59, 60, 62, 63, 64, 74, 77, 81, 82, 85, 168
Art. 42.2	15, 38, 39, 51, 64, 67, 75, 77, 81
Art. 42.2.3°	135
Art. 42.3	63, 64
Art. 42.3.1°	55, 64, 78, 89, 111, 168
Art. 42.3.2°	11, 25, 33, 37, 43, 48, 51, 52, 53, 54, 55, 65, 66, 81, 82, 111, 123, 131, 142, 165, 169

Constitution of Ireland 1937 (*contd.*)

Art. 42.3.4° 123
Art. 42.4 .... 13, 14, 16, 23, 24, 25, 31, 33, 34, 35, 36, 38,
42, 44, 53, 59, 68, 69, 75, 76, 78, 85, 89,
90, 111, 117, 125, 128, 144, 165, 169
Art. 42.5 .... 36, 47, 63, 69, 70, 71, 72, 168
Art. 43 .... 7, 72, 91, 147
Art. 43.2.2° 142
Art. 44 .... 72, 73, 90, 91, 131, 138, 139
Art. 44.1 138
Art. 44.1.2° 132
Art. 44.2.1° 138, 142, 148
Art. 44.2.2° 127, 128, 130, 132, 133, 138
Art. 44.2.3° 94, 109, 130, 135
Art. 44.2.4° 31, 89, 90, 93, 95, 99, 100, 101,
104, 128, 135, 139, 140, 160
Art. 44.2.5° 89, 90, 92, 94, 95, 99, 101, 147, 148, 160
Art. 44.2.6° 91, 93, 136, 137, 140, 142, 148
Art. 44.4 .... 75, 81, 84, 90
Art. 44.5 75
Art. 46 151
Art. 50 112

TABLE OF STATUTES

IRELAND

Pre-Union

An Act for the Erection of Free Schools 1570 (12 Eliz. 1, c. 1) 86

Parliament of the United Kingdom of Great Britain and Ireland

Agriculture and Technical Instruction (Ireland) Act 1899
    (62 & 63 Vict., c. 50) 107
Children's Act 1908 (8 Edw. 7, c. 67)
    s.58 63
Educational Endowments (Ireland) Act 1885 (48 & 49 Vict., c. 18) ... 105, 106
Government of Ireland Act 1914 (4 & 5 Geo. 5, c. 90) 127
Government of Ireland Act 1920 (10 & 11 Geo. 5, c. 67) 127, 128
    s.5 133
Intermediate Education (Ireland) Act 1878 (41 & 42 Vict., c. 66) 105,
    s.5 (3) 109
Intermediate Education (Ireland) Act 1914
    (4 & 5 Geo. 5, c. 41) 105, 106, 109
Intermediate Education (Ireland) Act 1900
    (63 & 64 Vict., c.43) 105, 106, 109
Irish Universities Act 1908 (8 Edw. 7, c. 38)
    s.7 127
Offences Against The Person Act 1861 (24 & 25 Vict., c. 100) 2
Prevention of Cruelty to Children Act 1904 (4 Edw. 7, c. 15) 40, 111, 112
Public Libraries (Ireland) Act 1855 (18 & 19 Vict., c. 40) 106
Public Libraries (Ireland) Amendment Act 1877 (40 & 41 Vict., c. 15) 106
Criminal Law Amendment Act 1885 (48 & 49 Vict., c. 69) 2
Irish Education Act 1892 (55 & 56 Vict., c. 42) 11
Technical Instruction Act 1889 (52 & 53 Vict., c. 76) 107

Acts of the Oireachtas

Adoption Act 1988 (No. 30)
    s.3 (1) 72
Adoption Act 1952 (No. 25) 163
Aliens Act 1935 (No. 14) 146
Child Care Act 1991 (No. 17)
    ss.13, 17, 46 64

Table of Statutes

Children's Act 1941 (No. 12)
    s.10 63
Courts of Justice Act 1924 (No. 10)
    ss.90, 91 163
Eighth Amendment of the Constitution Act 1983 69
Electoral (Amendment) Act 1959 (No. 33)
    ss.3(1), 4 68
Finance Act 1987 (No. 9)
    s.18 150
Finance Act 1990 (No. 10)
    s.26 150
       (1) 150
Fourteenth Amendment of the Constitution Act 1992 69
Guardianship of Infants Act 1964 (No. 7)
    s.6(a) 61
Higher Education Authority Act 1971 (No. 22)
    s.1(1)(b) 134
Intermediate Education (Amendment) Act 1924 (No. 47) 105, 106, 109
Ministers and Secretaries (Amendment) Act 1924 (No. 36) 29, 107
Offences Against The State Act 1939 (No. 13) 126
    s.34 .... 126, 143
    s.52(1) 150
School Attendance Act 1926 (No. 17) 62
Status of Children Act 1987 (No. 26) 61
Statute of Limitations Act 1957 (No. 6)
    s.11(2) 126
Thirteenth Amendment of the Constitution Act 1992 69
Unfair Dismissals Act 1977 (No. 10) 97
Vocational Education Act 1930 (No. 29) 12, 62, 168
    s.21 109
Vocational Education (Amendment) Act 1970 (No. 15) 108

ENGLAND

Education Act 1944 (7 & 8 Geo. 6, c. 31)
    s.8 26
Race Relations Act 1976 (c. 74) 98
Sex Discrimination Act 1975 (c. 65) 98

Chapter 1

Unenumerated/Implied Constitutional Rights

Irish citizens[1] enjoy two classes of constitutional rights, those which are enumerated in the 1937 Constitution (Bunreacht na hÉireann) and those which are not. This second category of rights are termed unenumerated or implied constitutional rights. The courts have the role of interpreting and applying the Constitution and the exercise of this function has led to the courts being the sole arbiter of whether an unemunerated constitutional right exists or not.

Unenumerated/Implied Rights

The basis for the existence of these rights is either that they are implied from the provisions of the Constitution itself or that they follow from natural law or the Christian and democratic nature of the State. Most lawyers would find the first basis more attractive than the latter two. However, Chief Justice Finlay has stated:

> "The unenumerated rights are to be found, not by the transient needs or moods of society, but rather by a consideration of the fundamental nature of the society envisaged by the Constitution itself. In a sense they can be said to be *ejusdem generis* with the rights expressly provided for in the Constitution. This conclusion arises, I think, not only from the terms in which these rights have been recognised and the principles underlined, but also in the nature of the rights which have been identified."[2]

Natural law was cited by Walsh J. in *McGee v. Attorney General*[3] where he stated: "The individual has natural and human rights over which the State has no authority; and the family, as the natural and primary and fundamental unit group of society, has rights as such which the State cannot control."[4]

The Christian and democratic nature of the State was cited by Kenny J. in the seminal case of *Ryan v. Attorney General*,[5] by Finlay P. in *The State (K.M.)*

---

1. As to the rights of non-citizens see Chap. 15 below.
2. The Hon. T.A. Finlay, Chief Justice, *The Constitution: Fifty Years On* (1988) pp. 11–12.
3. [1974] I.R. 284.
4. *ibid.* at 310. As to the rules of Natural Justice see Farry, *Vocational Education and the Law* (1996).
5. [1965] I.R. 294.

v. *Minister for Foreign Affairs*[6] and by Hamilton P. (as he then was) in *Kennedy v. Ireland*.[7]

In the *Ryan* (water fluoridation) case Kenny J. in the High Court referred to many personal right which follow from the Christian and democratic nature of the State.[8] In *The State (K.M.) v. Minister for Foreign Affairs*[9] (the right to travel case) Finlay P. stated:

> "... it appears to me that the citizens of the State may have a right (arising from the Christian and democratic nature of the State – though not enumerated in the Constitution) to avail of the existing facilities (for the purpose of travelling outside the State) without arbitrary or unjustified interference by the State."[10]

In *Kennedy v. Ireland*[11] (the telephone tapping case) Hamilton P. said: "Though not specifically guaranteed by the Constitution the right of privacy is one of the fundamental personal rights of the citizen which follow from the Christian and democratic nature of the State."

On the other hand the Christian nature of the State was a factor in the Supreme Court's decision in *Norris v. Attorney General*[12] (the gay rights case) when they held that having regard, *inter alia*, to the Christian nature of the State the right to privacy claimed by the plaintiff could not prevail against the sanctions imposed by sections of the Offences Against the Person Act 1861 and a section of the Criminal Law Amendment Act 1885.

The identification of constitutional rights by reference to natural law and to the Christian and democratic nature of the State is problematic. The difficulty with natural law as a source of personal rights is the uncertainty as to its content. This difficulty of what exactly natural law is and what precisely it imports was raised by Walsh J. in *McGee v. Attorney General*.[13] The difficulty with the Christian nature of the State is that it excludes non-Christian beliefs. In the *Norris* case point 9 of the Supreme Court judgment specifically cites the Christian nature of the State.[14]

In 1995, however, the Supreme Court rejected the superior status of natural law in a case involving the constitutional validity of the Information (Termination of Pregnancies) Bill 1995.[15] It held that the Constitution was the fundamental and supreme law of the State, representing as it did the will of the people

---

6. [1979] I.R. 73.
7. [1987] I.R. 587.
8. See full quotation on p. 6 below.
9. Above, n.5.
10. *ibid.* at. 80-81.
11. Above, n.6.
12. [1984] I.R. 36.
13. Above, n.2 at 318.
14. Above, n.11 at 37.
15. *Re Article 26 and the Regulation of Information (Termination of Pregnancies) Bill 1995* [1995] 1 I.R. 1.

and it rejected the argument that "natural law" was the fundamental law of the State and was antecedent and superior to all positive law including the Constitution. The Court also rejected the argument that it was impermissible for the People to exercise the power of amendment of the Constitution unless such amendment was compatible with the natural law and the existing provisions of the Constitution. Significantly the Court also held that:

> ". . . from a consideration of all the cases which had recognised the existence of a personal right not specifically enumerated in the Constitution, it was manifest that the Court in each such case had satisfied itself that such personal right was one which could be reasonably implied from, and was guaranteed by, the provisions of the Constitution, interpreted in accordance with the ideas of prudence, justice and charity; and that courts had at no stage recognised the provisions of natural law as superior to the Constitution."[16]

From a legal perspective the attempt to resolve the uncertainty of natural law by recourse to the concepts of prudence, justice and charity is fraught with difficulty. These concepts are not narrowly defined and are no more precise than "natural law". An individual judge's understanding of them is subjective and may culminate in a subjective interpretation of the most fundamental laws of the State, a matter which is scarcely desirable. It may be asked if future litigants face the vagaries of a constitutional lottery?

In relation to the concept of justice, O'Higgins C.J. in *The State (Healy) v. Donoghue*[17] stated:

> "In the first place the concept of justice, which is specifically referred to in the Preamble in relation to the freedom and dignity of the individual, appears again in the provisions of Article 34 which deal with the courts. It is justice which is to be administered in the Courts and this concept of justice must import not only fairness and fair procedures . . . but also regard to the dignity of the individual. No court under the Constitution has jurisdiction to act contrary to justice."[18]

In relation to charity, Walsh J. in *McGee v. Attorney General*[19] referred to the esteem which both Aristotle and the Christian philosophers had for the virtues of justice and prudence and added: "the great additional virtue introduced by Christianity was that of charity". This was "not the charity which consists of giving to the deserving, for that is justice, but the charity which is called mercy."[20]

---

16. *ibid.* at 4. Note that the Preamble to the Constitution refers to ". . . seeking to promote the common good, with due observance of Prudence, Justice and Charity." Note also the criticism of this approach to constitutional interpretation in the Report of the Constitution Review Group (Dublin, May 1996) at pp. 251-252. See Ch. 14 below.
17. [1976] I.R. 325.
18. *ibid.* at 348.
19. Above, n.2.
20. *ibid.* at 319. Finlay C.J. interpreted the Constitution in *Attorney General v. X.* [1993] 1 I.R. 1 in accordance with this explanation at 53.

The Report of the Constitution Review Group[21] in reference to the use of the concepts of prudence, justice and charity in constitutional interpretation states:

> "Clearly, there is a real potential for judicial subjectivity in this approach. The idenfication of rights by reference to broadly defined and potentially competing concepts such as prudence, justice, charity, freedom, dignity and the common good is unsatisfactory since these are concepts which are capable of different interpretations, depending upon the context, and if the application of these concepts produces conflicting results, it is unclear how such a conflict is to be resolved."[22]

This decision of the Supreme Court "to discount natural law in interpreting the constitution" has been criticised by Archbishop Desmond Connell in a homily in the Pro-Cathedral on July 7, 1996[23] while the philosophic pedigree of the Irish judiciary to interpret the constitution has reportedly been questioned by Professor William Binchy, Regius Professor of Law in TCD and legal adviser to the Pro-Life Campaign[24] who claimed that the judges of the Supreme Court:

> "don't seem to have the philosophic resources and philosophic ability to be able to see what is in the Constitution . . .and have practically wrecked the fundamental rights provisions of the Constitution, and specifically the protection for the unborn . . . ."

The first intimation of constitutional rights being implied by the courts, in modern times, occurred in relation to the enumerated right of freedom of association under Article 40.6.1° (the right of citizens to form associations and unions) in the case of *Educational Co. of Ireland v. Fitzpatrick*[25] where Budd J. stated:

> ". . . if it is a liberty that is guaranteed, that means that the citizen is free to form and I think that must include join such associations and unions...Apart from authority, therefore, I would myself construe the words of the Article as meaning by implication that a citizen has the correlative right not to form or join associations or unions if he does not wish to do so. . . . I hold therefore, in accordance as I believe with the views of the Supreme Court, that under the Constitution a citizen is free to join or not to join an association or union as he pleases."[26]

Further he could not be deprived of the right to join "or not to join such

---

21. See above, n.15.
22. At p. 252 of the report.
23. See *Irish Independent*, July 8, 1996.
24. See *Irish Times*, August 12, 1996 (report on Pro-Life Campaign Seminar at All Hallows College on August 10, 1996).
24. [1961] I.R. 345.
26. *ibid.* at 362-365.

association". This implied (unenumerated) right of disassociation was later upheld by the Supreme Court in *Meskell v. C.I.E.*[27] where the plaintiff refused to accept a special condition of re-employment to be "at all times" a member of a trade union. The court stated that the right to form associations and unions guaranteed by Article 40.6.1.iii, necessarily recognised a correlative right to abstain from joining associations and unions. Thus the concept of implied unenumerated rights was born.

Ryan v. Attorney General and after

The first case in which a constitutional right was actually implied by the courts was the case of *Ryan v. Attorney General*[28] which involved a claim that the fluoridation of drinking water was an interference with the claimant's constitutional rights, in violation of her rights and those of her children under Article 40.3.1°. It was also claimed that there had been a violation of the authority of the family under Article 41, and a violation of the family's right to physical education of the children under Article 42. The Supreme Court held that although not expressed in the Constitution, the citizen had a right of bodily integrity implied under Article 40.3.2°. The Court decided that "personal rights" mentioned in Article 40.3.1° of the Constitution are not exhausted by the enumeration of "life, person, good name, and property rights" in 40.3.2°, as is shown by the use of the words "in particular" in that section, nor by the more detached treatment of specific rights in the subsequent sections of Article 40. The Court considered that it was unnecessary, in this case, to attempt to list the rights which properly fall within the category of "personal rights".

The constitutional justification for implying that there are additional, unenumerated rights, is derived in the *Ryan* case, from the interpretation that the use of the words "in particular" in Article 40.3.2° which alludes to those particular rights specified, indicates that other rights have not been specified.

Note that since this decision, other rights including the following have been held to exist:

– to litigate (*Macauley v. Minister for Posts and Telegraphs*[29])

– to one's good name (*Re Haughey*[30])

– to earn a livelihood (*Murtagh Properties v. Cleary*[31])

– to marital privacy (*McGee v. Attorney General*[32])

---

27. [1973] I.R. 21.
28. Above, n.4.
29. [1966] I.R. 345.
30. [1971] I.R. 217.
31. [1972] I.R. 330.
32. Above, n.12.

- to legal aid, to justice and fair procedures (*The State (Healy) v. Donoghue*[33])
- to travel (*The State (K.M.) v. Minister for Foreign Affairs*[34])
- to custody of an illegitimate child by the child's unmarried mother (*G. v. An Bord Úchtála*[35])

For a more extensive list of rights which have been recognised see *Constitutional Law in Ireland* by Casey.[36]

The Role of the Courts

As to who should declare these constitutional rights, Kenny J. in *Ryan v. Attorney General* stated:

> "in modern times this would seem to be the function of the legislature rather than of the judicial power but it was done by the courts in the formative period of the Common law and there is no reason why they should not do so now."[37]

Chief Justice Finlay, states that if one can conclude that the Constitution has been reasonably adaptable to the changes in society:

> "That fact may owe much to the doctrine of the unenumerated personal Constitutional right first identified by the late Judge John Kenny in *Ryan v. Attorney General*, endorsed on appeal by the Supreme Court and subsequently adopted by the Courts."[38]

The rationale of the decision as stated by Kenny J. was that:

> "there are many personal rights of the citizen which follow from the Christian and democratic nature of the State which are not mentioned in Article 40 at all, the right to free movement within the State and the right to marry are examples of this. This also leads to the conclusion that the general guarantee extends to rights not specified in Article 40."[39]

This case has led to the classification of constitutional rights under two headings, enumerated rights, *i.e.* rights specifically written in the Constitution and unenumerated rights, *i.e.* rights not written in the Constitution. The Constitution Review Group[40] point out that while the development of its unenumerated rights doctrine has proved beneficial in many respects, unease has been

---

33. Above, n.16.
34. Above, n.5.
35. [1980] I.R. 32.
36. (1st ed., 1987), pp. 306–307.
37. Above, n.4, at 313.
38. Above, n.1, at 11.
39. Above, n.4, at 313.
40. See above, n.15.

expressed that the language of Article 40.3.1° offers no real guidance to the judiciary as to what these personal rights are. The Report states: "The experience of thirty years or so since *Ryan* has demonstrated that there does not appear to be any objective method of ascertaining what these personal rights are".[41]

The Constitution and Education

The constitutional provisions which deal with education are contained in Article 42 but an early indication that the judiciary considered that the Kenny dictum was not confined to Article 40 was given by Walsh J. in *McGee v. Attorney General*[42] when he stated that Articles 41, 42 and 43 of the Constitution "emphatically reject the theory that there are no rights without laws, no rights contrary to the law and no rights anterior to the law."[43]

This statement anticipated the path of a future judicial decision in relation to education under Article 42 which occurred in *Crowley v. Ireland*[44] six years later. The case arose out of the nomination of a Principal of Drimoleague National School, whom the INTO alleged was not eligible for consideration under Rule 76 of the Rules for National Schools, because he had not got sufficient years service. As a result of the dispute, the organisation withdrew the services of its members from three national schools in the parish of Drimoleague, and later issued a directive to its members in schools in neighbouring parishes not to enrol pupils from Drimoleague parish in their schools. This directive was withdrawn in June 1977 but the plaintiffs being dissatisfied with the alternative arrangements made by the State claimed an order directing the provision of free primary education within the parish of Drimoleague and damages for a conspiracy to deprive them of their constitutional rights to free primary education. This case is fully discussed below in Chapter 3.

The Constitution Review Group

The Constitution Review Group made the following recommendations and reached the following conclusions in relation to Article 40.3.1° and 40.3.2°:

Recommendation

Article 40.3.1° should not be retained in its present form.

---

41. At pp. 214–215 of the report.
42. Above, n.8.
43. *ibid.* at 310.
44. [1980] I.R. 102.

Recommendation

On balance, the Review Group favours an amendment of Article 40.3.1° which would provide a comprehensive list of fundamental rights which could specifically encompass the personal rights which have been identified by the Irish courts to date, and which might also include those set out in the European Convention on Human Rights and the International Covenant on Civil and Political Rights, so far as may be considered appropriate, and other personal rights which might be particularly appropriate in an Irish context, and which should confine further recognition of fundamental rights by the courts to those necessarily implicit in the rights expressly listed.

Recommendation

In general, personal rights should not be confined to citizens but should be extended to all human persons. There may be some rights which should be confined to citizens.

Recommendation

The existing qualifying clauses contained in Article 40.3.1° and Article 40.3.2° should be replaced by a general and more comprehensive qualifying clause along the lines of Article 10(2) of the European Convention on Human Rights. Certain rights – such as the right to life and freedom from torture and slavery – may call for special treatment.

Conclusion

There should be no express obligation in the Constitution on anyone other than the State to respect, defend and vindicate the personal rights of the citizen. However, an individual should not be precluded from seeking to enforce such rights against another person.

Conclusion

The State ought to be accountable for omissions to legislate resulting in failure to vindicate an individual's personal rights. However, the accountability of the State for omissions to legislate ought probably to be confined to declaratory judgments to that effect and/or to an entitlement to damages. It ought not to result in the courts effectively ordering the State to legislate in particular areas, because of the infringement of the principle of separation of powers. Constitutional amendment may not be required having regard to the developed state of the law in this difficult area.

Chapter 2

Primary Education and Constitutional Rights

The present Constitution, unlike its predecessor, the Constitution of the Free State of Ireland 1922, does not expressly provide that there is a right to free primary education. The framers of the 1937 Constitution deliberately decided that a right to free primary education should not be included in the text of the Constitution. This decision was initially taken by the constitutional committee which De Valera had established in 1934. He wrote to the committee on May 24, 1934,[1] asking them to examine the 1922 Constitution, to ascertain which of its Articles should be regarded as fundamental and to submit a recommendation as to which Articles should be retained.

Drafting Decision

Due to the view of the Department of Education, the committee did not recommend the inclusion of Article 10 of the 1922 Constitution which provided:

> "All citizens of the Irish Free State (Saorstát Éireann) have the right to free elementary education."

In a submission the Department pointed out that Article 10 had never been formally invoked, that there was no legal interpretation of it, or of the obligations it imposed. Apart from the obligation that elementary education should be free other claims could possibly arise. These included:

- whether a small number of children living a long distance from a National School could successfully claim a right to transportation, or their own school; and
- whether the Article could be construed to oblige the State not alone to pay teachers, but also to build, equip and maintain schools, and provide free books and requisites.

In the opinion of the Secretary of the Department, the position was: "that the principle underlying the Article is fundamental and should be preserved if

---

1. 1074/77 De Valera Papers, Franciscan Institute of Celtic Studies and Historical Research, Killiney, Co. Dublin.

possible". In the absence of a clear designation of the State's obligation under the Article it would: "be undesirable to put it in such a position as to make it more difficult to deal by legislation with any problem that might arise."[2]

Criticism of Article 10 of 1922 Constitution

Article 10 had been criticised by N. Umis who claimed that:

> "The whole Article smells a little of State omnipotence: it seems to be based on the idea that education is primarily a matter for the State, and that if the State gives free education it has a right to give whatever sort of education it likes – a pernicious idea, utterly at variance with right reason."[3]

The author suspects that Umis was a pseudonym, but E. Brian Titley suggests that Umis was: "perhaps an extreme case. . . . An even more intransigent upholder of the tradition of private schooling"[4] than Rev. Lambert McKenna S.J., Chairman of the National Programme Conference on Primary Education and author of the article "State Rights in Education" published in 1927.[5]

The author suggests that a number of passages in this article, cited elsewhere, apparently had a significant influence on the framers of the educational provisions in the 1937 Constitution. The first section of Article 38 of the first English draft[6] of the Constitution in 1934 (which later became Article 42) provided: "All citizens have the right to free elementary education." Mr. T.J. O'Connell INTO had pointed out in the Dáil debate on the draft Article 11 of the Irish Free State Constitution that the word elementary would lead to confusion "because it would be necessary to define what elementary means in this connection, and at the present time it is rather undecided."[7]

The second section of Article 38 of the first English draft provided "Primary instruction is obligatory . . .". The Irish version refers to both elementary education and primary instruction as bunoideachas. In addition another early draft[8] went so far as to state: "Primary education is compulsory, and the right to free primary education is guaranteed."

1922 Constitution

During the 1922 debates T.J. O Connell T.D. (INTO General Secretary) had proposed that the draft Article 11 of the 1922 Constitution which stated that:

---

2. ibid.
3. Umis, "What's Wrong with the Secondary System?", *Irish Monthly*, 57, No. 674, August, 1929, p. 412.
4. Titley, *Church, State, and the Control of Schooling in Ireland, 1900–1944* (1983), p. 123.
5. L. McKenna S.J., M.A., "State Rights in Education", *Studies* XIV, p. 220.
6. 1060/1 De Valera Papers, *op. cit.*, above, n.1.
7. *Dáil Debates* Col. 1697, October 18, 1922.
8. 1078/1b De Valera Papers, *op. cit.*, above, n.1.

"All citizens of the Irish Free State have the right to free elementary education" should be amended to: "Provision shall be made by the State for the free education of the young up to an age to be prescribed by law. School attendance shall be compulsory." This amendment was defeated. The then Minister for Education, Professor MacNeill, pointed out that the right of education, in the first place belonged to the parents:

> ". . . we must be extremely careful in anything that we lay down as a general principle that we do not say or appear to say that the control of education belongs as by right to the State."

He thought that parents had a right to consider themselves capable of educating their children at home. Mr. O'Higgins pointed out[9] that the Article in the Draft defined the right of the citizen, as against the State. The proposed amendment took a somewhat different angle and stated: "that as between certain ages, up to an age to be prescribed by law, the State must make provision for the free education of the young".

1937 Drafts

Specific mention of a right to free elementary or primary education was not made in either the Jesuit or McQuaid submissions in relation to the present constitution. It had disappeared completely from the drafts before 1936 and was never reinstated. An Article making primary education compulsory, inserted in the Jesuit submission of 1936 was not accepted by De Valera possibly because of the reservations of the constitutional committee and the Department of Education. In the final version neither the right nor the compulsory aspects appeared. The Department's reservations were based on the recognition that with the giving of a right the initiative passed to the donee to enforce it. They desired that the initiative should lie with the State. The power of the State in Article 42.3.2° to require that children receive a certain minimum education encompasses both aspects.

Compulsory School Attendance

It is noteworthy that when the English Cabinet sought to introduce a legal obligation to send children to school, in the Irish Education Act 1892 the Irish Catholic Bishops protested that they did not approve of the principle of direct compulsion. An Episcopal meeting on April 5, 1892, passed a resolution:

> "That, whilst on more than one ground we feel unable to express approval of those provisions of the Education Bill which apply to Ireland the principle of

---

9. *Dáil Debates* Col. 1702, October 18, 1922.

direct compulsion, we should highly approve of any reasonable measure of indirect compulsion."[10]

In the same article published 10 years prior to the Constitution, the Rev. L. McKenna S.J. also pointed out that at one period: "when some ecclesiastics sought to impose an obligation on parents to send their children to church schools, Pope Alexander III vindicated the liberty of parents, and strictly forbade that any person of good character and sufficient learning should be prevented from opening a school."[11]

By June 1923, however, Catholic primary school managers, who were in the main parish priests were calling for compulsory school attendance.[12] The Hierarchy also opposed the compulsory powers of the Minister under the draft Vocational Education Act 1930 and these were dropped as a consequence. In any event it would have been thought superfluous to give a right to primary education if it was being made compulsory to receive it. The High Court, however, in the case of *Crowley v. Ireland*[13] has held that there is such a constitutional right to free primary education (see Chapter 3 below). In doing so it has merely continued a process initiated by the Supreme Court in the case of *Educational Company of Ireland v. Fitzpatrick*[14] and in *Ryan v. Attorney General*.[15]

The Constitution Review Group

The Constitution Review Group in their report[16] state: "There is a potentially important diffference between the wording of the 1922 Constitution and the 1937 Constitution in relation to education."[17]

---

10. See above, n.5, p. 216.
11. *ibid.*, p. 220.
12. *Irish Catholic Directory 1924*, p. 580; See Titley, *op. cit.* above, n.4, p. 104.
13. [1980] I.R. 102.
14. [1961] I.R. 345.
15. [1965] I.R. 294.
16. *Report of the Constitution Review Group*, May 1996.
17. *ibid.*, p. 343

Chapter 3

The Constitutional Right to Free Primary Education

The provision of the Constitution which is relevant to the right to free primary education is Article 42.4 which provides: "The State shall provide *for* free primary education . . ." (emphasis added). In the draft Constitution as revised on the instructions of the President on March 31, 1937 the wording was: "The State shall provide free primary education . . .". The preposition "for" was inserted into the draft of Article 42.4 by De Valera in his own handwriting in a re-draft made on April 7.[1] The duty imposed on the State and the meaning of this provision was considered by the High Court in 1978, and on appeal by the Supreme Court in 1979, in *Crowley v. Ireland*.[2]

Crowley v. Ireland

The *Crowley* case arose out of a strike over the appointment of a individual whom it was alleged, His Lordship, the Bishop of Cork and Ross, had directed should be appointed principal teacher to a primary school in Drimoleague, County Cork. The individual concerned was ineligible for permanent appointment and was appointed on a temporary basis initially. The INTO regarded the managers failure to make a permanent appointment as an attempt to give the post to an ineligible teacher at the expense of eligible and suitable INTO members. They ballotted teachers in the Drimoleague area and with the exception of M (the individual concerned) the teachers were unanimously in favour of strike action. On March 16, 1976, the INTO sent strike notice to the manager for failing to make a permanent appointment and on April 1, 1976, and the teachers in schools under the manager went on strike. On August 20, 1976, the INTO sent a directive to teachers in schools adjoining Drimoleague Parish instructing them not to enrol Drimoleague pupils who might seek admission because of the strike in their own schools. This circular was withdrawn on June 13, 1977.

The plaintiffs claimed damages against the INTO by reason of a conspiracy

---

1. 1079/3 De Valera Papers, Franciscan Institute of Celtic Studies and Historical Research, Killiney, Co. Dublin.
2. *Crowley v. Ireland* [1980] I.R. 102.

to deprive them of their constitutional right to free primary education. It was submitted that the means adopted by the INTO, *i.e.* the issuing of the directive, was unlawful and a conspiracy to deprive the children of their constitutional right in order to bring pressure to bear upon the manager of the Drimoleague school.

The High Court Judgment

In the High Court judgment McMahon J. held that Article 42.4 which directed the State expressly to provide for free primary education conferred by implication on those for whose benefit the direction was made a corresponding right to receive such instruction. In the course of his judgment McMahon J. said:

> "It is not seriously disputed that the constitutional duty of the State to provide for free primary education creates a corresponding right to receive primary education on the part of those for whom it is designed."[3]

The Supreme Court judgment

This view that the duty on the State created a corresponding right to primary education was endorsed by O'Higgins C.J. when the High Court judgment was later appealed to the Supreme Court where he stated:

> "Article 42. s.4, of the Constitution lays down that 'the State shall provide **for** free primary education . . .' These words impose an obligation on the State which is of general application to all citizens. Article 10 of the Constitution of the Irish Free State provides expressly for the citizen's rights rather than for the State's duty.
>
> That Article of the former Constitution stated: 'All citizens of the Irish Free State (Saorstát Éireann) have the right to free elementary education.' However, the imposition of the duty under Article 42, s.4, of the Constitution creates a corresponding right in those in whose behalf it is imposed to receive what must be provided.
>
> In my view, it cannot be doubted that citizens have the right to receive what it is the State's duty to provide for under Article 42, s.4. . . . What was involved was the denial of a constitutional guarantee given to the children attending the affected schools and the breakdown of the arrangements which the Minister had made for the honouring of this guarantee."[4]

The version of Article 42.4 in Irish the first official language of the State is: "Ní foláir don Stát socrú a dhéanamh chun bunoideachas *a bheith ar fáil* in aisce," while the English version is: "The State shall provide for free primary

---

3. *ibid.* at 108.
4. *ibid.* at 121–122.

The Supreme Court Judgment

education . . .". The Irish version clearly imposes an obligation on the State to make arrangements that primary education is available free of charge. There are no guidelines as to the nature of these arrangements, whether they are to be financial, administrative or legislative or indeed all three.

Airteagal 42:

> 1. "Admhaíonn an Stát gurb é . . . ná ar dhualgas doshannta tuistí chun oideachas de réir a n-acmhainne *a chur ar fáil* dá gclainn. . . .
>
> 2. Tig le tuistí an t-oideachas sin *a chur ar fáil* dá gclainn ag baile . . .".

In Article 42.1 and 2 the words "a chur ar fáil" are presented in the English text as "to provide". Is there a difference between "a chur ar fáil" and "a bheith ar fáil"? In the present writers opinion the phrase "a chur ar fáil" involves taking positive action whereas "a bheith ar fáil" is more passive. Significantly O'Higgins C.J. referred to the Irish version and commented:

> "In the portion of Article 42, s.4 which deals with free primary education the State's duty is declared to be, in the English text, "to provide for" and in the Irish text "socrú a dhéanamh chun bunoideachas a bheith ar fáil in aisce." If there were a conflict between the English and Irish texts such must be resolved upon the proper interpretation of the Irish text. In my view the difference indicated is more apparent than real."[5]

Kenny J. in the Supreme Court (with whom a majority of the judges agreed) stated:

> "The distinction between providing free education and providing for it is brought out vividly in the Irish version which is 'ní foláir don Stát socrú a dhéanamh chun bunoideachas a bheith ar fáil in aisce' whose agreed literal translation is: 'The State must make arrangements to have basic education available free'."[6]

Kenny J. then continued:

> "I think that the change from Article 10 of the Constitution of the Irish free State: 'All citizens of the Irish Free State (Saorstát Éireann) have the right to free elementary education' was intended to emphasize that the State's obligation was not to educate but to provide for it . . .

> The trial judge (Mr. Justice McMahon) held that the circular was an unlawful interference with the constitutional rights of the infant plaintiffs to free primary education.

---

5. *ibid.* at 122.
6. *ibid.* at 126. The present writer would point out that the word socrú is singular and arrangement is also singular. My own translation would be: "The State must make an arrangement/provision towards elementary education being available free (as a boon)."

I think that he was right in doing so: it is significant that INTO and the members of its central executive have not appealed against this finding. Therefore, INTO have been held to have caused an unlawful interference with the constitutional rights of the infant plaintiffs . . .".

It was in this manner that the provisions of Article 42.4. of the Constitution were held to confer on the plaintiffs a right to receive free primary education. The existence of the constitutional right as distinct from whether the INTO action amounted to a lawful or unlawful interference with that right, were separate issues.

Constitutional Interpretation

The late Professor John Kelly referring[7] to the technique of constitutional interpretation used by the Irish courts, even in relation to the fundamental rights Articles, stated that the methods adopted by the courts in interpreting the Constitution were not above criticism. He stated:

> "I think the Supreme Court has in some cases gone much too far in its over-literal interpretation of a document not originally intended to be so minutely parsed and scrutinised.
>
> Indeed, in one case, the court put itself in the really unsustainable position of deciding a point on the ground that the Irish verb used to render an English phrase was in the future rather than in the present tense, while the English phrase was open to either a present or a future construction, and that the future sense of the Irish must therefore prevail, although plenty of other examples showed that the present construction was the one that accorded with actual known practice."[8]

This of course, is a subjective view. The reason cited by Professor Kelly for this conclusion is that the Irish version of the text arrived later in the Dáil than the original draft in English. He also claimed that the Irish version was scarcely debated at all, let alone properly analysed and that the "possible divergent implications of Irish usage" were not examined. These observations are undoubtedly correct in relation to the sequence of introduction and the debate but there is no basis for concluding that the Irish version was not properly analysed or understood.

1937 Drafts

A study of the drafts of the 1937 Constitution and of the correspondence associated with its drafting contained in the De Valera Papers, indicates that

---

7. Kelly, "Fundamental Rights and the Constitution" in Farrell, ed., *De Valera's Constitution and Ours* (1988) p. 170.
8. Kelly, *The Irish Constitution* (1st ed., 1980), pp. 140-141 referring to *The State (Ennis) v. Farrell* [1966] I.R.107.

the framers were conscious that it would be subject to careful scrutiny. Professor Kelly,[9] however, states it should be borne in mind, that at the time, no one thought it necessary to scrutinise closely or indeed at all the linguistic usage of Irish. In relation to the fact that in the case of conflict the Irish text must prevail Professor Kelly suggests that:

> "... one ought not to look for conflicts needlessly; one should I think, bend over backwards to reconcile what may be apparent conflicts by looking at what common sense and practice suggest the drafters and the Dáil intended."[10]

Taken to its conclusion this argument comes perilously close to negativing the primacy of the Irish text, as specified in Article 25.5.4° in the event of conflict with the English version.

In relation to the Irish interpretation in *Crowley* the courts seem to have done as Professor Kelly has suggested but the present writer considers that this may not accord with what the drafters of the Constitution intended *viz.*, that there should only be an obligation on the State to make an arrangement that primary education be available free of charge and not a right or entitlement to it.

The Judges

That Kenny J. endorsed the view of Mc Mahon J. is scarcely surprising given the fact that the judicial extension of constitutional rights had virtually been initiated by him in *Ryan v. Attorney General*[11] and continued by Ó Dálaigh and Walsh J. during the 1960s and 1970s. Having succeeded in introducing new rights on a basis of non-interpretative review it was an even easier task in *Crowley* which was closer to interpretative review.

Existence of Right Acknowledged

Besides from the beginning the existence of the constitutional right had been virtually conceded. Even at first instance McMahon J. in the High Court remarked: "*It is not seriously disputed* that the constitutional duty of the State to provide for free primary education creates a corresponding right to receive primary education on the part of those for whom it is designed"[12] and in the Supreme Court it was submitted on behalf of the INTO, that there was no evidence that INTO intended to injure the children, that the teachers had a constitutional right to withdraw their services that: "the injury to *the children's constitutional right* was merely incidental to the exercise by INTO members of

---

9. Above, n.7.
10. *ibid.*, p. 171.
11. [1965] I.R. 294.
12. Above, n.2, at 108 (emphasis added).

their constitutional rights."[13] As a consequence, it may be that the existence of the right received a somewhat cursory examination, the main judgments being directed towards liability in damages and the obligation on the State.

In the circumstances, the right to free primary education was a constitutional right recognised more by consensus than by determination of law. The High Court merely recorded that consensus as a finding in its judgment.

That fact that the INTO did not dispute the existence of the right is consistent with the policy of that organisation as first expressed by its general secretary T.J. O'Connell in the Dáil in 1922 when he sought to have school attendance at free primary education made compulsory throughout the whole of the Free State.[14] The decision of the INTO in the *Crowley* case fifty odd years later not to contest the existence of a constitutional right to free primary education may have been based on a determination that it was unwise for them to do so or to be seen to do so. The acquiescence of the State is more difficult to understand.

The State acknowledgment of the existence of the right must, however, have received a slight set-back after the McMahon judgment, even though counsel would have envisaged the matter eventually being resolved by the Supreme Court. Acknowledgment of the right was one thing, acceptance of liability another. Acquiescence in the acknowledgment of the right was alright if it accorded with the *de facto* position which after all was the basis of state expenditure on primary education as justified in the estimates.

De Valera Papers

The decision in *Crowley v. Ireland* was handed down in 1980, some years before the release of the De Valera papers, which in the author's opinion clearly indicate that there was no intention to confer a right to free primary education. The statement of McMahon J.[15] that it was not seriously disputed that the duty imposed on the State created a corresponding right to receive such education anticipated the judgment (in part) and had the De Valera papers been available they may not have influenced the court or contributed significantly to the judgment.

Subsequent events seem to indicate that most if not all of the De Valera papers would not have been regarded as being of legal significance in determining the issue. In 1988 the Supreme Court considered the admissibility of some of the De Valera Papers when counsel sought to introduce them to elucidate the meaning of the words 'inalienable' and 'imprescriptible' in the Constitution in a case entitled *Re Article 26 and the Adoption (No. 2)*

---

13. *ibid.* at 109 (emphasis added).
14. *Dáil Debates*, Cols. 224-225, November 17, 1922.
15. Above, n.2, at 108.

Bill 1987.[16] In the event they were ruled inadmissible as merely reflecting the views of one individual.

The conclusion reflected in the title of Brian Farrell's book, *De Valera's Constitution and Ours*, did not, apparently, carry any significance for the judges. But Professor Kelly's advice in reference to the divergent implications of the Irish text that "one ought not to look for conflicts needlessly" was obviously adopted by the Court.[17]

The INTO

It was also considered significant by both the Supreme Court in *Crowley*[18] and by Carroll J. in *Hayes v. Ireland*[19] that the INTO did not appeal the decision of McMahon J. that the directive of August 1976 issued by the INTO to all their members in the areas adjoining Drimoleague, directing them not to enrol pupils from Drimoleague was an unlawful interference with the constitutional rights of the infant plaintiffs to free primary education.

Chief Justice Finlay in *Conway v. INTO*[20] commented that while Ireland, the Minister for Education and the Attorney General did appeal a finding of liability in the Crowley case, the INTO did not, and he was satisfied, having regard to what was clearly *the acceptance of liability*, that the defendants were bound by the findings made by McMahon J. in the High Court in *Crowley v. Ireland*.

Depending on one's point of view the decision of the Supreme Court results from either the failure of the constitutional draftsmen to correctly state or reflect the intention of De Valera not to give a right to free primary education, by negativing his use of the preposition for or the wrongful interpolation of such a right by the courts.

The Role of the Courts

The questions raised by non-interpretative review, *i.e.* "the elaborating and enforcing by the Courts of various values not expressly included in the constitution" in the words of Peter Sutherland, S.C.[21] "give rise to greatest difficulty

---

16. [1989] I.L.R.M. 266. See *Student Law Reporter* [1990] at p. 63: See also *Wavin Pipes Ltd. v. Hepworth Iron Co. Ltd.*, unreported, High Court, Costello J., May 8, 1981, where the Parliamentary history of the Patents Act, 1964 was used as a guide to statutory interpretation; *Bourke v. Attorney General* [1972] I.R. 36 where the Supreme Court examined the *travaux preparatoires* of the European Convention on Extradition in the interpretation of a statute and *Attorney General v. S.I.T. Ltd* (1960) 94 I.L.T.R. 161 where the preamble to the Constitution was used as an interpretation aid. Chap. 14 below.
17. Above, n.7, p. 171.
18. Above, n.2, at 128.
19. [1987] I.L.R.M. 651 at 654.
20. [1991] I.L.R.M. 497 at 500–501.
21. Sutherland, "Twin perspectives" in Farrell (ed.), *De Valera's Constitution and Ours* (1988).

regarding the permissible limits of judicial intervention." The decision in *Crowley v. Ireland* must inevitably raise questions not just about the correctness of the court's decision but also about the parameters and extent of the court's constitutional function.

Professor James Casey states:

> "Judicial review is built into Bunreacht na hÉireann in the plainest terms.... Its operation in practice may have produced some controversial results, but those results are based upon principles stated or implicit in the text. So it can hardly be said that judicial review is undemocratic."[22]

As an issue of fact, the power of judicial review (at present) extends to implying constitutional rights and not merely to interpreting the correct meanings. Whether it should do so is a separate issue.

Richard F. Humphreys commenting on literalism has stated:

> "To by-pass the literal meaning of a text by some form of harmonious, purposive or originalist interpretation is in a sense to create a parallel and intangible text alongside the tangible one. It is to encourage the view that the task of the courts is to refine judicial doctrines rather than elucidate the positive law. It is to create the danger that a word means what the interpreter chooses it to mean, neither more or less."[23]

The suggestion, so beloved of academic constitutional commentators, that the judicial activism of the Supreme Court during the 1960s and 1970s in interpolating constitutional rights from the Constitution, filled a lacuna created by the inactivity of the legislature, may raise the spectre of the doctrine of the separation of powers and the parameters of legitimate judicial activity in this regard. This is a matter which has yet to receive the attention it deserves in this jurisdiction.

In relation to the constitutional right to education. In the author's view the De Valera papers reflect more than the opinion of one man. They contain the submission from the Department of Education and the conclusion of the constitutional commission not to include a right to free primary education.

Chief Justice Finlay[24] referring to the role of the courts in constitutional matters has quoted former Chief Justice O'Higgins delivering the judgment of

---

22. Casey, "Changing the Constitution" in Farrell (ed.), *op. cit.* above, p. 160. Article 34.3.2 of the Constitution states: "Save as otherwise provided by this Article, the jurisdiction of the High Court shall extend to the question of the validity of any law having regard to the provisions of this Constitution ..." and this is the meaning of judicial review in this context. It does not embrace the wider meaning of a jurisdiction exercised by declaratory order against administrative bodies or the scrutiny of administrative determinations. See J.M. Evans, *de Smith's Judicial Review of Administrative Action* (4th ed., 1980) p. 28.
23. Humphreys, "Reflections on the role and functioning of the Supreme Court" (1990) 12 D.U.L.J (N.S.) 127 at p. 132.
24. "The Constitution, Fifty Years On", *Supplement to Irish Law Times*, February 1988, p. 14.

the Court of Criminal Appeal in *The People v. Madden*[25] which noted with approval the views of Chief Justice Carroll in *Youman v. The Commonwealth* that:

> "... in the exercise of their great powers courts have no higher duty to perform than those involving the protection of the citizen in the civil rights guaranteed to him by the Constitution and if at any time the protection of these rights should delay or even defeat the ends of justice in the particular case it is better for the public good that this should happen than that a great constitutional mandate should be nullified."[26]

One wonders if pragmatism and expediency has a role in constitutional interpretation? Critics of the *Crowley* judgment may conclude that it has.

Gerard Hogan writing about constitutional interpretation points out that the lack of consistency applied in the theory or method of constitutional interpretation has been so prevalent that individual judges have utilised whatever method might seem to be most convenient or to offer adventitious support for conclusions they had already reached. He concludes:

> "The task is to find a method of constitutional adjudication that allows the courts to create new rights under the Constitution, if these can be shown to be enduring rather than ephemeral and to respect fundamental community values that transcend pragmatic political judgment."[27]

The Constitution Review Group

The Review Group addressed the issues of providing a more explicit statement of:

1. the obligations on the State to provide free education;
2. the rights of the child to education.

They considered removal of the word "for" but agreed to adopt the alternative approach of enshrining the right of the child to free primary education in the Constitution.

Recommendation

The right of every child to free primary education should be explicitly stated in the Constitution. The Oireachtas should also seriously consider extending this right to second level education as this may be defined by law. If the right is so extended, the new Article might read as follows:

---

25. [1977] I.R. 336.
26. 189 Ky 152.
27. Hogan, *The Constitution of Ireland 1937–1987* (1988) p. 188.

"Every child has a right to free primary and second level education. The State shall provide for such education and shall endeavour to supplement and give reasonable aid to private and corporate educational initiative, and, where appropriate, provide other educational facilities or institutions with due regard, however, for the rights of the parent, especially in the matter of religious and moral formation."

Chapter 4

The Extent of the State's Obligation

Article 42.4 of the Constitution states:

> "The State shall provide for free primary education and shall endeavour to supplement and give reasonable aid to private and corporate educational initiative, and when the public good requires it, provide other educational facilities or institutions with due regard, however, for the rights of parents, especially in the matter of religious and moral formation."

The inclusion of the preposition *for* was of major significance to the Supreme Court in *Crowley v. Ireland*[1] when they held that the relevant obligation of the State under that section was "to provide for" such education and not to supply it. When the plaintiffs in the *Crowley* case applied for a mandatory injunction McWilliam J. accepted the argument that "provide for education" meant effectively provide for education.[2] Some 25 years previously Dr Alfred O'Rahilly wrote in what seems a reasonable interpretation that:

> "the version in the Irish language (Ní foláir don Stát socrú a dhéanamh chun bunoideachas a bheith ar fáil in aisce...) removed any ambiguity: The State must arrange that primary education is available gratuitously. This did not imply that the State, directly or through local bodies must itself undertake primary education, but only that it must make such education available gratuitously, e.g., by subsidising parental enterprise...".[3]

The early drafts of the 1937 Constitution contain an Article stating: "The State shall provide free primary education. ..." the preposition *for* was inserted by De Valera in the April 7, 1937, draft[4] for the reasons so accurately stated by Kenny J. in the Supreme Court judgment which was given before the De Valera papers and the drafts of the Constitution were accessible to the public.

The Irish version states that there is an obligation on the State to make an arrangement. Could it be argued that the obligation is disposed of once the arrangement has been made? Given the constitutional right to free primary

---

1. [1980] I.R. 102.
2. *Crowley v. Ireland*, unreported, High Court, McWilliam J., December 1, 1977, at p. 7 of the judgment.
3. O'Rahilly, *The Constitutional Position of Education in the Republic of Ireland* (1952).
4. 1079/3 De Valera Papers. Franciscan Institute of Celtic Studies and Historical Research, Killiney, Co. Dublin.

education held to exist in the *Crowley* case it would seem that while the State can delegate the provision of free primary education to individuals, groups or private bodies, it cannot absolve itself from responsibility should these fail to provide free primary education sufficient to satisfy the constitutional right of the individual. The provision of buildings and the payment of teachers are aspects of the States obligation that have been referred to in this respect. Vincent Grogan, S.C in 1970 stated: "The State binds itself to provide for free primary education- which would include, where necessary, the provision and maintenance of school buildings and payment of teachers."[5]

Irish Version

Kenny J. delivering the majority judgment of the Supreme Court in the *Crowley* case some years later referred to Article 42.4 and concluded:

> "The effect of this is that the State is to provide the buildings, to pay the teachers who are under no contractual duty to it but to the manager or trustees; to provide means of transport to the school if this is necessary to avoid hardship, and to prescribe minimum standards."[6]

He then referred to the Irish version and to what he called its agreed literal translation:

> "The State must make arrangements to have basic education available free. I think that the change from Article 10 of the Constitution of the Irish Free State-'All citizens of the Irish Free State (Saorstát Éireann) have the right to free elementary education' – was intended to emphasize that the State's obligation was not to educate but to provide for it. Thus, the enormous power which the control of education gives was denied to the State: there was interposed between the State and the child the manager or the committee or board of management."[7]

State Subsidy

The extent of the State's financial arrangements was a matter of concern to another commentator who is reported as stating:

> "There is nothing in the Constitution which says or requires the State to massively fund the educational system and leave control of it, at least in the case of the national school sector, in the hands of the Churches . . . 'Provide for free primary education' can mean, at its lowest level, that the State is only obliged to organise a system to ensure that pupils have access to a school which will educate them at no charge. It does not mean that the State has to finance the system, either partially or totally, so that, for instance, teacher's salaries do not have to be paid for out of the public purse. In the organisation of the system the

---

5. Grogan, "Schools under the Constitution", *Studies*, Winter, 1970.
6. Above, n.1, at 126.
7. Above, n.1, at 126–127.

State need do no more than establish a curriculum and provide an inspectorate to ensure a minimum standard of teaching and academic achievement."[8]

Sweet music indeed to the ears of the Department and the hard pressed taxpayer. Unfortunately the extent of the obligation depends on the existing circumstance. The author doubts that the State would fulfil its obligation to "provide for" were it merely to do the above.

A case can be made, and indeed has been made that Irish primary schools are under-funded. The INTO has claimed that the full cost of primary education should be borne by the State.[9] In a submission to an OECD team the union stated that the current capitation grant per pupil was £24 from the Department of Education and £6 from local sources: ". . . the combined contributions fell short of the running costs of the schools." The union submission quoted a survey conducted by school managers in the Dublin area which showed that there was a shortfall of £8.90 per pupil between the actual per capita cost and the capitation grant.

Judicial Opinions

In the *Crowley* case the argument was advanced on behalf of the State that if the State had set up the necessary machinery to provide for free primary education, as it had done, that was all that was required of it. This argument was rejected by McWilliam J. on the basis that it was clearly the constitutional duty of the State to see that children did receive it by virtue of Article 42.3.2° although the qualification "in view of actual conditions" might have been relevant to the case. The late Professor Kelly stated: "the requirements of actual conditions are the only standard by which not merely the level, but also the kind of compulsory education can, in reason or in law, be determined."[10]

The obligation imposed on the State to provide for free primary education was referred to in the *Crowley* case in terms of effectiveness by Chief Justice O'Higgins who thought:

> "If what has been provided proves ineffective or unworkable due to a change in circumstances, it seems to me that this does not relieve the State or the Minister from seeking alternative or other means or methods to provide what is guaranteed to children by the Constitution."[11]

O'Higgins C.J. accepted that the correct meaning of the words used in Article 42.4 was to oblige the State to see that machinery exists under which and in

---

8. McKillen, Campaign to Separate Church & State, Letters to the Editor, *Irish Times*, December 2, 1988.
9. See *Irish Independent*, December 19, 1988. In 1995 capitation grants were increased from £28 to £38 per child.
10. Kelly, "Education and the Irish State" (1994) XXXIV Ir. Jur. 85-86 (*N.S.*).
11. Above, n.1, at 124.

accordance with which such education is in fact provided. He stated:

> "The State discharges this obligation by paying teachers in national schools owned by the Churches, by making grants available for the renovation, repair, and at times, building of national schools, by paying for teaching and for school books and by the provision of a proper curriculum and appropriate supervision. It is only when such assistance to the church schools is not possible or cannot succeed in providing what is required, that the State must act directly to do so."[12]

In the event the majority of the Supreme Court, held that the absence of free primary education in an area for a considerable period of time furnishes prima facie evidence that the State is not performing its duty and imposes on the State the onus of rebutting that evidence. The total evidence in the *Crowley* case established that the State had not failed to provide for free primary education for the benefit of the plaintiffs. This decision has been described as "a most unsatisfactory decision" by Professor James Casey:[13] "Its result is to validate total Ministerial inactivity in such circumstances."

Comments

Professor Osborough commented:

> "Not even what is called 'the minimum tolerable response' above, namely, insistence on the provision of transport facilities to neighbouring schools, thus in the end received a constitutional buttress and 'a majority appended their *imprimatur* to a substantial limitation on the right of the citizen to secure redress'."[14]

Gerry Whyte states: "the majority judgment in Crowley provided a constitutional *imprimatur* for the inactivity of the Department of Education in the face of industrial action."[15]

The fact that McWilliam J. in the High Court ordered that the Minister provide transport to the neighbouring schools, did seem to indicate that the Minister was remiss in not doing so previously, but this had no consequence for the State. A clue to the Supreme Courts attitude may be found in the emphasis placed on the length of the dispute. McMahon J. stated in the High Court[16] that

---

12. Above, n.1 at 122–123.
13. Casey, *Constitutional Law in Ireland* (2nd ed., 1987), pp. 518–519.
14. Osborough, "Education in the Irish Law and Constitution" (1978), xiii Ir. Jur. 145 (*N.S.*) at p. 166 and D.U.L.J. (1979–80) at 101.
15. Whyte, "Education and the Constitution" in Lane, *Religion Education and the Constitution* (1992), p. 93.
16. Above, n.1, at 112. Note that the statutory duty imposed on every LEA by s. 8 of the English Education Act 1944 has not been considered to be absolute. In *R. v. ILEA, ex parte Ali, The Times*, February 21, 1990, the judgment of a Queen's Bench Divisional Court states: "A local education authority, faced with a situation where, without fault on their part, they had not complied with the standard which the section set for a limited period of time, were not automatically in breach of the section."

if it could be foreseen that the breakdown was merely temporary, the State might be justified in taking no action. Counsel had contended that the period from March 1976, to December 1977, amounted merely to a temporary breakdown in the system but did not constitute a denial of the children's right to free primary education having regard to the nature of the system. The Supreme Court held that:

> "the absence of free primary education in an area for a considerable period of time furnishes prima facie evidence that the State is not performing its duty to provide for that education in that area, and imposes on the State the onus of rebutting the evidence"[15]

and Kenny J. concluded that:

> ". . . the whole of the evidence must be looked at and it may show that the minister has not been at fault. In the present case I think the totality of the evidence, oral and written, and the inferences that are to be drawn from it, fail to establish that there has been a breach of the constitutional duty imposed on the State."[18]

It should be remembered that the minister had provided transport to neighbouring schools from January 1978 albeit, as a result of a mandatory injunction by McWilliam J. requiring him to do so. The appeal to the Supreme Court was in part against the finding that the State had been in default of a constitutional obligation during the period from April, 1976, to December, 1977 when transport was not provided and although the "bussing" has been described by Professor Osborough[19] as the minimum tolerable response its implementation meant that the minister had not been completely inactive in the dispute at the time of the Supreme Court judgment.

The minister has been faulted for not freely taking this initiative[20] yet, it must have been an option considered by the Department, who were probably dissuaded by the possibility of the escalation of the strike if they did so. Similar considerations would undoubtedly have influenced the minister in refusing to accede to the parents requests to change the Rules for National Schools to permit parents to employ unqualified teachers, provide parents with money to employ new teachers or from taking the initiative of establishing a model school.

In addition the bussing of children to school was one of the obligations foreseen by the Department in 1934, which might arise if a right to free primary education were enshrined in the 1937 Constitution, and therefore one of the

---

17. *ibid.* at 103.
18. *ibid., per* Kenny J. at 129–130.
19. Above, n.14.
20. *ibid.* at 166 Professor Osborough states: "Twenty months of apparent official inactivity led in the end only to the inauguration of a taxi-service to adjacent schools, and the Department of Education had had to be brought to court before they would agree even to that . . .".

reasons why the right to free elementary education enunciated in Article 10 of the 1922 Constitution was dropped. It could also be argued that the acceptance by the Department of an obligation to bus would have been tantamount to accepting that a right to free primary education existed before the issue had been legally adjudicated.

The desire to bring about a quick resolution of the dispute inspired the INTO directive not to enrol Drimoleague students in the neighbouring schools whereas in retrospect the escalation by strike action would have been the safer legal option. The method used went further than a conflict of two constitutional rights and indeed in *Hayes v. Ireland* [21] Carroll J. opined that the union had made an error of judgment in the method they chose and added:

> ". . . perhaps if the INTO had chosen the wider non- discriminatory weapon of a country-wide strike which would have affected all the children of the State, they would probably not be here today. In a very difficult and frustrating situation they came to the wrong decision." [22]

Rules for National Schools

An action against the Minister on the basis of the National School Rules may have been considered prior to the issue of the directive but was probably discarded because of the long time delay in getting the matter before the courts. Significantly McWilliam J. in his judgment in the *Crowley* case on December 1, 1977 stated:

> "I have been referred to the Rules for National Schools under the Department of Education given under the hand and seal of the Minister for Education on 22nd., January, 1965, and those of the Minister for Finance on 11th., February, 1965 . . . as no party has contested their validity, I will accept that they are binding. Certainly, until revoked or altered, it appears to me that they should be observed by the Minister for Education." [23]

He then commented:

> "An affidavit filed on behalf of the first three defendants (*Ireland, The Minister for Education and The Attorney General*) is vague as to the implementation of these rules by the Minister, either in this case or generally."

The legal status of the Rules and Regulations as they affect national teachers came before the Supreme Court in two earlier cases. In the first case *McEneaney v. Minister for Education*,[24] it was held that they constituted representations legally binding on the Minister for Education, made to both managers and teachers as to the application of the funds entrusted to the Minister by the

---

21. [1987] I.L.R.M. 651.
22. *ibid.* at 654.
23. Above, n.2, at p. 3 of the judgment.
24. [1941] I.R. 43.

Oireachtas. In the second case of *O'Callaghan v. Minister for Education*[25] it was declared that the representations contained in the 1932 version of the Rules were binding on the Minister and that the Rules and Regulations governing the position, duties, rights and emoluments of national teachers which were in operation when a national teacher entered the national education service formed part of a continuing contract of employment which persisted so long as the teacher remained in the service. Kingsmill Moore J. delivering the judgment of the Supreme Court stated: "If the rules in force when a teacher enters the service are to be represented to him as to the conditions of service, he should be able to rely on the continuance of such conditions subject to such provisions for change as are contained in the Rules themselves."[26]

McWilliam J. in the *Crowley* case stated that if the Minister consented to the permanent appointment, it would appear that he had overlooked breaches of the spirit and intention of his own rules.

Stanley's letter of 1831[27] providing for the formation of a Board of Commissioners of National Education to administer state aid to schools stated that the Board would have complete control over schools erected under its auspices or which placed themselves under its management. The letter also provided: "A full power will, of course, be given to the board to make such regulations upon matters of detail, not inconsistent with the spirit of these instructions, as they may judge best qualified to carry into effect the intentions of the government and the legislature." There is no record of any statutory assignment of such powers to the Board. In 1832 Regulations were drawn up by the Board and submitted to the government authorities but these were replaced by what were called Regulations and Directions adopted in October 1833. These latter Regulations were appended to the reports of the Lord Lieutenant and were put before Parliament and Government in various forms.[28]

The Ministers and Secretaries Act 1924 transferred and continued the powers, duties and functions of The Commissioners of National Education in Ireland and of The Commissioners of Education in Ireland (endowed schools) in relation to primary education and provided that they should be assigned to and administered by the Minister for Education. These powers, duties and functions included those of making rules and regulations prescribing the conditions upon which State aid would be provided to schools. The 1924 Act

---

25. Unreported, Supreme Court, Kingsmillmoore J., March 31, 1955.
26. *ibid.*, p. 3 of the judgment.
27. Akenson, *The Irish Education Experiment* (1990), App., pp. 392–402 and Hyland and Milne, *Irish Educational Documents* (1987) pp. 105–107.
28. See 1834 Parliamentary Papers, Vol. 40 and 1837 Parliamentary Papers, Vol. 9, p. 36. They contained sections dealing with Building School Houses, Assistance towards the Construction of Schools. Tuition and Attendance, Books to be used, Teachers and Miscellaneous matters. Note that *Twelve Practical Rules for the Teachers of National Schools*, were published in App. XXVII to the Thirteenth Report of the Commissioner of National Education in Ireland in 1846.

affected a transfer and assignment of the power to make Rules but it does not provide a statutory basis for them and the Constitution of 1937 has not altered their status. Sean P. MacCarthy (TUI) in the Report of the Primary Education Review Body,[29] pointed out that doubts were cast on the legal standing of rules and circular letters and recommended that the matter be referred to the Law Reform Commission. The most recent edition of the Rules for National Schools was published in 1965 and subsequent amendments by way of Circular letter have been sent to each Board of Management. It is suggested that new education legislation should specifically give the Minister for Education statutory power to make such rules and regulations.

The Kenny Judgment

Professor Osborough states:

> "The second ground in the (Crowley) judgment was Kenny J.'s assertion that the right in the citizen correlative to the State's duty in regard to primary education would only be justiciable as against the State where it could be shown that the latter had failed to vindicate that right by *law* (Article 40.3.1): no valid claim, therefore, could be brought against the State where, in essence, the complaint concerned ministerial inactivity . . .".[30]

It should be noted that the Kenny judgment does not state that a claim can never lie against the State it merely states that the claim against the State under Article 40.3.1°, would only be justiciable as against the State where it could be shown that the State had failed to vindicate that right by *its laws*.

The word used in Article 40.3.1° is "laws" and subsequent to the publication of Professor Osborough's article Kenny J. in *The People v. Shaw* explained:

> "The obligation to implement this guarantee is imposed not on the Oireachtas only, but on each branch of the State which exercises the powers of legislating, executing and giving judgment on those laws: Article 6. The words 'laws' in Article 40. s.3 is not confined to laws which have been enacted by the Oireachtas but comprehends the laws made by judges and by Ministers of State when they make Statutory Instruments or Regulations."[31]

The Contra–Kenny Interpretation

A number of very cogent arguments against Kenny J.'s interpretation and emphasis on the word "laws" have been advanced by Hogan and Whyte in the third edition of J.M. Kelly's *The Irish Constitution*.[32] They submit that:

---

29. See Minority Report, December, 1990, p. 122.
30. Above, n.14, at 180 (emphasis added).
31. [1982] I.R. 1 at 62.
32. Hogan and Whyte, *Kelly: The Irish Constitution* (3rd ed., 1994) pp. 788–789.

The Contra-Kenny Interpretation

1. On a number of occasions the courts have accepted that the State's duty may be discharged through the law of torts.[33]
2. A number of personal rights have been successfully asserted against the State in a non-statutory context.[34]
3. Article 40.3 has been used in private law disputes.[35]
4. "laws" should include a duty to remedy legislative omissions.

The present writer would endorse this view and suggest that the word "laws" should be interpreted in a general sense rather than in the sense of legislation. If the word "law" rather than "laws" had been used the meaning might have been clearer. The thrust of the Article could well be to cover situations where the position is such that no legal remedy is available under the existing law either in contract, tort, criminal law, etc. It is also suggested that had the framers of the Constitution intended the word "laws" to mean legislation, they would have used the word legislation as they did in Article 44.2.4°. Also of significance is the Irish text having regard to the fact that under Article 25.4 in case of conflict between the texts of the Constitution, the Irish language version shall prevail. The Irish text uses the word "dlíthe" and not "reachtaíocht" (legislation).

A claim in the *Crowley* case under Article 42.4 of a right correlative to the duty imposed, was a different matter to a claim under Article 40. It may be that some comments take the judgment too far and discount the element of fault which the court significantly introduced in relation to the duty under Article 42. The risk of the Minister provoking a country-wide strike, if he took any direct action or recruited non INTO teachers and the misapplication of public moneys had he paid unqualified teachers were considered by the court in arriving at the conclusion that he was not in default and that the State had not failed to discharge the duty, to provide for free primary education, imposed on it by Article 42. The idea that the nomination of the principal could have been withdrawn by the manager or that the Minister could have withheld his approval (Rule 15) does not seem to have been considered.

The Department's recognition of Fr Crowley's nominee as temporary principal might have been open to legal challenge particularly since they sub-

---

33. See *Hanrahan v. Merck Sharpe and Dohme* [1988] I.L.R.M. 629 and *Sweeney v. Duggan* [1991] 2 I.R. 274.
34. *Kennedy v. Ireland* [1987] I.R. 587.
35. *Educational Company of Ireland v. Fitzpatrick* [1961] I.R. 345. (Note that Finlay C.J. delivering the Supreme Court judgment in *Re Article 26 and the Adoption (No.2) Bill, 1987* [1989] I.L.R.M. 266 stated: "The State would, in any event, by virtue of Article 40.3 of the Constitution be obliged as far as practicable to vindicate the personal rights of the child whose parents have failed in their duty to it."

sequently acknowledged that one of the applicants did possess the desired standard of general suitability.[36] Had the Minister withheld consent the appointment of a temporary principal may not have been expedient. In *Phelan v. Co. Laoise VEC & Parsons*[37] a case involving a similar dispute within the vocational system the minister withheld consent and McWilliam J. in the High Court said:

> "In the absence of the Minister's consent, Mr. Parsons was not appointed Principal and the subterfuge of appointing him acting Principal and leaving him in that position without the consent of the Minister was wholly improper."

He also pointed out that once a vacancy for a Principal existed a VEC had a statutory obligation to fill it and if they failed to do so, and adopted the subterfuge of appointing an unqualified person as "acting" until such time as he did qualify, an affected party could apply for a mandatory injunction directing them to fill the position forthwith.

Is the State's duty an Absolute One?

If the duty imposed on the State to provide for free primary education does not translate to the State being liable if it is not available in all circumstances, the corresponding right is not an absolute one. In relation to the State's duty McWilliam J. clearly suggests that this is the case:

> ". . . although the State is bound to provide proper free primary education, it seems to be obvious that circumstances could arise when it would be unreasonable to insist that this duty should be performed under the actual conditions existing at any particular time."[38]

He examined the conditions which existed in the parish and concluded that the State should provide transport to other schools. Two aspects of the McWilliam J. judgment attract one's attention namely:

1. the omission of reference to the preposition *for* and;

2. his use of the words "actual conditions" in the context of this section of Article 42.

Both of which will be considered later.

His view of the obligation imposed on the State was supported later by McMahon J. who stated:

> "It appears to me that the State is not necessarily in breach of its constitutional obligation when there is a breakdown in the system in any parish, and that the matter will depend on the circumstances and causes of the breakdown. Where the breakdown is due to a dispute between teachers and management, then it appears to me that, if it can be foreseen that the breakdown is merely temporary,

---

36. *Hayes v. Ireland* [1987] I.L.R.M. 651 at 653, *per* Carroll J.
37. Unreported, High Court, McWilliam J., February 28, 1977.
38. Above, n.2, at p. 8 of the judgment.

the State may be justified in taking no action and in allowing the parties involved in the dispute to settle their differences."[39]

His Lordship considered that when the obligation to provide for free education was not being discharged, the onus was on the State through the Minister for Education to show that the absence of free primary education was not due to a breach of obligation on the part of the State. He then concluded that:

> "the state of affairs which prevailed in Drimoleague schools from March, 1976 to December, 1977, provides prima facie evidence of a breach of obligation on the part of the State, and that the Minister has failed to displace the prima facie interference that the State was in default of its constitutional obligation."[40]

The Supreme Court rejected the finding that the State was not fulfilling its constitutional obligation and placed even greater emphasis on the question of fault. Kenny J. stated:

> "The failure of the Minister to call evidence does not of itself establish that he had committed a breach of his constitutional obligation. I agree that when free primary education has not been provided for an area for a considerable period, that fact, if looked at in isolation, may be taken as prima facie evidence of a failure to carry out the constitutional obligation so as to cast on the Minister a duty to show that he has not been at fault."[41]

The court explained that the whole of the evidence must be looked at and that it might show that the Minister had *not been at fault*. Kenny J. stated:

> "In the present case I think the totality of the evidence, oral and written, and the inferences that are to be drawn from it, fail to establish that there has been a breach of the constitutional duty imposed on the State. The Minister's sole duty in this case is to provide for free primary education for those who want it."[42]

The constitution does not require that the State shall provide for free primary education "having regard to actual conditions" nonetheless, if the State is just a facilitator, it appears that it may discharge its duty once it has made provision for primary education even if such is not available. Such would probably be the case in the event of a nation-wide strike by teachers.

"Actual conditions" This term was used by McWilliam J. in relation to the State's duty to provide for free primary education although it is not a term used in Article 42.4. These words are used in 42.3.2° in relation to the State requiring that children receive a certain minimum education. Was this an attempt by McWilliam J. to import this clause from section 3 into section 4 or was it just a coincidental choice of language?[43]

---

39. Above, n.1, at 112.
40. *ibid.* at 112.
41. *ibid.* at 129.
42. *ibid.* at 130.
43. See Chap. 7 below, Rights and Duties of the Family and Parents.

Article 42.4:

> "The State shall provide for free primary education and shall endeavour to supplement and give reasonable aid to private and corporate educational initiative and, when the public good requires it, provide other educational facilities or institutions with due regard, however for the rights of parents, especially in the matter of religious and moral formation."

"shall" The word "shall" is mandatory. It is also noteworthy that the word shall is not repeated in the Irish text before the word "iarracht".

"Endeavour" indicates that supplementing and giving reasonable aid is an aspirational provision. In relation to the use of the word "endeavour" in Article 41.2.2°, Dr Alfred O'Rahilly described it[44] as a phrase which was not susceptible of precise appraisment. Certainly the phrase is weaker than "shall ensure." *The Shorter Oxford English Dictionary* Volume 1 describes endeavour as: "The action of endeavouring; effort directed to attain an object; a strenuous attempt; to do one's utmost; to try to fulfil (a law)." *Collins English Dictionary* defines it as: "to attempt, to try, to strive, to aim, to exert physical strength or intellectual power for the accomplishment of an object." The Irish version is "iarracht a dhéanamh", in the writer's opinion "make an attempt or effort".

On one reading of Article 42.4 namely: "That the State . . . and shall endeavour to supplement . . ." means that while an endeavour *must* be made to supplement, it need not lead to success in doing so. It is suggested that such an interpretation is probably in keeping with the Irish version of the text. It has also been suggested that the use of the word "endeavour" enables the State to refuse claims for financial assistance towards the establishment of private schools if it wishes to do so. (See, however, comments of Michael McDowell, S.C., below in Chapter 13.) Until now the State has refused to supplement or give reasonable aid to schools which do not follow the prescribed curriculum and this interpretation has never been legally challenged. If it is correct, and this provision allows the State a discretion to impose conditions, there is no reason why compliance with the specified curriculum should be the only condition. Why not add adopting a specified management model as another requirement which must be met. This would have significant repercussions in the area of control of education. See Chapters 8–10 below.

To the present writer the use of the word "endeavour" seems to indicate that this provision *is merely aspirational* and not obligatory. But if money has been voted for this general purpose from central government funds, is it still merely aspirational? Does it then become obligatory on the Minister to give aid? It could be suggested that it does.

The Irish version is: "agus *iarracht a dhéanamh chun cabhrú* go réasúnta

---

44. O'Rahilly, *Thoughts on the Constitution* (1937) p. 62. See also *Monkland v. Jack Barclay* [1951] 2 K.B. 252.

Is the State's duty an absolute one?

agus chun cur le tionscnamh oideachais idir phríobháideach agus chumannta . . .". A literal translation of the Irish version is: "and make an attempt to give reasonable help and to assist educational initiatives both private and corporate." This offers no additional assistance as to whether the State is "bound" to, or "obliged" to, give financial aid? How genuine must the "endeavour" be, to prevent the courts intervening?

"private and corporate educational initiative" A small number of primary schools are owned by the State but for the most part our primary/national schools and our secondary schools are part of the private and corporate educational initiative referred to in Article 42.4. They are not in public ownership, they are not managed by central or local government. They are privately owned and managed. Dr. Alfred O'Rahilly has stated that their status is really that of parental or family schools."[45] This provision is the legal authorisation for the payment of grants and public funds towards the support of such schools and it has been suggested that in endowing such schools the State is indirectly endowing religion.[46]

"public good" "and when the public good requires it, provide other educational facilities or institutions with due regard, however for the rights of parents, especially in the matter of religious and moral formation." Michael Forde, in *Constitutional Law of Ireland* states: "It is the legislature which is the principal organ of State to decide what the public good demands in this context."[47] In the event of a challenge the High or Supreme Court would have to decide if the public good did require the provision of other educational facilities or institutions. In *Buckley v. Attorney General*[48] the question of "the exigencies of the common good" was held not to be peculiarly a matter for the legislature, the decision of the legislature thereon, being capable of review by the courts. See Chapter 15 below, "The Common Good".

"provide other educational facilities or institutions" The omission of the preposition "for" after the word provide is of similar significance as its inclusion was in the "provide for" primary education aspect of the *Crowley* case. If the public good requires it, it is mandatory on the State to provide other educational facilities or institutions.

---

45. O'Rahilly, *The Constitutional Position of Education in the Republic of Ireland* (1952) p. 6. Louis McRedmond in a review of Alfred O'Rahilly 111, *Catholic Apologist*, by Anthony Gaughan, Dublin, 1993, in *Studies*, Spring 1994, Vol. 83, No. 329, pp. 112–114 says of O'Rahilly "he traded in polemics, abusive, sarcastic strung together with references culled from writers of whom he approved . . . if the human weakness of a fine mind became evident in disputation, the positive record stood untarnished."
46. UN Report E/CN. 4/1989/44. See the discussion on this topic by Gerry Whyte in "Education and the Constitution", above, n.15, pp. 98–107.
47. Forde, *Constitutional Law of Ireland* (1987) p. 731.
48. [1950] I.R. 67.

In *F.N. v. Minister for Education*[49] Geoghegan J. based his decision on Article 40, Article 42.5 and section 58 of the Childrens Act 1908 that the State was under a constitutional obligation towards the applicant to make suitable arrangements for his containment with treatment. He did not refer to the obligation on the State under Article 42.4 to provide other educational facilities or institutions. The State did not appeal this judgment and in the case of *D.D. (a minor) v. EHB*[50] it was accepted that the State owed a constitutional duty to the applicant to make suitable arrangements to meet his special needs and that it was in breach of this constitutional duty. Costello J. ordered the EHB to care for and accommodate D and also ordered that in the interests of his welfare the Board be authorised to detain him.

Vincent Grogan[51] seems to take the view that the latter part of the section which obliges the State when the public good requires it to provide other educational facilities or institutions relates to secondary, vocational and higher education. The author would suggest that secondary education comes within the ambit of the previous part of the section relating to the giving of reasonable help and assistance to educational initiatives.

Vocational schools, community schools and NIHEs were provided by the State on the basis that the public good required them. In matters of education the Minister for Education is the agent of the State charged with discharging the State's duties and it is on the basis of his/her decision that the requirement of the public good is established. Incidentally, could this be used to justify the paying of chaplains in schools?

The State is obliged to endeavour to give reasonable aid to private primary and secondary schools. The words used in Article 42.4 are "shall endeavour" which would suggest that an endeavour is mandatory. Article 2 of Protocol No 1 of the European Convention on Human Rights[52] stipulates:

> "No person shall be denied the right to education. In the exercise of any functions which it assumes in relation to education and to teaching, *the state shall respect the right of parents to ensure such education and teaching in conformity with their own religious and philosophical convictions*." (Emphasis added. See Chapter 8 below, "Control and Parents").

The right envisaged in this provision is concerned primarily with elementary education but does not require the State to organise its educational system in accordance with a certain religious or philosophical conviction of parents,[53] or to subsidise a particular form of education: it is enough if a State respects these convictions within the existing and developing system.[54]

---

49. Unreported, High Court, Geoghegan J., March 24, 1995.
50. Unreported, High court, Costello J., May 3, 1995.
51. Grogan, "Schools under the Constitution", *Studies*, Winter, 1970 p. 378.
52. Signed on November 4, 1950; ratified February 25, 1953; came into force September 3, 1953.
53. Reference to the case of *Kjeldsen*, ECHR, D 75277/76 (UK) July 5, 1977, 11/147.
54. D 7782/77 (UK) May 2, 1978, 14/179.

Is the State's duty an absolute one?

In *Campbell and Cosans v. U.K.*[55] it was stated that although this right extended primarily to curriculum content and the manner in which the education was conveyed, it also covered the organisation and financing of public education.

"due regard": see Chapter 8 below.

Compulsory School Attendance

A further obligation is imposed on the State under Article 42.3.2° which provides:

> "The State shall, however, as guardian of the common good, require that the children receive a certain minimum education, moral, intellectual and social."

The State carries out this obligation by means of the School Attendance Acts which provide for the compulsory school attendance of children up to age 15. Unless there is reasonable excuse the parent of a child is obliged under the Acts to cause the child to attend a national or other suitable school, *i.e.* a school certified by the Minister. See Chapter 7 below, "Rights and Duties of Family and Parents".

The Constitution Review Group

The Constitution Review Group considered the use of the words: "when the public good requires it" in Article 42.4 and decided that the use of these words might unduly constrain the rights of the State to provide "other education facilities or institutions" and that the words "when the public good requires it" should be replaced with "where appropriate".

Their suggested wording for the new Article is as follows:

> "Every child has a right to free primary and second level education. The State shall provide for such education and shall endeavour to supplement and give reasonable aid to private and corporate educational initiative, and, where appropriate, provide other educational facilities or institutions with due regard, however, for the rights of the parent, especially in the matter of religious and moral formation.

---

55. (1981) 3 E.H.R.R. 531.

Chapter 5

The Meaning of Education

In *Ryan v. Attorney General* [1] the plaintiff claimed that provisions of the Health (Fluoridation of Water Supplies) Act 1960 were void on the grounds, *inter alia*, that they violated the family's right to physical education of the children under Article 42 of the Constitution. In the High Court Kenny J. held, *inter alia* that the word "education" in Article 42.1 of the Constitution is not used in its former sense which included 'rearing and nurturing'. The education referred to in Article 42.1, he stated, having regard to the words of Article 42.2: "Parents shall be free to provide *this* education in their homes or in private schools or in schools recognised or established by the State." must be of a scholastic nature. Therefore the fluoridation of the public water supply (even if it were harmful) did not interfere with or violate the rights given to the family and to parents by Article 42 of the Constitution.

The Irish Version

The Irish version of Article 42.2 is:

"Tig le tuistí an t-oideachas *sin* a chur ar fáil. . . ." The word "sin" means "that" and in the present writer's opinion the English version is incorrect. The translation of the word "sin" as "that" would seem to indicate that the education referred to in section 2 is clearly referable to that in section 1. The word "seo" would have been used to indicate "this".

Counsel for the plaintiff had argued that the word "education" in this Article should be given a wide meaning so that it would include rearing and nurturing. Kenny J. accepted that the word undoubtedly had this meaning at one time but that in 1937 when the Constitution was enacted, this meaning had become obsolete. In the *Shorter Oxford Dictionary 1932*, the meaning, "the process of nourishing or rearing" was marked with a sign to show that this meaning was obsolete in 1933. He commented:

> "Moreover, it seems to me that the terms of this Article show that the word 'education' was not used in this wide sense in the Constitution. Section 1 of the Article recognises the 'right and duty of parents to provide, according to their means, for the religious and moral, intellectual, physical and social education

---

1. [1965] I.R. 294.

of their children', but in section 2 it is provided that the parents are free to provide *this* education in their homes or in schools recognised or established by the State. The education referred to in section 1 must, therefore, be one of a scholastic nature."[2]

Professor Niall Osborough[3] states that Kenny J. may have subscribed unwittingly to the fallacy of *unum nomen unum nominatum*. His logic that the use of the demonstrative adjective *this* before education in section 2 appeared to imply, that the word education was being used in the same sense in both sections 1 and 2 and that the emphasis on a scholastic definition for "education" in the latter half of section 2 meant that the same definition was intended for education in section 1, could be challenged. It would be equally possible to maintain that the word *"this"* indicated that it was not intended to refer to education of an identical type to that in section 2, that it meant education of the kind mentioned in section 1, in so far as it is capable of being imparted by scholastic method.

In the Supreme Court Ó Dálaigh C.J. also rejected the contention that the provision of suitable food and drink for children was physical education. According to Ó Dálaigh C.J.:

> "education essentially is the teaching and training of a child to make the best possible use of his inherent and potential capacities, physical, mental and moral. To teach a child to minimise the dangers of dental cavities by adequate brushing of his teeth is physical education for it induces him to use his own resources. To give him water calculated to minimise the danger of dental cavities is in no way to educate him, physically or otherwise, for it does not develop his resources."[4]

Thus O'Hanlon J. in *O'Donoghue v. Minister for Health*[5] points out: "the Supreme Court adopted a definition of the word 'education' as used in the Constitution which appears to be wider in scope than that referred to by the High Court Judge".

Landers v. Attorney General

Some 10 years after the *Ryan* case in *Landers v. Attorney General*[6] Finlay J. referred to the definition of education in it and commented:

> "This definition in his (Mr. Justice Kenny's) judgment comes at the end of a careful and full analysis of the terms of the Article and of the meaning of the word education, which I would, if it stands unaffected by a decision of the

---

2. Above, n.1, at 310.
3. Osborough, "Education in the Irish Law and Constitution" (1978) XIII Ir. Jur. 145 (*N.S.*) at 170.
4. Above, n.1, at 350–351.
5. Unreported, High Court, O'Hanlon J., May 27, 1993.
6. (1975) 109 I.L.T.R. 1.

Supreme Court, find both an extremely persuasive and entirely acceptable authority.

It is suggested to me on behalf of the plaintiff that the references..in the report of the judgment of the former Chief Justice O'Dalaigh to teaching and training of a child so as to make the best possible use of his potential talents was in some way to be taken as departing from or partly overruling the definition of Mr. Justice Kenny. I do not construe this part of the judgment of the Supreme Court in *Ryan v. Attorney General* in that way nor do I find it in any way inconsistent with the express definition contained in the judgment of Mr. Justice Kenny."[7]

Because of the foregoing Finlay J. then concluded that the proper definition of education as provided for in Article 42 of the Constitution did not, whatever else it included, include the public singing career of a child between the age of seven and ten years, and he explained:

"If the subsections challenged in this case in any way inhibited the training or practice of Michael Landers in his musical accomplishment then a question of his education and the rights guaranteed by the Constitution to the family and to his parents in regard to his education might arise."

Finlay J. found that the restriction imposed by the 1904 Act being challenged in the proceedings, did not touch on the education of Michael Landers as a musician or singer or on any part of his education but only upon his professional public appearance at his then age, and therefore Article 42 was in no way applicable to the proceedings.

O'Donoghue v. Minister for Health

In *O'Donoghue v. Minister for Health*,[8] the State had claimed that such training as could be given to the applicant and benefit him, was not properly describable as "education", and could not be regarded as "primary education" within the meaning of that expression as used in Article 42 of the Constitution. The free primary education guaranteed, was the conventional type of primary education, scholastic in character, exemplified in the curriculum of the national schools, and such education could not be of any benefit to the applicant.

O'Hanlon J. considered[9] that this argument was undermined by the fact that special schools, integrated and recognised as part of the National School system had been established and a special curriculum largely concerned with personal and social development, under such headings as mobility, dress, food and drink, hygiene, health and safety, locomotion, orientation and function had been drawn up. The ordinary national school curriculum always had a significant "non-academic" content. In special schools for the handicapped the emphasis was

---

7. *ibid.* at 5.
8. Above, n.5.
9. *ibid.* at p. 96 of the judgment.

laid on a limited group of subjects, to the exclusion of subjects which would make too great a demand on the intellectual powers of the mentally handicapped.

When one compared the Curriculum for Schools for the Severely and Profoundly Handicapped outlined in Professor Hogg's work on Profound Retardation and Multiple Impairment[10] with the Curriculum "Towards Independence" drawn up by the Department of Education for pupils with moderate mental handicap the actual content of the curriculum put forward as appropriate for schools in each category was largely the same and "is directed towards the promotion of the child's physical, intellectual, emotional, social, moral and aesthetic development to the maximum extent possible"[11] having regard to the child's handicap.

O'Hanlon J. then addressed the difficulty in reconciling the *O'Donoghue* claim with the finding by Kenny J. in *Ryan v. Attorney General* (discussed above) that the word "education" in Article 42.1 of the Constitution is not used in its former sense which included "rearing and nurturing" that it must be of a scholastic nature. He stated:

> "I believe that it has now come to be accepted that trained teachers and the schools environment can make a major contribution to this process (*education of the handicapped*) which cannot – with the best will in the world – be provided as effectively or as successfully by parents and family in the home.
>
> I therefore come to the conclusion that the education to which the Plaintiff in the present case lays claim, in reliance on rights derived from the provisions of Article 42 of the Constitution can be corrrectly described as 'primary education' within the meaning of that phrase as used in Article 42.3.4°."[12]

The State (C.) v. Frawley

The comparable situation in *The State (C.) v. Frawley*[13] regarding the obligation on the State with regard to the provision of special medical attention (see Chapter 6) does not appear to have been considered or referred to in the *O'Donoghue* case but it was considered in 1995 by Geoghegan J. in *F.N. (A minor suing by his next friend M.M.) v. Minister for Education*[14] where he held that on the balance of probabilities the provision of the necessary accommodation and services necessary to meet the requirements of the applicant were "not so impractical or so prohibitively expensive as would come within any notional limit on the State's constitutional obligations."[15]

---

10. Hogg and Sebba, Hester Adrian Research Centre, University of Manchester, 1986.
11. Above, n.5, at pp. 97–98 of the judgment.
12. *ibid.*
13. [1976] I. R. 365. For the facts of the *Frawley* case see Chap. 6, "Children with Special Needs", below.
14. Unreported, High Court, Geoghegan J., March 24, 1995.
15. *ibid.* at p. 9 of the judgment.

Significantly the *Report of the Committee on the Constitution*[16] when considering Article 42.4 felt that the word "primary" should be "deleted and replaced by some clause which would have the effect of imposing on the State the obligation to provide, up to a minimum standard laid down by law, the education needed by the individual to enable him to play a normal role in society."[17] The Committee sought the advice of the Attorney General as to whether it was desirable to alter the existing wording.

The European Commission on Human Rights in *Campbell and Cosans v. U.K.*[18] pointed out that the term "education" is generally understood to mean not only theoretical instruction in a strict sense, but also generally the development and moulding of a childs character and mental powers. In the opinion of the Commission the disciplining of children "must also be considered to form a natural and even inseparable part of the parental duties to educate and teach their children."[19]

The Constitution Review Group

The Constitution Review Group considered whether a definition of education should be included in the Constitution but considered it better "not to attempt to itemise the various aspects of education (for example, 'religious', 'intellectual', 'social') and that Article 42 should simply refer to education". Special arrangements should be made – in relation to state intervention – in respect of religious and moral education.

---

16. 1967.
17. *ibid.*, p. 144.
18. (1981) 3 E.H.R.R. 531.
19. *ibid.* at 538.

Chapter 6

The Quality of Primary Education

In addition to the obligation to provide for free primary education in accordance with Article 42.4 the State also has a duty under Article 42.3.2° which provides:

> "The State, shall, however, as guardian of the common good, require in view of actual conditions that the children receive *a certain minimum education*, moral, intellectual and social." (Emphasis added.)

Factors which influence Quality

In *Crowley v. Ireland*[1] McWilliam J. was satisfied that a form of makeshift education provided by the parents was not sufficient to satisfy the minimum required by modern standards, and this led to him ordering that the children be "bussed" to adjoining schools. McMahon J. dealt with the claim regarding defective primary education received by the Drimoleague children at neighbouring schools mainly under three headings as follows:

1. It was complained that the children were not given remedial treatment to compensate for the loss of schooling which they had suffered.
2. It was complained that the teachers gave preference in the form of more attention to their own children.
3. While the approved pupil-teacher ratio was not exceeded. the teachers in the neighbouring schools could not give as much individual attention to the Drimoleague children as these had been accustomed to receive in their own schools before the strike.[2]

McMahon J. accepted that *class sizes* in the neighbouring schools were virtually doubled by the influx of Drimoleague children and that it was probable that there had been a falling off in the quality of the education received by the children. He also accepted that the physical effects of *travelling longer distances* by bus must have affected the children's performance in school (In some cases children had to travel up to 14 miles by bus, were collected as early as 8.30 a.m. and did not arrive home until 4 p.m.) The question of whether the

---

1. Unreported, High Court, McWilliam J., December 1, 1977.
2. [1980] I.R. 102 at 114.

buses provided a reasonably accessible system of primary education could not be decided merely on the basis of the hardship caused to very young children. There was no evidence to suggest that it was necessary for a child to start primary school at the age of four-and-a-half years in order to get an adequate primary education.

He concluded that it was very probable that the children did not get as much *individual attention* as they would had they continued to attend the parish schools. However he held that such deficiencies in the education of the children as were attributable to the fact that the children were travelling out of the parish of Drimoleague to outside schools were *not such* as to justify the Court in saying that the children were not receiving primary education as ordinarily recognised in this country and notwithstanding the undoubted disabilities from which the children suffered. they were receiving the free primary education to which they were entitled under the Constitution. The State was discharging its constitutional obligations in regard to the provision of such education. A different situation would arise were the buses discontinued or if the bus service was so altered that schools were no longer reasonably accessible for the children.

Children with Special Needs

Is the State obliged to take account of the special needs of handicapped or retarded children? Undoubtedly they have the same right to free primary education as normal children but is the State obliged to provide special education, or facilities for them because of their disabilities?

The constitutional right of the applicant and the provision of *special medical care* in a special institution was litigated in the *State (C.) v. Frawley*[3] referred to earlier. A *habeas corpus* application under Article 40.4.2° of the Constitution, the prosecutor claimed that the State had failed in its duty to protect his right to bodily integrity because he was not provided with the specialised treatment which he needed. Finlay P. held that the executive's failure to provide him with specialised treatment in an institution not existing in the State did not in all circumstances of the case constitute a breach of duty. The duty was not an absolute one. Finlay P. stated:

> "The right to bodily integrity as an unspecified constitutional right is clearly established by the decision of the Supreme Court in *Ryan v. Attorney General*[4] by which I am bound and which I accept. . . . The real failure in this duty alleged against the respondent is that he has failed to provide the special type of institution and treatment which was recommended . . . as a long term treatment and that, to an extent, imprisonment in any other form is directly harmful to the progress of the prosecutor's condition of personality disturbance. *A failure on the part of the Executive to provide for the prosecutor treatment of a very special*

---

3. [1976] I.R. 365.
4. [1965] I.R. 294.

> kind in an institution which does not exist in any part of the State, does not, in my view constitute a failure to protect the health of the prosecutor as well as possible in all the circumstances of the case . . .".[5]

Finlay P. perceived that it was not the function of the court to recommend to the Executive what was desirable or to fix the priorities of its health and welfare policy. The function of the court was confined to identifying, and, if necessary, enforcing the legal and constitutional duties of the Executive. He explained:

> "I cannot conscientiously hold that an obligation to provide for prisoners in general the *best* medical treatment *in all the circumstances* can be construed as including a duty to build, equip and staff the very specialised unit which Dr. McCaffrey has recommended and which might be appropriate to the needs of the prosecutor and four or five other persons."[6]

O'Donoghue v. Minister for Health

In *O'Donoghue v. Minister for Health*[7] it was claimed that there was no institution in the State to educate a seven year old quadriplegic and severely mentally handicapped child and that he had the same constitutional right to free primary education as normal children. O'Hanlon J. concluded that the constitutional obligation on the State to provide for free basic elementary education of all children involved giving each child, such *advice, instruction* and *teaching* "as will enable him or her to make the best possible use of his or her inherent and potential capacities, physical, mental and moral, however limited these capacities may be". Or, to borrow the language of the United Nations Convention and Resolution of the General Assembly: "such education as will be conductive to the child's achieving the fullest possible integration and individual development; such education as will enable the child to develop his or her capabilities and skills to the maximum and will hasten the process of social integration and reintegration."[8]

O'Hanlon J. explained:

> "This process will work differently for each child, according to the child's own natural gifts, or lack thereof. In the case of the child who is deaf, dumb, blind, or otherwise physically or mentally handicapped, a completely different programme of education has to be adopted and a completely different rate of progress has to be taken for granted, than would be regarded as appropriate for a child suffering from no such handicap."[9]

---

5. Above, n.3, at 372–373 (emphasis added).
6. Above, n.3, at 372–373.
7. Unreported, High Court, O'Hanlon J., May 27, 1993. See also *Irish Times*, June 26, and July 1, 1992 and *Cork Examiner*, May 28, 1993.
8. *ibid.* at p. 94 of the judgment.
9. *ibid.* at p. 95 of the judgment.

The State

He then opined that the State had responded generously to its obligations in relation to virtually all of these categories of handicapped children but had clearly lagged behind other developed countries in what it had done for the most seriously handicapped, which included the plaintiff. Research now indicated that education in a formal setting, involving school, equipment and teachers, and integrated as far as possible in the conventional school environment could be of real benefit to the severely and profoundly handicapped. (The State had claimed that the plaintiff was ineducable by reason of being profoundly mentally and physically disabled but O'Hanlon J. rejected this contention.)

Once that was established, and O'Hanlon J. concluded[10] that it had been, then, in his opinion, it gave rise to a constitutional obligation on the part of the State to respond to such findings by providing for free primary education for this group of children "in as full and positive a manner as it has done for all other children in the community."[11]

The position according to O'Hanlon J. was not unlike that envisaged by the Supreme Court in *Ryan v. Attorney General*[12] where it concurred in the finding of fact by Kenny J. in the High Court that it had not been demonstrated by the evidence adduced, that the introduction of minimal quantities of fluoride into drinking water presented any danger to health. Chief Justice Ó Dálaigh stated, however, that if further advances in scientific knowledge in the future should support a contrary conclusion, a claim of the same nature as put forward by Mrs Ryan would not be foreclosed. O'Hanlon J. held that the Minister for Education was failing to provide free primary education for the infant plaintiff, thus depriving him of his constitutional rights.

The divergent approach adopted by O'Hanlon J. in the *O'Donoghue* case, from that of Finlay P. in *The State (C) v. Frawley*, raises important considerations relating to the separation of powers and the role of the courts in constitutional interpretation. Undoubtedly a certral issue which will be addressed by the Supreme Court when the *O'Donoghue* case is appealed.

Circumstances

The particular circumstances in each case are crucial in relation to the power of the courts to review the conduct or policy of the government. Fitzgerald C.J. in *Boland v. An Taoiseach* stated:

> "The courts have no power . . . to supervise or interfere with the exercise by the Government of its executive functions, unless the circumstances are such as to amount to a clear disregard by the government of the powers and duties conferred on it by the Constitution".[13]

---

10. *ibid.*
11. *ibid.*
12. Above, n.4.
13. [1974] I.R. 338 at 362.

Did the circumstances in the *O'Donoghue* case amount to: "a clear disregard by the government" of the duties conferred on it by the Constitution, and to what extent may the courts prescribe the action to be taken by the executive?

Article 42.5

In *F.N. (A minor) v. The Minister for Education*[14] Geoghegan J. referred to *G. v. An Bord Úchtála*,[15] *Re Article 26 and the Adoption (No. 2) Bill, 1987*[16] and *M.F. v. Superintendent Ballymun Garda Station*[17] and stated:

> "Having regard to the principles enunciated in these cases, I would take the view that where there is a child with very special needs which cannot be provided by the parents or guardian there is a constitutional obligation on the State under Article 42 section 5 of the Constitution to cater for those needs in order to vindicate the constitutional rights of the child. It is not necessary for me to determine how absolute that duty is; conceivably there may be very exceptional circumstances where there is some quite exceptional need of the child which the State cannot be expected to provide. In this connection the case of *The State (c) v. Frawley* [1976], I.R. 365 was relied on by counsel for the State. But it would seem to me that on the balance of probabilities the provision of such necessary accommodation, arrangements and services by the State as might meet the necessary requirements of this applicant is *not so impractical or so prohibitively expensive* as would come within any notional limit on the State's constitutional obligations."[18] (Emphasis added.)

Geoghegan J. took the view that the State was under a constitutional obligation to establish as soon as reasonably practicable, either by use of section 58(4) of the 1908 Act, or otherwise, suitable arrangements of containment with treatment for the applicant. This judgment was not appealed and the State in *D.D. (a minor) v. EHB*[19] accepted that they owed a constitutional duty to D to make suitable arrangements to meet his special needs and they accepted that they were in breach of this constitutional duty.

In a judgment in the case of *G.L. (a minor) v. The Minister for Justice*[20] delivered the same day, Geoghegan J. stated that he was quite satisfied that, in general, there ought to be a certified industrial school or some such institution to accommodate a child with similar needs to the applicant and of the applicant's age. He referred to *O'Donoghue v. The Minister for Health* and added:

> "I accept the views expressed in that judgment and that being so, I could not

---

14. Unreported, High Court, Geoghegan J., March 24, 1995.
15. [1980] I.R. 32.
16. [1989] I.R. 656.
17. [1991] 1 I.R. 189.
18. Above, n.14, at pp. 8-9 of the judgment.
19. Unreported, High Court, Costello J, May 3, 1995.
20. Unreported, High Court, Geoghegan J., March 24, 1995.

accept that on the basis of the principle which was applied in *The State (O.) v. Frawley* there is no constitutional obligation to meet the educational requirements of this child."

In a third judgment that same day, *D.T. (a minor) v. The Eastern Health Board*,[21] the same judge stated he was satisfied that for the reasons which he indicated in the N. case that the State owed a constitutional duty to D.T. to cater for her needs. The applicant was a 12 year old girl of such an unruly disposition that she needed to be cared for in some kind of suitable confinement. A serious aspect of her case was that she had suicidal tendencies and unless kept in proper confinement there was apparently grave danger that she would take her own life. He gave the State a reasonable opportunity to provide suitable arrangements for her upbringing as far as practicable and he added: "This is a case where conceivably all potential schemes might fail and the question of limits on the constitutional duty might arise. But that stage has not been reached yet." He adjourned the case for a period to be agreed with counsel.

Article 42.3.2°

> "The State, shall, however, as guardian of the common good, require in view of actual conditions that the children receive a certain minimum education, moral, intellectual and social."

"The State shall . . ."

The first thing to note is that this provision is mandatory, *i.e.* the State must require, in view of actual conditions, that children receive a certain minimum education. How is it to go about requiring a certain minimum?

Referring to this certain minimum education the Supreme Court in *Re Article 26 of the Constitution and the School Attendance Bill, 1942*[22] stated "We are of the opinion that the State, acting in its legislative capacity through the Oireachtas, has power to define it . . ." In other words the State has power to enact legislation requiring that children receive a certain minimum education.

Gerry Whyte writing in his article "Education and the Constitution", interprets this as an exclusive power which prohibits prescription by the Minister. He states:

> "One point about which we can be fairly definite is that the State's power to prescribe a minimum standard of education can *only* be exercised by the Oireachtas through legislation."[23]

On the previous page of his article Mr Whyte states that in recent times the

---

21. Unreported, High Court, Geoghegan J., March 24, 1995.
22. [1943] 77 I.L.T.R. 96; I.R. 334.
23. Lane, ed., *Religion, Education and the Constitution* (1990) p. 90 (emphasis added).

argument has been advanced that: "content and manner of education are not separate and that any power to prescribe a minimum standard of education must necessarily encompass both content and method of education."[24] He points out that even if this were so, such a power on the part of the State is: "Cabined, cribbed, confined" by the express constitutional rights and freedoms of parents. It is undoubtedly true that the constitutional rights of parents cannot be infringed by the State in carrying out its constitutional obligation but this does not absolve the State from failing to do so.

"A Certain Minimum"

The Supreme Court has suggested in *Re Article 26 of the Constitution and the School Attendance Bill, 1942*,[25] that this phrase means "a minimum standard of elementary education of general application". The late Professor J.M. Kelly states: "The Court's paraphrase of 'a certain minimum education' is not very helpful, since its interpretation could be just as controversial as that of the words which it was intended to explain."[26] Whyte describes it as: "a proposition which is scarcely enlightening."[27] With regard to determining the level of the "certain mimimum education" which children must receive Professor Kelly stated:

> ". . . the requirements of actual conditions provide the yardstick . . . the requirements of actual conditions are the only standard by which not merely the level, but also the kind of compulsory education can, in reason or in law, be determined . . . actual conditions do not require and the State would have absolutely no right to enforce, university education for all . . . the State has no right to enforce the learning of subjects which cannot reasonably be thought to belong to a minimum moral, intellectual and social education . . . I say that if the State imports into the structure of that minimum education which it claims to be entitled to enforce, any element or any subject which cannot be justified by reference to actual conditions, the State is exceeding its constitutional power and is therefore doing something unlawful."[28]

It must be pointed out that other subjects may be in addition to the minimum rather than part of it. The State may see that these other subjects are provided but may not require that they be received as part of the minimum as they may with subjects which do form part of the minimum. In other words the certain minimum education which children must receive may differ significantly from that which the State provides or requires to be provided in order to qualify for State aid.

---

24. *ibid.* p. 89.
25. Above, n.22, at 345.
26. Kelly, *Fundamental Rights in the Irish Law and Constitution* (1961) p. 166.
27. Above, n.23, at 90.
28. Kelly, "Education and the Irish State", App. to Whyte, "Education and the Constitution: Convergence of Paradigm and Praxis" (1990–1992) XXV-XXVII Ir. Jur. 69 (*N.S.*).

Professor Kelly opined that although there is no theoretical compulsion to send a child to a state primary school if the curriculum prescribed in the national school includes elements dictated by anything except actual conditions, or goes beyond what actual conditions require, that curriculum is unlawful. Gerry Whyte states:

> "While one could easily accept that the State may only require children to receive a certain minimum education determined by reference to actual conditions, it does not follow that the State may not support educational initiatives which exceed that standard. [A view expressed earlier by the present writer] And yet, if Kelly is right, the Constitution would appear to veto such support unless it can be shown that the initiative in question is optional, both in form and in reality."[29]

Section 4 of the School Attendance Bill 1942 provided:

> "A child shall not be deemed for the purposes of this Act to be receiving suitable education in a manner other than by attending a national school, a suitable school, or a recognised school unless such education and the manner in which such child is receiving it, have been certified under this section by the Minister to be suitable."

At issue was the power which the section purported to give the Minister to certify the education and the manner in which it was imparted. Did this come within the power of the State under Article 42.3.2° to require that children receive a certain minimum education, moral, intellectual and social?

1. It was possible under the section to set a standard much higher than the minimum permitted under Article 42.3.2°.

2. That standard might be made to vary from child to child and was therefore not a standard of general application as envisaged under Article 42.3.2°.

3. The section of the Bill purported to give the Minister power to prescribe even the manner in which the certified suitable education was given.

4. Parents would be in default if they continued educating pending certification which would inevitably involve some delay in implementation.

The fourth ground could simply have been covered by a clause to exempting parents in such cases. Academic legal commentators[30] point out that the relevance of this judgment has been overtaken by subsequent judicial development of constitutional principle. In relation to point No. 1. in 1970 the Supreme Court in *East Donegal Co-Operative v. Attorney General*[31] stated that: "An

---

29. *ibid.* at 76.
30. Osborough, "Education in the Irish Law and Constitution" (1978) XIII Ir. Jur. 173 (*N.S.*); Casey, *Constitutional Law in Ireland* (1987) p. 520; Lane (ed.), *Religion, Education and the Constitution* (1992) p. 90, *per* Whyte.
31. [1970] I.R. 317.

Article 42.3.2°

Act of the Oireachtas, or any provision thereof, will not be declared to be invalid where it is possible to construe it in accordance with the Constitution . . . and that an interpretation favouring the validity of an Act should be given in cases of doubt."[32] In relation to point No. 3 Professor Osborough comments:

> "Points in the Supreme Court's reasoning appear *at this distance* of time less than convincing. A modern approach to syllabus, even in regard to subjects of elementary education, requires concern as much with teaching method as with teaching content; a regulation as to teaching method broadly defined, would nowadays surely be felt to fall within any legal power to prescribe any standard of education. Of necessity, practical difficulties of surveillance would arise where, as the Constitution permits, a child is educated in his own home, but the language of the Supreme Court *sounds* altogether too bald."[33]

Professor Casey states[34] that the decision now has *a very old fashioned air* from both a legal and educational viewpoint and that the presumption of constitutionality expounded in *East Donegal Co-Op.* would cover the fear of the court that the Minister might prescribe a standard higher than the constitution permits. In relation to the minimum standard he points out that this is not static, that a minimum standard thought appropriate for the 1940s might be altogether inappropriate for the 1980s. He also states that it would not be accepted nowadays that educational content and teaching methods are separable in the way the Supreme Court seem to think. He concludes that the *School Attendance Bill* case: "*may* have little long term effect on Irish educational provision; afterall, the whole system has been transformed since then."[35]

Both commentators appear to have carefully qualified their comments. Gerry Whyte[36] refers to the argument of both that content and manner of education are not separable and then refers to the parent's rights under Article 42.2 as to provision of the education in their homes or in schools. There seems to have been a difference in interpreting the word "*manner*" as used by the Supreme Court. Did the court intend it to indicate the primacy of parental choice as to how, when and where parents discharge their duty to educate their children? Under Article 42.2: "Parents shall be free to provide this education in their homes or in private schools or in schools recognised or established by the State." (See Chapter 7 below, "The Manner of Education at Home").

Vincent Grogan[37] certainly interpreted it as meaning location rather than referring to prescription by the State of pedagogue. He states: "This would appear to provide an effective protection for denominational schools as being

---

32. *ibid.* at 341 *per* Walsh J.
33. Above, n.30, at 173.
34. Above, n.30, at 520.
35. *ibid.* at 521 (emphasis added).
36. Above, n.30, at 89.
37. Schools under the Constitution, *Studies*, Winter, 1970, p. 378.

the means chosen by parents for their children's education." The present writer subscribes to this interpretation. Other commentators seem to interpret it as a prohibition on the State prescribing the teaching methods to be adopted. Gerry Whyte points out and the present writer agrees that it is not necessary to deny the State the power to regulate the manner of education in order to protect the parent's right to educate at home. Gerry Whyte concludes: ". . . the decision of the Supreme Court offers us very little guidance as to the extent of the State's powers to prescribe a minimum standard education."[38]

The Report of the Committee on the Constitution in December 1967 points out[39] that subsequent to the Supreme Court decision, an attempt was made to redraft the legislation to bring it into conformity with their interpretation. Serious difficulties arose in this connection, however, in ascertaining the full significance of the Supreme Court interpretation and the legislation was accordingly abandoned. The Committee suggested that the existing subsection 2 of Article 42.3 might be replaced by a provision on the following lines:

> "Laws, however, may be enacted to oblige parents who have failed in their duty to provide for the education of their children to send their children to schools established or designated by the State."[40]

"in view of actual conditions"

Mr Justice Brian Walsh has written:

> "What does or does not constitute primary education will be decided in the light of the circumstances and conditions prevailing at the time the question was raised and not those prevailing at the time the Constitution was enacted . . . the basic minimum requirements of primary education naturally become greater with the progress of society and increasing standards of living and improvement in the quality of life."[41]

In the Summer 1994 edition of *Studies* the present writer wrote:

> "The expression 'in view of actual conditions' should be interpreted as referring to conditions prevailing in society at the particular time when the Constitutional guarantee is invoked. . . . It imposes an obligation on the State to take cognisance of the actual conditions and to relate the requirement that children receive a certain minimum education to the actual conditions prevailing at that time. Thus the process of ongoing review of what constitutes a minimum education at any particular time means that curriculum changes and changes in the school leaving age can be effected."[42]

---

38. Above, n.30, at 90.
39. at para. 132, p.46.
40. *ibid.* at para. 133, p. 47.
41. Walsh, "Existence and Meaning of Fundamental Rights in Ireland" (1980) 1 *Human Rights Law Journal*, at p. 178.
42. Farry, "Education and the Irish Constitution", *Studies*, Vol. 83, 174.

J.M. Kelly[43] wondered if the Irish version "toísc cor an lae" which might be paraphrased with: "because of the turn the world has taken" did not make its meaning plainer than the English version. He added: "It follows after this as a corollary that, since nothing but actual conditions can justify the State in prescribing compulsory education, the State is only justified in prescribing such minimum compulsory education as these conditions require."[44]

"moral, intellectual and social"

Religious and physical education are not included in this section as they are in Article 42.1 in relation to the rights and duty of parents. The distinction is relevant in so far as it highlights that both of the omitted types of education are outside the area of state compulsion and the State cannot require that a child must receive them and consequently attend at them. The Campaign to separate Church and State[45] have pointed to this distiction between moral and religious education/instruction and to the fact that at present moral education is provided within the framework of religious instruction. They call for the introduction of secular ethics as a mandatory subject and contend that it would not undermine separately given religious education. "Therefore while the State guarantees primary education, it does not expressly guarantee secondary or higher education" according to Walsh J.[46]

In the *O'Donoghue* case[47] O'Hanlon J. was not convinced that the State was meeting the specific obligation imposed on it by Article 42.4 of the Constitution to provide for free primary education, in the case of the applicant. A much greater deployment of resources was required for the provision of free primary education for severely or profoundly handicapped children.

Resources Required

The applicant in the *O'Donoghue* case had been offered a place in the Cope Foundation (a Cork institution for persons suffering from severe mental and physical handicap, administered by the Cork Polio and Aftercare Association) in reliance on the apointment of one additional teacher to undertake responsibility for a further 12 pupils, but O'Hanlon J. opined that this ratio far exceeded the work load deemed appropriate for a teacher in an ordinary primary school where the pupils were not mentally or physically handicapped. Evidence had been given that the pupil teacher ratio in the U.K. was two to five and in Denmark two teachers and one assistant for seven pupils.

---

43. Kelly, *op. cit.* above, n.28, at 85–86.
44. *ibid.* at 86.
45. Colgan, *Minimum Requirements for Education Act(s)* (1989) para. 2(c).
46. *op. cit.*, above, n.41, at p. 178.
47. Above, n.7.

The length of the school day and the school week was also a concern. A new approach was required to meet the special needs of the applicants category. O'Hanlon J. then proceeded:

> "(a) Age of Commencement: Early intervention and assessment being of vital importance if conditions of mental and physical handicap are not to become intractable.
>
> (b) Duration of Primary Education: As this category will, in all probability, never proceed further, and is unlikely to proceed far up the ladder of primary education itself, the process should, ideally, continue as long as the ability for further development is discernible. Professor Hogg suggests that the age of 18 may not be unrealistic in this context.
>
> (c) Continuity of Education: The lengthy holiday breaks which take place in the life of the ordinary primary school appear likely to cause serious loss of ground which may never be recovered, in the case of children with severe or profound handicap. Accordingly, to deal adequately with their needs appears to require that the teaching process should, so far as practicable, be continuous throughout the entire year.
>
> These factors lead me to believe that the Respondents are misled in their belief that the arrangements already made to provide a place for the applicant in the Cope Foundation are sufficient of themselves to satisfy any claim that may arise in his favour under the provisions of the Constitution to have free primary education provided for his benefit."[48]

Since the *O'Donoghue* judgment there have been significant improvements in the State's provision for children with severe or profound mental handicap. The pupil teacher ratio has been improved from 12:1 to 6:1, Child Care Assistant support has been improved to a similar level and capitation funding increased from £92.70 to £341 per child.

The Constitution Review Group

The Review Group considered two phrases used in Article 42.3.2°, *viz.*, "a certain minimum education" and "in view of actual conditions".

"*a certain minimum education*"

In a submission to the Constitution Review Group, the Department of Education stated that the absence of a more precise definition of these words could leave the State vulnerable, in enacting any future school attendance legislation, to a charge that it is seeking to impose a level of education greater or lower than the minimum envisaged by the Constitution.

The Review Group conceded that the term was susceptible to a variety of interpretations but considered "that the Constitution should, where possible,

---

48. *ibid.* at 102.

endeavour to state propositions at a sufficient level of generality to permit a evolution and development." The Oireachtas should have the express power to define by law the meaning of the term.

Recommendation

The Review Group recommend that Article 42.3.2° might be amended to read:

> "The State shall require that children receive a certain minimum education as may be determined from time to time by law, provided that the State shall at all times have due regard to the right of parents to make decisions concerning the religious and moral education of their children".

"in view of actual conditions" (Article 42.3.2°)

The Review Group state that the meaning of this phrase is obscure and difficult to interpret but that it *seems* to mean that the minimum education which the State can require that a child receive may vary. According to the Review Group this variation may be according to circumstances prevailing in the family environment and in society at large. The Review Group considered that the rights of parents should where necessary, give way to the right of the State to insist on a certain minimum education and that this should not be contingent on "actual conditions".

Recommendation

The Review Group recommend that:

> "In the case of Article 42.3.1°, no change is proposed. However, the words "in view of actual conditions" should be deleted from Article 42.3.2° and, following the discussion at Issue 7 below, further amendments to this provision are suggested".

Chapter 7

Rights and Duties of the Family and Parents

Significantly the first section of Article 42 of the Constitution is the acknowledgment of the Family as the primary and natural educator of the child and a guarantee to respect the inalienable right and duty of parents to provide for the education of their children according to their means.

Article 42.1

> "The State acknowledges that the primary and natural educator of the child is the Family and guarantees to respect the inalienable right and duty of parents to provide, according to their means, for the religious and moral, intellectual, physical and social education of their children."

This was not contained in the first drafts and is undoubtedly of clerical origin. Rev. Cahill S.J. in response to a letter from Eamonn De Valera in 1936, asking for his ideas of what should be in the new Constitution suggested as a fundamental principle that: "primary responsibility and control of the education of the young belong inalienably to the parents and the Church, it is a function of the State to assist where necessary and supplement their efforts..."[1] The first of the draft articles submitted by the Jesuits omitted any mention of the Church and dealt with provision rather than control of the education of the young. It states: "It is the natural right as well as the duty of parents to provide, as far as in them lies, for the education of their children."[2]

The function of the State was transcribed into the article as: "the duty and the right to assist in the work of education...". The authority for this submission was partly the 1929 Papal Encyclical "Divini Illius Magistri", of Pius XI, but also the Polish, Austrian and Belgian Constitutions. This right of parents was "recognised" in another draft[3] and ultimately in the McQuaid draft[4] became "The State acknowledges the Family as the primary and natural educator of the child." It was probably felt that the word "recognise" was more neutral, whereas "acknowledge" connotes recognising as genuine.

---

1. De Valera Papers 1095/29.
2. *ibid.* 1095/53.
3. *ibid.* 1078/1B.
4. *ibid.* 1078/4.

Writing in 1927 Rev. Lambert McKenna cited[5] St. Thomas, *Summa Contra Gentiles* L.111., Chapter 123 and *Summa Theologica* P.111., Q.lxviii, art.10 for the assertion that it is a principle of natural law that the right of educating children belongs to children's parents. He commented: "The right, therefore, as well as the duty, of educating children belongs to parents, and this right implies of course, a duty on the part of others not to interfere with its exercise." The right and duty phrase was to be repeated in the 1937 Constitution. The Church according to Rev McKenna "is the authorative interpreter of the Natural Law as well as the Divine Law".[6]

The public statements of the Catholic Church had always extolled the rights of parents in the matter of education.[7] At a local level the public utterances of clerics asserting parental rights contrasts stangely with the decision of the Catholic Managers Association, adopted by the Bishops at a meeting of the Hierarchy on October 9, 1934 as official church policy that: "No lay committee of any kind is to be associated with the manager in school management."[8] This meant that parents were to be excluded by local church policy, from being associated with, not to mention partaking in the management of primary schools. Despite the knowledge of this policy it may be significant that the 1937 Constitution asserted and enshrined the right of parents and of the family in regard to education of children.

The state attitude toward parents is illustrated to some extent, by the controversy over the use of Irish as a medium of instruction in the early 1930s when Thomas Derrig was Minister for Education. When parental dissatisfaction was cited by James Dillon, T.D., the Minister stated: "I cannot see that parents as a body can decide this matter . . . : Parents are always free to make representations on this matter."[9] In this context, E. Brian Titley concluded that "Parental rights in education was as much a slogan of convenience for the State as it was for the Church."[10]

Parent's Right and Duty

The right of parents to the custody and control of their children has long been recognised by the courts as a common law right. In *The Queen v. Barnardo (Jones's)* case[11] the Court of Appeal cited *R. v. Clarke*[12] and approved of Lord

---

5. McKenna, "State Rights in Education, *Studies* 1927 Vol. XVI, at 215.
6. *ibid.*, 219.
7. See *Encyclicals Divini illius Magistri and Catechesi Tradendae*. Bishops Pastoral, IER, 1867, Vol. 111.
8. Dept. of Finance DF, S22/4/37 and Ó Buachalla, *Education, Policy in Twentieth Century Ireland* (1988). See also chap. 8, "Control of Education and Parents", below.
9. 59 *Dáil Debates* Col. 2197, December 10, 1935.
10. Titley, *Church, State, and the Control of Schooling in Ireland, 1900–1944* (1983) p. 137.
11. [1891] Q.B. 194.
12. 7 L.& B. 186.

Coleridge's statement that: "If a guardian by reason of nurture, delivers the infant to another for his instruction he may afterwards retake the infant. This last position is as old as the Year Book."[13] In 1889 when Dr Bernardo refused to return a young boy to his mother who wished to place him in a Roman Catholic institution, it was argued that the wishes of the mother of an illegitimate child were at most only one element to be considered in deciding what was for the child's best interest. This was rejected by the court holding that it would, in a proper case, give the same effect to the mother's wishes in respect of the care, maintenance and education of the child as it gave to the wishes of the father of a legitimate child.

The right and duty of parents to provide for, and to prescribe the manner of education as well as religious instruction of their children, has been upheld by the courts prior to the enactment of the Constitution in a number of cases on the grounds of public policy.[14] Subsequent to the enactment of the Constitution the right of parents under Article 42 has been upheld in *Burke v. Burke*[15] and *Re Blake decd.*[16] In *Burke v. Burke* a testatrix by will left property on trust for the purpose of maintaining and educating her sister's godson as a Roman Catholic. The selection of the Roman Catholic school to be attended by the infant was at the absolute discretion of the trustees of the estate. Gavan Duffy P. held that this discretion was inoperative and must be ignored since it tended to override the parental authority and right and duty of education declared by Article 42. He added:

> "Now, while the father may at any time, if he sees fit, be guided by the trustees in his choice of school for his son, the decision must rest with the father alone, the boy's mother being on the evidence excluded from a practical voice in the events which have occurred. Miss Burke here made a bad mistake, for the will at this point would override the sacred parental authority and defy the parental right and duty of education under Article 42 of the Constitution. Consequently, this clause in the will, however wellmeaning from the standpoint of an anxious benefactor, is inoperative and must be ignored."[17]

In the *Blake* case the testator bequeathed a legacy to trustees to apply the income for the maintenance and education of the children of his daughter provided they should be brought up in the Roman Catholic faith. The children had been baptised in the Church of Ireland and were being reared in that tradition. Dixon J. followed the decision in *Burke v. Burke* and held that the condition that the children should be brought up as Roman Catholic faith was

---

13. Illich 8 Edw.1V, fol B.2; Year B. Mich 8 Edw. IV.
14. See *Re Westby Minors (No. 2)* [1937] I.R. 311, *Public Trustee v. Bryant* [1936] 2 All E.R. 878; *Re Borwick* [1917] 2 Ch. 126; *Re Sandbrook* [1912] 2 Ch. 471.
15. [1951] I.R. 216.
16. [1955] I.R. 89.
17. Above, n.15, at 222.

Article 42.1

void as an attempt to restrict or fetter the right and duty of parents to provide for the education of their children declared by Article 42. Referring to this right he stated:

> "It is clear that any attempt to restrict or fetter that right would be contrary to the solemnly declared policy and conceptions of the community as a whole and therefore such as the courts established under the Constitution could not and would not lend their aid to . . . a provision such as the present could only operate, as an inducement to the parents and a form of indirect pressure on them to change the religion of their children from that which they themselves professed or had adopted and in which they had baptised the children."

"acknowledges"

Admits as true or recognises as genuine.

"primary"

In *O'Donoghue v. Minister for Health*[18] O'Hanlon J. states that the adjective given as equivalent to *primary* in the Irish version of this Article is *"príomha"* meaning *"principal"* or "foremost" and he cites the dictionary definition of education contained in *Chambers Twentieth Century Dictionary* (1981): "Bringing up or training, as of a child; instruction; strengthening of the powers of body or mind; culture." It is not significant that the Irish text clearly shows a different meaning for the word primary in Article 42.1 to that in Article 42.4 where primary education is bunoideachas in Irish.

"and natural"

The Irish version of the text is "múinteoir príomha dúchasach"; it is not "múinteoir príomha agus dúchasach". It could be suggested that the addition of the word "and" in the English text of Article 42 is not compatable with the Irish version and serves to distort the meaning of the English version There is no conjunctive *and* in the Irish version. There is a difference between the State acknowledging the Family as the primary natural educator of the child (one aspect of the Families power) and the State recognising the Family as the primary *and* natural educator of the child (two aspects). However, the omission of "agus" in the Irish version is of no special significance because "agus" is not normally used between attributive adjectives in Irish.

"Inalienable"

In 1867 the Catholic Bishops stated: "that education is not a function of the State, but an *inalienable* office of the parents . . . nature has given to the parents

---

18. Unreported, High Court, O'Hanlon J., May 27, 1993 at p. 93 of the judgment.

the right of educating that offspring. And not only has it given the right, but it has imposed the duty: and a right which is bound up with a duty is altogether *inalienable*."[19]

The word "inalienable" is defined in *Collins English Dictionary* as meaning: "incapable of being separated or transferred". In *Ryan v. Attorney General*[20] Kenny J. interpreted it to mean: "that which cannot be transferred or given away". In *G. v. An Bord Úchtála*[21] however, Walsh J. in reference to Article 42.1 and the State guarantee to respect the inalienable right and duty of parents to provide in accordance with their means for the religious and moral, intellectual, physical and social education of their children, stated: "It is also to be borne in mind that some inalienable rights are *absolutely inalienable* while others are *relatively inalienable*."[22]

This would seem to be borne out by the judgment of Finlay C.J. *Re Article 26 and the Adoption (No. 2) Bill, 1987*[23] where the Supreme Court rejected the submission that the nature of the family as a unit group possessing inalienable and imprescriptible rights made it constitutionally impermissible for a statute to restore to any member of an individual family constitutional rights of which he had been deprived by a method which disturbed or altered the constitution of the family, if that method was necessary to achieve that purpose.

"family"

The Constitution in the words of Murnaghan J. in *The State (Nicolaou) v. An Bord Úchtála*[24] "recognises only 'the family', founded on the institution of marriage". A natural father, mother and child do not constitute a family within the meaning of Articles 41 and 42. Henchy J. stated:

> "I am satisfied that no union or grouping of people is entitled to be designated a family for the purposes of the Article if it is founded on any relationship other than that of marriage . . . For the State to award equal Constitutional protection to the family founded on marriage and the "family" founded on an extra marital union would in effect be a disregard of the pledge of the State in Article 41.3.1° to guard with special care the institution of marriage."[25]

Henchy J. in *Re J., an Infant* stated: "The Constitution gives no definition of the family, but it does recognise in Article 41.3.1° that it is founded on the

---

19. "The Right to Educate to whom does it belong?" (1867) 111 I.E.R. 282.
20. [1965] I.R. 294 at 308.
21. [1980] I.R. 32.
22. *ibid.* at 79.
23. [1989] I.R. 656; [1989] I.L.R.M. 266.
24. [1966] I.R. 572 at 590. See also *G. v. An Bord Úchtála* [1980] I.R. 32.
25. *ibid.* at 622.

institution of marriage."[26] Gerry Whyte opines in his article, "Education and the Constitution",[27] that it is inconceivable that other families should be treated any differently in respect of the education of their children. Michael Staines[28] has stated that the use of the two particular adjectives "inalienable" and "imprescriptible", has led to unfortunate consequences for the rights of the marital family and that its seemed illogical and unjust to him, to exclude the natural family from the protection of Articles 41 and 42 "merely as a result of an injudicious choice of words by Mr De Valera in framing the Constitution." He also points out that in the course of the Dáil Debate on Article 41 De Valera stated: "we want to stress the fact that these inalienable and imprescriptible rights cannot be invaded by the State".[29] A married couple without children is a "family" within the meaning of Article 41 and according to Costello J. in *Murray v. Ireland*[30] is entitled to the same constitutional protection under Article 41 as a married couple with children.

The opinions of both Whyte and Staines were subsequently vindicated in *Keegan v. Ireland*[31] when the European Court of Human Rights in Strasbourg held that the notion of "family" is not confined solely to marriage based relationships and may encompass other *de facto* "family" ties, where the parties are living together outside marriage. The Court stated:

> "A child born out of such a relationship is *ipso jure* part of that family unit from the moment of his or her birth, and by the very fact of it. There thus exists between the child and the parents a bond amounting to family life even if at the time of the child's birth the parents are no longer co-habiting if their relationship has then ended."[32]

Section 6(a) of the Guardianship of Infants Act 1964, inserted by the Status of Children Act 1987 permitted a court on the application of an unmarried father, to appoint him to be a guardian of his child. Whereas a married father was a joint guardian of an infant without application.

Mr. Keegan claimed that there had been a violation of his right to respect for family life (Article 8 of the Convention) in that his child had been placed for adoption without his knowledge or consent, that Irish law did not even give the father of a child born out of wedlock, a defeasable right to be appointed guardian, that he had no *locus standi* in the Irish Adoption Board proceedings, and that he had been discriminated against in the exercise of his rights when his position was compared to that of a married father. He also claimed a breach of Article 6 (Entitlement to a hearing).

---

26. [1966] I.R. 295 at 306.
27. Lane (ed.), *Education and the Constitution, Religion Education and the Constitution* (1992), p. 111.
28. "The Concept of the Family under the Irish Constitution" (1976) XI Ir. Jur. 239 (*N.S.*).
29. 67 *Dáil Debates* Col. 1888, June 4, 1937.
30. [1985] I.R. 532.
31. (1994) E.H.R.R. 342.
32. *ibid.* at 360.

The Court held that both Articles had been violated and that Ireland must pay Mr Keegan £12,000 in respect of non-pecuniary and pecuniary damage in addition to costs and expenses. The Irish Government claimed that there was no period during the life of the child in which a recognised family life involving her had been in existence. In their view neither a mere blood link nor a sincere and heartfelt desire for family life were enough to create it. In the event this argument was rejected by the court.[33]

As a result of the decision in the *Keegan* case the Government initiated the Adoption (No. 2) Bill, 1996 which provides for the introduction of a statutory procedure and an obligation to consult the father of a child born outside marriage before the child is placed for adoption. The father may then exercise his right to apply for guardianship and/or custody of the child.

"parents"

According to Michael Staines[34] the acknowledgment of the family and its definition does not restrict the definition of parent in the remainder of Article 42.1. However it should be noted that in the *Nicolaou* case Henchy J. stated:

> "It seems to me unthinkable that the Constitution should guarantee to the putative father of an illegitimate child the rights over the child referred to in Article 42.1 even in cases where the sole nexus between the father and the child may have been the rape of the mother."[35]

"Parent" is defined in both the School Attendance Act 1926 and in the Vocational Education Act 1930 in very similar terms. In the School Attendance Act the word "parent" in relation to a child means the person having the legal custody of the child and where owing to the absence of such person or for any other reason the child is not living with or is not in the actual custody of such person, includes the person with whom the child is living or in whose actual custody the child is. In the 1930 Act the word "individual" is used instead of "person". The common law right of parents to the custody and control of their children arose in *The Queen v. Barnardo*[36] where the mother of a child who had undertaken not to take the child away from Dr Bernardo's home sought to break the agreement and retake her child. It was held that she was entitled to do so.

The common law was perfectly clear that parents who agreed not to take back children whom they had placed in schools or homes could not be bound by such an agreement. "No such agreement can deprive a parent of the right of

---

33. The existence of a family life falling within the scope of Art. 8 of the Convention depends on a number of factors of which co-habitation in only one. "The application of the principle has been found by the Commission to extend equally to the relationship between natural fathers and their children born out of wedlock." *Keegan v. Ireland*, above, n.31, at 354.
34. Above, n.27.
35. Above, n.24, at 623.
36. Above, n.11.

absolute control over his or her own child" stated Lord Esher M.R. in *The Queen v. Barnardo*.[37] This common law right of parents could be overcome by a statutory provision. This would have been the situation in *Re Doyle (an Infant)*[38] had section 10 of the Children's Act 1941 been passed before the enactment of the 1937 Constitution. Section 10 enabled parents (in cases of mental incapacity or desertion of one parent) to consent to a child under 15 being the subject of a detention order for teaching and training at an Industrial School whereas, a sole parent did not have the right to demand the discharge of the child even though their circumstances had improved. Chief Justice Maguire pointed out that the makers of the Constitution by the provisions of Article 42.1 and 42.3 deliberately preserved this common law principle and put it beyond the reach of ordinary legislation.

It should be noted that the court also expressed the view that Article 42.5 does not enable the legislature to take away the right of a parent who is in a position to do so, to control the education of their child, where there is nothing *culpable* on the part of either parent or child. It seemed clear to the court that where such a surrender of parents rights (under Article 42.1) to the State was sanctioned it could be for a period limited by the parent's inability to provide for the education of a child.

The constraints which the provisions of the new Constitution relating to the family and parents would impose on the State were recognised, and illustrated by the fact that during the drafting of the Constitution the Department of Education drew the attention of De Valera to the likelihood that sections of the Children's Act, 1908 would be unconstitutional in so far as they gave the Minister power to retain a child in an industrial school on the ground of poverty.[39]

In the event, in 1955 the Supreme Court[40] did hold that section 10 of the Children Act 1941 (which amended section 58 of the Children Act 1908) was invalid as being repugnant to the Constitution, in as much and in so far, as it deprived a parent with whose consent a child had been sent to a certified industrial school (the consent of the other party having been dispensed with for desertion) – of the right to resume control of the child so as to provide for its education, when that parent was willing and able to do so.

Specific mention of a right to free elementary education was not made in either the Jesuit or McQuaid submissions for the Constitution submitted to De Valera. It had disappeared altogether from the drafts before 1936 and was never reinstated. In *Campbell and Cosans v. United Kingdom*[41] the European Commission of Human Rights stated: "the disciplining of children must also be

---

37. *ibid.* at 207.
38. [1989] I.L.R.M. 277.
39. See Ref; 1037 De Valera papers. Franciscan Institute of Celtic Studies and Historical Research, Killiney, Co. Dublin.
40. *Re Doyle (an Infant)*, above, n.38.
41. (1980) 3 E.H.R.R. 531.

considered to form a natural and even inseparable part of the parental duties to educate and teach their children."[42]

Maguire C.J. in *Re Doyle (an Infant)* referring to Article 42.1 stated:

> "it cannot be that the mere fact that parents are at a given time unable to support their child would entitle the parents to surrender and the State to accept a surrender of the parent's rights or would enable the parents by agreement with the State to rid themselves of the duty so plainly stated in Article 42.1 It seems clear that where such a surrender is sanctioned it can be for a period limited by the parents' inability to provide for the education of a child."[43]

Provision is made in the Child Care Act 1991 for emergency care orders (section 13) and interim care orders (section 17) placing a child under the care of a health board for a maximum period of eight days. Under section 46 any person having the actual custody of a child who fails or refuses to comply with a District Court order to deliver up a child removed from care, is guilty of an offence.

Article 42.2

> "Parents shall be free to provide this education in their homes or in private schools or in schools recognised or established by the State."

In *Re Doyle* the Supreme Court stated that Article 42.2 and 42.3 appeared in their view, expressly to secure to parents the right to choose the *nature* of the education to be given to their children and the schools at which such education should be provided. This right was a continuing right. The Court stated: "Parents must be entitled to change and substitute schools as in their judgment they think proper and to hold that a choice once made is binding for the period of a child's education would be to deny such right."[44]

Article 42.3.1°

> "The State shall not *oblige* parents in violation of their conscience and lawful preference to send their children to schools established by the State, or to any particular type of school designated by the State."

Is the State obliging parents, in breach of Article 42.3.1°, to send their children to schools under the management of different religious denominations, in violation of their conscience and lawful preference, in rural areas where there is no choice of school?

"Conscience" is normally thought of as ingrained moral values of right and wrong or of what is fair and just. The meaning of the word was not addressed

---

42. *ibid.* at 538.
43. Above, n.38, at p. 280.
44. *ibid.* See also McDowell on catchment areas, p. 78 below.

Article 42.3.1° 65

by the Supreme Court in *Re Article 26 and School Attendance Bill, 1942*.[45] A conscientious objector was defined in *Newell v. Gillingham Corporation*[46] as "one who on religious grounds thinks it wrong to kill and to resist by force." In *Hynds v. Spillers French-Baking*[47] the phrase "grounds of conscience" in section 9 of the English Industrial Relations Act 1971 were held to refer to religious conviction in the broadest sense as opposed to personal feeling or intellectual need.

Bona fide parental objection to the administration of corporal punishment to school children was held in *Campbell and Cosans v. United Kingdom*[48] to be "views of a clear moral ordering concerning human behaviour and, being philosophical convictions of parents were entitled to respect in accordance with Article 2 of the First Protocol".[49]

Article 42.3.2°

> "The State shall, however, as guardian of the common good, require that the children receive a certain minimum education, moral, intellectual and social."

Article 2 of the first English draft in 1934 provided that primary instruction was obligatory while Article 6 stated that the teaching of religion was compulsory for all pupils in all schools and educational establishments for the instruction of young persons who had not reached the age of 18 years. The same two matters were dealt with in the 1936 Jesuit submission which provided that. "The teaching of religion within school hours, and as part of the curriculum, shall be obligatory in all schools, maintained or subsidised by the State"[50] and that primary education was compulsory on all Irish citizens.[51]

Although Dr Dermot Keogh[52] has referred to the modest role played by the Irish Jesuit community he later argues[53] that the Jesuit draft Constitution was quite influential in a number of different ways and he refers to the interesting correlation between it and the structure of Articles 41 to 45. He concludes:

> "... the Jesuits were more indirectly influential than I had at first thought. They produced the first draft in the areas where the 1922 Constitution was not particularly expansive. Having set the context and the topics for discussion, the Jesuits were thus quietly influential in the drafting process."[54]

---

45. [1943] I.R. 334.
46. [1941] 1 All E.R. 552 at 553.
47. [1974] I.T.R. 261.
48. Above, n.41.
49. *ibid.* at 531.
50. Para. d, p. 46 Ref 1095/De Valera papers.
51. Para. f, p. 54 Ref 1095/De Valera papers.
52. Keogh, "The Jesuits and the 1937 Constitution", (1989) *Studies*, Vol. 78, No. 309, p. 82.
53. *ibid.* p. 91.
54. *ibid.* p. 94. See also Keogh, "Church, State and Society" in Farrell (ed.), *De Valera's*

The Article as eventually adopted is a more subtle and diplomatic expression of the sentiments contained in Article 6 of the first draft and the Jesuit submission.

School Attendance

The State carries out its obligation under Article 42.3.2° by requiring school attendance under the School Attendance Acts or requiring parents to prove that their child is receiving a suitable elementary education in some other manner. In relation to school attendance, a parent is obliged under the Acts to cause a child over six and under 15 years of age to attend a national or other suitable school on every day on which the school is open for the time prescribed or sanctioned by the Minister, unless there is a reasonable excuse for not doing so. In the words of the *School Attendance/Truancy Report*, published by the Department of Education in April 1994[55]: "The State must, if it is to discharge its constitutional duty, be in a position to verify if children are achieving minimum standards, whether they are educated at home or in schools."

This however, does not mean that a parent can insist on their child attending a primary school which refuses to enrol him or her. (See *Carmody v. Meehan and Cullen*[56] where an injunction was granted to prevent parents trespassing on school premises and leaving their children at a Celbridge school.)

Time Prescribed

The attendance required by the Act must be attendance for the periods prescribed. In *Hinchley v. Rankin*[57] it was held that even if the boy had regularly arrived only a minute or two late, *by "late" was meant the time the attendance register was closed*, there would be a failure to attend regularly within the meaning of the Act because he should have been present for the commencement of instruction.

Section 55 of the Rules for National Schools 1965 provides that a roll-call shall take place at each school meeting and be completed not later than 40 minutes after the commencement of instruction.

Reasonable Excuse

Section 4(2) School Attendance Act 1926 states:

Constitution and Ours, pp. 109–110 and Keogh, *The Vatican, the Bishops and Irish Politics, 1919–1929* (1986), pp. 208–209 and n.33, p. 275.
55. At p. 5.
56. Unreported, High Court, Morris J., September 14, 1993; see *Irish Times*, September 15, 1993. See also settlement of dispute in *Irish Times*, October 15, 1993.
57. [1961] 1 W.L.R. 421.

"Any of the following shall be a reasonable excuse for failure to comply with this section, that is to say:

(a) that the child has been prevented from attending school by the sickness of the child, (Any physical or mental malady or injury is included in this term);

(b) that the child is receiving suitable elementary education in some manner other than by attending a national or other suitable school. This provision was to take account of parent's rights under Article 42.2 to provide the education themselves;

(c) that there is not a national or other suitable school accessible to the child which the child can attend and to which the parent of the child does not object on religious grounds, to send the child;

(d) that the child has been prevented from attending school by some other sufficient cause."

When a child attending a school is absent for a day his parent is obliged to communicate the cause of such absence either in writing or in person to the school Principal within three days. A parent may be fined up to £10 under the Act. This is scarcely a significant fine and the fact that this amount was fixed in 1956 and has not been increased since must raise questions about the State's bona fides to enforce school attendance.

Education at Home

The reasonable excuse (b) that a child is receiving suitable elementary education in some manner other than by attending a national or other suitable school, covers the situation where a child is being educated at home either by a tutor or by parents or in a private school. Under Article 42.2 parents are free to educate their children in their home.

In the English case of *Bevan v. Shears*[58] it was held that a 13 year old boy educated by a private teacher was receiving the *efficient* education required by statute. The court had jurisdiction to decide this without deciding if it was as efficient as he would have received at a public elementary school. The teacher's own statement that it was not as efficient was not admitted. The fact that the boy received no education at all on one particular day did not weigh with the justices.

Manner of Education at Home

Section 4(1) of the School Attendance Bill 1942 provided that a child should not be deemed to be receiving suitable education in a manner other than by attending a school (other than a national school, a suitable school, or a recog-

---

58. [1911] 2 K.B. 936.

nised school) unless such education and the manner in which the child was receiving it had been certified by the Minister to be suitable.

The Supreme Court held:

> "The State is entitled to require that children shall receive a certain minimum education. So long as parents supply this general standard of education we are of opinion that *the manner in which it is being given and received is entirely a matter for the parents and is not a matter in respect of which the State under the Constitution is entitled to interfere.*" (Emphasis added.)

The role of the State is thus confined to assessing and verifying standards, however the point made in the *School Attendance/Truancy Report*[59] that: "These constitutional restrictions would not, however, prevent the State from offering guidance, on a purely voluntary basis, to parents who are educating their children at home" is well taken.

Article 42.4

The first part of Article 42.4: "that the State shall provide for free primary education" has been dealt with in Chapter 3 above.

Article 42.4 continues:

> "... and shall endeavour to supplement and give reasonable aid to private and corporate educational initiative, and when the public good requires it, provide other educational facilities or institutions with *due regard however, for the rights of parents*, especially in the matter of religious and moral formation." (Emphasis added.)

"due regard for rights of parents"

Before attempting to define the meaning and parameters of the phrase it is suggested that the "due regard" in Article 42.4 relates to the "other educational facilities or institutions" which the State may provide. Both phrases are contained in the same clause. Arguably it does not relate to the free primary education which the State must *provide for* or to the private or corporate educational initiative supplemented or given reasonable aid by the State. It relates specifically to the *other* educational facilities or institutions which the State *may provide*.

In the case of *O'Donovan v. Attorney General*[60] it was held that in enacting the Electoral (Amendment) Act 1959 the Legislature when revising the constituencies did not have *due regard* to the changes in the distribution of the population as they were obliged to do under Article 16.2.4° of the Constitution. Subsection 1 of section 3 and section 4 of the Act were declared to be repugnant

---

59. Published by the Department of Education in April 1994 p. 6.
60. [1962] I.R. 114.

to the Constituion and invalid. The interpretation and meaning of the phrase "due regard" in Article 40.3.3° as inserted into the Constitution by the Eight Amendment of the Constitution arose in the case of *Attorney General v. X*.[61] This subsection states: "The State acknowledges the right to life of the unborn and, with due regard to the equal right to life of the mother, guarantees in its laws to respect, and, as far as practicable, by its laws to defend and vindicate that right."[62]

The late Mr Justice McCarthy asked: "What does the term 'due regard' mean?" and John Rogers, S.C. submitted: "It means appropriate and proper in the circumstances of the case and the background of the Constitution."

There may be two aspects of having "due regard", a positive and a negative. In some instances the State may be obliged to do or provide something and in others to refrain from doing or providing something.

It has been held that the State by paying the salaries of chaplains in community schools is having regard to the rights of parents *vis-à-vis* the religious formation of their children and enabling them to exercise their constitutionally recognised rights. See Costello P. in *Campaign to Separate Church and State Ltd v. Minister for Education*.[63]

Incidentally, it is not clear to the author whether the word *"other"* in Article 42.4 means extra, additional or different. Indeed under Article 42.4 in relation to education *other* than primary education the State is obliged to have "due regard to the rights of parents, *especially* in the matter of religious and moral formation." According to E. Cahill S.J.[64] this was inserted as a safeguard against the liberalist principles of laicism and secularism in education and what he termed the awesome ideal of L'Ecole Unique which was upheld in Europe and America in the 1930s.

"religious and moral formation"

See Chapter 8 below.

Article 42.5

> "In exceptional cases, where the parents for physical or moral reasons fail in their duty towards their children, the State as guardian of the common good, by appropriate means shall endeavour to supply the place of the parents, but always with due regard for the natural and imprescriptible rights of the child."

---

61. [1992] I.R. 1.
62. Note that two other subsections were subsequently added, one by the Thirteenth Amendment of the Constitution Act 1992 and another by the Fourteenth Amendment of the Constitution Act 1992.
63. Unreported, High Court, Costello P., January 17, 1996.
64. 100/1095 Cahill File, DeValera Papers, *op. cit.*

Parental Right and One Parent

In the *Doyle* case[65] it was argued that Article 42 did not apply in the case of a broken or disrupted family. The Supreme Court approved of the manner in which Ó Dálaigh J. (as he then was) dealt with this argument. He had stated: "Mere recital of these provisions is enough to demonstrate that desertion on the part of a mother without just cause leaves the authority of the family unimpaired and in no way diminishes the parental right with regard to the education of the children." In many cases family authority and parental rights would be asserted by parents jointly; but the assertion of that authority and of those rights could not be less effective because of desertion on the part of one parent. This of course was in accord with the judgment in 1967 of *R. v. Clarke*.[66]

The Supreme Court in *Re Article 26 and the Adoption (No.2) Bill, 1987*[67] held that Article 42.5 is not to be construed as being confined to a failure by the parents of a child to provide for their education. In the exceptional cases envisaged therein, the States shall supply not only the parental duty to educate but *any other duty* to cater for the personal rights of a child.

In the view of the Supreme Court in the *Doyle* case, Article 42.5 did not enable the legislature to take away the right of a parent who was in a position to do so to control the education of his child, where there is nothing culpable on the part of either parent or child.

The Hosford case

In *Hosford v. John Murphy and Sons Ltd*,[68] the plaintiffs claimed compensation for being permanently deprived of the love affection guidance, etc., of their father who was rendered unable to communicate following a severe electric shock, received while working for the defendants. In addition to claiming liability in tort they also claimed that the defendants' careless act amounted to an infringement of the rights conferred on each of the plaintiffs by Article 41 (the Family) and Article 42 (Education) of the Constitution which guaranteed that the State would protect the family and respect the right and duty of parents to educate their children. The plaintiffs contended that they were entitled to be compensated for the injury suffered by virtue of the infringement of these rights.[69]

Referring to Article 42 and to the State guarantee "to respect the inalienable right of parents to provide for the education of their children", Costello J. in the High Court acknowledged that Mr. Hosford was unable to exercise this right

---

65. Above, n.38.
66. 7 L&B 186.
67. Above, n.23.
68. [1987] I.R. 621.

because of the injuries he sustained and that his children's rights to be educated by their father (which he thought were implied from this Article) had been impaired by the negligent act which caused those injuries. He considered that whether these rights had been unconstitutionally infringed would depend on whether the negligent act constituted a breach of constitutional duty imposed by Article 42. He concluded:

> "I do not think it did. The State has given a "guarantee to respect" Mr. Hosford's right to educate his children, but I do not think that by these words the rights which Mr. Hosford enjoyed under this provision included an ancillary right not to be injured by a negligent act which interfered with his ability to exercise his rights *vis-à-vis* his children. His children would not therefore enjoy any implied ancillary right that their father would not be negligently injured. This being so, the defendant's negligent act did not infringe any of their Article 42 rights."[69]

In relation to interpretation Costello J. stated that the rights which the family enjoys *vis-à-vis* the State are rights which are correlative to the duties imposed and are ascertained by reference to those duties and he added:

> "It must be remembered that the Court is construing a constitutional document whose primary purpose in the field of fundamental rights is to protect them from unjust laws enacted by the legislature and from arbitrary acts committed by State officials."

Article. 42.5 and Adoption

In *Re Article 26 and the Adoption (No. 2) Bill 1987*[70] the Bill provided for the adoption under certain circumstances, of any child, whether born in wedlock or not, and whether one or both parents survive or not, where parents for physical or moral reasons have failed in their duty towards their children It also provided for adoption of children without the consent of their parents or guardian. The Bill was held not repugnant to the Constitution or any provision of it.

Counsel for the Attorney General placed considerable reliance on Article 42.5 as justifying the proposals in the Bill and submitted that the State had the duty and the right to protect and to vindicate the rights of a child who by reason of its parents' failure has lost, and is likely to permanently to lose, not only its rights as identified in Articles 41 and 42 of the Constitution but also other personal rights which, though unenumerated derive from the Constitution.

In the opinion of the court Article 42.5 should not be construed as being confined, in its reference to the duty of parents towards their children, to the duty of providing education for them. In the exceptional cases envisaged by

---

69. *ibid.* at 627.
70. Above, n.23.

that section where a failure in duty has occurred, the State by appropriate means shall endeavour to supply the place of the parents. This must necessarily involve supplying not only the parental duty to educate but also the parental duty to cater for the other personal rights of the child.

The court accepted that the right and duty of the State to intervene upon the failure of parents to discharge their duty to a child could be considered under both Article 42.5 and Article 40.3. By the express provision of Article 42.5, the State is endeavouring to supply the place of the parents and is obliged to have due regard for the natural and imprescriptible rights of the child.

Section 3(1) Adoption Bill 1987 (now section 3(1) Adoption Act 1988) In an application under paragraph (a) or (b) of section 3 one of the matters required to be shown to the satisfaction of the court is that "by reason of such failure, the State, as guardian of the common good, should supply the place of the parents." This requirement raised two issues for determination by the court:

1. whether the place of the parents required to be supplied; and

2. if it did whether it would be appropriate for the State to supply their place.

In relation to whether the place of the parents required to be supplied, an example of a case where it might not, would be of a 16-year-old child who was found to have sufficient maturity not to require the replacement of the parents' duty to it. In relation to whether State intervention would be appropriate, a case might occur in which there was evidence of persons suitable and available to act in *loco parentis* to a child which would make the intervention of the State unnecessary and, therefore, inappropriate.

The Supreme Court concluded that Article 42.5 of the Constitution was not limited to cases where parents had failed in their duty to provide education for their children. Where a failure in duty has occurred the State may supply the parental duty to cater for the personal rights of the child, including those rights identified in Articles 40, 43 and 44, and the unenumerated personal rights of the child. Despite the *inalienable and imprescriptible rights of the Family*, under Article 41.1 of the Constitution the State could vindicate and restore the personal rights of a member of a family by altering the constitution of that family if necessary.

Addressing the issue of culpability (a matter in relation to Article 42.5 raised by Maguire C.J. in the *Doyle* case) the Supreme Court stated that the failure of the parents had to arise for physical or moral reasons but *this did not mean that the failure must necessarily, in every case be blameworthy*. It does mean that a failure due to externally originating circumstances such as poverty would not constitute failure within the meaning of the subclause.

Parents and Syllabi

Mr Justice Brian Walsh,[71] has suggested that: "As taxpayers, parents should be free to require that some of their tax be devoted to the teaching of what they wish their children to learn." that if parents wish it for their children, there seems to be no objection to the State providing religious education of the type requested by the parents.

This suggestion was advanced in the context that in doing so the State would not be endowing religion contrary to the provision of Article 44. The present author suggests that such a proposition if valid in relation to one subject would also be valid in relation to any other, leading to the ultimately determination of subject syllabi by parents. What are the parameters of such rights (given the claim by the Department of Education outlined in the next chapter) and how realistic is such a proposition is a matter for future consideration by the courts.

The Constitution Review Group

The Review Group dealing with the concept of "the family" points out[72] that the family recognised and protected in Articles 41 and 42 is the family based on marriage, and while they received many submissions to the effect that Article 41 should be amended so as to recognise in the Constitution, family units other than the family based on marriage, their preferred option is to retain the pledge by the State to protect the family based on marriage but also to guarantee to all individuals a right to respect for their family life, whether that family is, or is not, based on marriage.

The emphasis of Article 41 is the protection of the rights of the family as a unit rather than the protection of rights of individuals resulting from a family relationship. The Review Group considers that the rights of the family as a unit are emphasised in Article 41 and Article 42 to the possible detriment of individual members.[73] Article 8(1) of the European Convention on Human Rights provides: "Everyone has the right to respect for his private and family life, his home and his correspondence" and the Review Group point out that the focus of this provision is on the protection of an individual's right to family life as distinct from protection of the rights of a family unit.

The Group states that while the family should retain a certain authority and autonomy, this should not be such as to prevent the State from intervening where the protection of the individual rights of one member of the family requires this and it should not prejudice the rights of the individuals within the family.

---

71. Litton (ed.), *The Constitution and Constitutional Rights, The Constitution of Ireland 1937–1987* (1988) p. 99.
72. *Report of the Constitution Review Group* (1996), p. 321.
73. For family rights under Art. 41 see *Re a Ward of Court* [1995] 2 I.L.R.M. 401.

"natural", "inalienable"

The Review Group were concerned that giving the family rights which are described as "inalienable or imprescriptible", even if they are interpreted as not being absolute rights, potentially placed too much emphasis on the rights of the family as a unit as compared with the rights of the individuals within the unit. The Review Group considered that the description of any rights or duties specified in Articles 41 or 42 should not include the objectives "natural", "inalienable" or "imprescriptible".

Recommendation

The Review Group recommends:

> "Remove the adjectives 'natural', 'inalienable', 'imprescriptible' from Articles 41 and 42".

"parents"

The Review Group points out that the reference to parents in Article 42.1 is confined to the family based on marriage but considered it appropriate that the rights under Article 42 should apply to all non-marital parents, provided they have appropriate family ties and connections with the child in question.

Recommendation

The Review Group recommends:

> "Article 42.1 should be amended to apply to all non-marital parents, provided they have appropriate family ties and connections with the child in question".

Note there is no indication of this proposal in the wording proposed for Article 42.1.

"Religious", "intellectual", "social"

The Review Group considered it better not to attempt to itemise the various aspects of education and that Article 42 should simply refer to education.

Recommendation

The Review Group recommends that the section might thus be amended to read as follows:

> "The State acknowledges that the primary educator of the child is the family and guarantees to respect the right and duty of parents to provide, according to their means, for the education of their children".

Chapter 8

Control of Education and Parents

While the Constitution contains no specific provision dealing with control of education, various provisions have the effect of severely restricting the power of the State to control the Irish education system. In the main, we have a system which is state funded but not state controlled. The constitutional rights of:

(a) parents; and

(b) religious denominations,

constitute the main constraints on state control of the system. Article 42.2 refers to private schools and schools recognised or established by the State and Article 42.4 refers to private and corporate educational initiative as well as the provision of other educational facilities or institutions by the State. Article 42.4 of the Constitution states:

> "The State . . . shall endeavour to supplement and give reasonable aid to private and corporate educational initiative, and when the public good requires it, provide other educational facilities or institutions . . .".

The provision of "reasonable aid to private and corporate educational initiative" permits the continuation of funding for private secondary schools and the provision of "other educational facilities or institutions" covers the other post-primary types of school.

Article 44.4 refers to schools under the management of different religious denominations and Article 44.5 provides "every religious denomination shall have the right to manage its own affairs" and this would include managing schools.

Private Schools

Most primary and secondary schools are private schools, recognised by the State,[1] supplemented and given state aid[2] and under the management of different religious denominations.[3] In the primary sector there exists a small number

---

1. Art. 42.2.
2. Art. 42.4.
3. Art. 44.4.

of model schools controlled and managed by the State. In the secondary sector, secondary schools are schools given reasonable aid[4] as "private and corporate educational initiatives" and community and comprehensive schools schools as well as third level institutions are "other educational facilities or institutions" provided by the State.[5]

Primary Education

There are two types of primary school: privately owned and managed schools; and model schools. The present basis for this system is a letter from E.G. Stanley (Chief Secretary of Ireland) to the Lord Lieutenant in October 1831. There are two versions of this letter both of which are reproduced in the Appendix to Akenson, *The Irish Education Experiment*.[6]

The absence of any statutory enactment in relation to the primary education sector has been highlighted on a number of occasions.

Kenny J. in *Newell v. Starkie*[7] in 1916 reviewed the history of control of national education:

> "... in the year 1831 grants of public money for the education of the poor were entrusted to the charge of the Lord Lieutenant of Ireland,[8] to be expended on the instruction of the children of every religious denomination under the superintendence of Commissioners, then nine in number, appointed by the Crown, and styled 'The Commissioners of National Education.' In 1845 and 1861 Charters were granted, under which the Commissioners were created a corporate body, with power to hold lands and to make leases, to erect and maintain schools, to sue and be sued in their corporate name, and to have a common seal. The power of appointing and removing Commissioners was vested in the Lord Lieutenant, and the total number was limited to twenty. Apparently the Commissioners were left to prescribe the machinery for carrying out the beneficent objects of the charters according to their discretion at least I have not been referred to any statutory enactments or rules."

It was argued that the Board of Commissioners was not a creature of Statute, that it was an illegal body, and that its acts were absolutely without authority. Kenny J. held that while there was no statutory enactment, the contention that it was an illegal body was quite unsustainable having regard to the Charters. He stated:

> "This is an extreme proposition at the end of seventy-one years from the incorporation of a body that in numbers of Acts of Parliament during that period has been recognised as the established head and centre of our system of national education in Ireland, and, in my opinion, cannot be sustained."

---

4. Art. 42.4.
5. Art. 42.4.
6. Akenson, *The Irish Education Experiment* (1970) pp. 392–402, See also pp. 118–120.
7. [1917] 2 I.R. 73 at 77–78.
8. The year of Stanley's Letter.

He then went on to say that the board had been conducting business on settled and uniform lines, had been accepted by Parliament and the public as a legal body exercising its powers without protest and apparently in a legal and regular fashion.

Model Schools

In the pre-Constitution case of *Leyden v. Attorney General*[9] Murnaghan J. pointed out:

> "certain schools were not under the control or management of local patrons and managers. These were called Model Schools. . . . They have been built out of funds placed by Parliament at the disposal of the Commissioners, and are under their exclusive control. Rule 59 of the Rules (1911–12) reads; 'The chief objects of the Model schools are to promote united education, to exhibit to the surrounding schools the most improved method of literary and scientific instruction, and to educate candidates for the office of teacher. No religious instruction was provided in the Model Schools as in the National schools, but opportunity was given for pupils to receive religious instruction, if arrangements could be made for such, under Rule 32. No local patron or manager existed in the case of Model schools, and Rule 50 provides: 'The Commissioners (of National Education) are the patron and manager of the Model School'."

The Catholic Archbishop and Bishops in a pastoral letter issued at the Maynooth Synod[10] in 1900 commented:

> "the maintenance of the Model Schools, which violate the principle of local control and managership, which is the very essence of the whole system, is a wrong to Catholics and an unpardonable waste of public money."

Parents

The following Articles of the Constitution specifically refer to parents:

Article. 42.1

> "The State . . . guarantees to respect the inalienable right and *duty* of parents to provide . . . *for* the religious and moral, intellectual, physical and social *education* of their children."

Article 42.2

> "Parents shall be free to provide this education in their homes or in private schools or in schools recognised or established by the State."

---

9. [1926] I.R. 334.
10. See IER, 1900, p. 553.

Article 42.3.1°

> "The State shall not oblige parents in violation of their conscience *and* lawful preference to send their children to schools established by the State, or to any particular type of school designated by the State."

The State cannot oblige parents to send their children to any particular type of school designated by the State. The State may have a preference but it cannot designate this preference. Parents thus have the exclusive right to choose the type of school they wish their children to attend. Note that the wording of the Article is "*and*" lawful preference not "or" lawful preference despite the fact that the Irish version is "*nó* rogha dleathaí" which translates as "or".

Article 42.4

> "The State shall when the public good requires it, provide other educational facilities or institutions, with *due regard*, however, *for the rights of parents, especially* in the matter of religious and moral formation."

"Due regard" See Chapter 7 above.

"especially" The use of this word preceding "religious and moral formation" has specifically singled out these matters but they constitute only one of the rights of parents that the State must take into account in providing "other" educational facilities or institutions.

Michael McDowell, S.C., has commented:

> "It is only when 'the public good requires it' that the State is empowered to provide "other educational institutions". But State schools may only exist with due regard for parents rights and not in substitution for the State aid for private education."[11]

He argued that parents have a say in student admission and in teacher selection through those whom they choose to educate their children. Would this "say" theoretically exist regardless of the extent of the powers of those in charge of denominational schools? He also stated that in his opinion geographic catchment areas for private schools would be unconstitutional. On the basis that the State would then effectively be choosing the schools to which parents had to send their children. According to McDowell:

> "While undoubtedly the courts would uphold the State's right to maintain minimum standards in educational institutions aided by the State it does not follow that it can dictate entry to private secondary schools, or the content of State-aided education, or that schools receiving State aid must prepare students for particular examinations . . . it is clear from Articles 42 and 44 that parents

---

11. "Choice and the Constitution", *Sunday Independent*, September 26, 1993.

and private educators are entitled to agree student entry requirements, course content and school policy."[12]

He then concluded: "the fundamental question remains whether private education is entitled to public funding without public control, and on this Article 42 leaves no room for doubt."

The denominational system and the rights of parents in regard to the religious and moral formation of their children compliment each other. In the main parents send their children to denominational schools to partake as co-religionists and because of the particular ethos of a school. The protection of the ethos of a school and the admissions policy of a school are also complimentary. In order to safeguard the ethos of a denominational school the management would be entitled to insist that the majority of students admitted to their school are co-religionists. This would not necessarily rule out the admission of children of other religions persuasions but merely impose a limit on their numbers.

Admission Tests

In 1993 Minister Niamh Bhreathnach announced[13] that schools which awarded places on the basis of academic performance or socio-economic status would no longer be eligible for State grants paid to approved post-primary schools. Such tests denied some children the right to attend their local school and hit pupils from disadvantaged backgrounds. Some six months earlier Ms Bhreathnach had criticised the Irish model of education which delivered its full liberal benefits "only to an elite".[14] The Minister was concerned that in the past Irish education had paid less attention to its social effects and to its socio economic role. In a submission to the National Education Convention[15] in October, Ms Patricia O'Donovan of the ICTU supported the Minister's stand and claimed that tax payer's money should not be used to maintain barriers to social equity.

In relation to the proposal that selective admission tests be abolished and that funding be withheld from fee paying secondary schools which conduct admission examinations Mr McDowell in his article "Choice and The Constitution" stated:

> "Any attempt by the Minister to impose such a condition on State aid seems so obviously constitutionally infirm....any action taken on foot of such a circular would, in my view and in the view of many others, fall immediate victim to constitutional challenge."[16]

---

12. *ibid.* See Art. 42.2 and *Re Doyle*, p. 64 above.
13. At the Easter Teacher Congresses. See also *Irish Times*, August 13, 1993, "Minister warns Schools on entry tests", by Frank Kilfeather.
14. *Sunday Times*, March 7, 1993.
15. *Irish Times*, October 15, 1993.
16. Above, n.11.

He concluded that the implications of parental choice go further than the illegality of the Ministers proposal and that if schools receiving State funding were prohibited from allocating their places on the basis of academic capacity, or if subjective selection criteria were excluded, the next step would be geographic catchment areas, and that such a policy would also be unconstitutional and illegal. The Minister, however, obtained the agreement of the managerial associations to selection procedures which provide for the discontinuation of student selection on the basis of academic ability.[17]

Mr McDowell argued that if the State is dissatisfied that fee-paying schools are favouring the educationally advantaged the State can offer "other educational facilities" but that the State is not entitled to use economic muscle to force schools in receipt of State aid to implement Government policy on admission or to make those schools, in effect, "types of schools" designated by the State.

An editorial in the "Education and Living" supplement to the *Irish Times*[18] entitled "Climbdown on entry tests" stated that the financial threat had been removed and secondary management authorities had "agreed" on a voluntary basis to discontinue the tests. The editorial commented that it was precisely because the Minister did not have any legal power to influence admissions policy in secondary schools that the proposed financial sanctions were important. It was the only real power the Minister had.

A positive method by which the State might remedy a perceived inequity in regard to access to private schools might be by the introduction of an assisted places scheme similar to that established by section 17 of the United Kingdom Education Act 1980. This introduced a means-tested scheme to assist pupils academically able to benefit from an independent school education. The total number of assisted pupils per annum must at least include 60 per cent from publicly maintained schools.

Teacher Selection

In relation to teacher selection in private schools Mr McDowell reasons that if parents have an inalienable right to determine the content of education, and to choose who educates their children, any person to whom parents delegate their duty must retain the same right. He states:

> "Protection afforded by the Constitution for parents and proprietors of private schools also extends to teacher selection . . . A proposal that Local Education Authorities appoint or dismiss teachers in private schools funded by the State would also be unconstitutional."[19]

---

17. See CL 51, December 2, 1993, and Agreed Memorandum attached.
18. December 7, 1993.
19. Above, n.11.

Control of Syllabi

Syllabus content in private secondary schools is beyond State prescription other than for grant purposes, but syllabus content in primary schools is not. Article 42.3.2° provides:

> "The State shall, however, as guardian of the common good, require in view of actual conditions that the children receive a certain minimum education, moral, intellectual and social."

To date this provision has been used to oblige parents under the School Attendance Acts to cause their children to attend school. It cannot be used in relation to school syllabi because 'a certain minimum education, moral, intellectual and social' has never been defined.

One subject which the State cannot make obligatory on the syllabus is religious instruction because under Article 44.4 the State is prohibited from affecting prejudicially the right of a child to attend a school receiving public money without attending religious instruction. Plans to make religion an examination subject in the Leaving Certificate were reported[20] to require new legislation and possibly even a constitutional referendum before the subject could be nationally assessed. The late Professor J.M. Kelly, however, in his article "Education and the Irish State" stated that religious instruction could be seen as forming part of the minimum moral education which the State is entitled to demand.[21]

In its submission to the National Education Convention in October 1993 the Department of Education claimed[22] that it had established that the State has the right in law:

> ". . . to lay down a whole series of matters concerning the content of education and the manner of its delivery. This legislation could, therefore, cover *subject syllabuses*, the length of the school day and year, assessment of pupils and the inspection of teaching."

The position, however, may not be as straight forward as at first appears. To the extent that the State can require that children receive a certain minimum education, moral, intellectual and social under Article 42.3.2° it may prescribe what it considers that minimum to be but it cannot go further than that. Moral, intellectual and social education are the three components that parents have the right and duty to provide for under Article 42.1. But see Professor Niall Osborough's comment on the Kenny interpretation of education in Article 42.2 in *Ryan v. Attorney General*[23] contained in Chapter 5 above.

Does this State power only extend to literacy, numeracy social development,

---

20. Cullen, "Hitch in plans for religion in schools", *Irish Times*, May 26, 1994.
21. (1990–1992), XXV–XXVII Ir. Jur. at 87 *(N.S.)*.
22. See *Irish Times*, October 19, 1993.
23. [1965] I.R. 294.

etc.? Does it extend to syllabi or can it not go further? Does the power of the State in relation to the minimum mean a minimum in terms of subjects or a minimum in terms of syllabi or both? It would appear to the author that it extends to both.

In relation to subject syllabi the State has guaranteed in Article 42.1 to respect the inalienable right and duty of parents to provide for . . . the religious and moral, *intellectual*, physical and social education of their children. "Parents are free to provide *this education* in their homes or . . . in schools recognised or established by the State." Do parents have the constitutional right to determine the content of their children's education? It is suggested that the State's power in Article 42.3.2° has to be placed in the context of the unequivocal guarantee to parents in Article 42.1. To date, in prosecutions under the School Attendance Acts the courts have refused to adopt a hypothetical standard against which to assess children being educated at home or in private schools.

The right of parents would seem to extend to curricular matters, because parents are not without a say in relation to other subjects or in relation to a higher standard than the minimum required by the State. In addition Article 2 of Protocol No 1 of the European Convention on Human Rights referred to in Chapter 4 above stipulates that *the State shall respect the right of parents to ensure such education and teaching in conformity with their own religious and philosophical convictions.* In the *Campbell and Cosans v. United Kingdom* case[24] it was stated that this right extended primarily to curriculum content and the manner in which it was conveyed. It is the parents who are providing the education and they are recognised as the primary and natural educator of the child. The right of the State is also limited by the phrase "in view of actual conditions".

Representation of Parents

Examination results are not a criteria of receiving such education but of achieving a certain standard, therefore, monitoring of syllabi content and inspection are the methods the State should use to ensure that this requirement is met.

The concept of the Church acting on behalf of parents was explained by Fr Martin Brennan, Professor of Education in Maynooth, when he wrote in 1938:

> ". . . the Catholic people or parents of Ireland for whom the bishops and parish priests are trustees, submit their schools to a system of national education, as a result of which the State pays the teachers and gives other financial assistance."[25]

---

24. [1981] 3 E.H.R.R. 531.
25. Brennan, *The Catholic School System of Ireland* (1938) pp. 257–271. See also O'Buachalla, *Education Policy in Twentieth Century Ireland* (1988) pp. 215–216.

In 1953 De Valera stated:

> "There are few parents associations as such and parent participation in school activities is therefore usually in accordance with the desires of individual parents in this respect. The Constitution of Ireland however, lays down that the primary rights and responsibilities in education are those of the parents and our system of education is based throughout on this principle."[26]

In a statement issued by Patrick Hillery Minister for Education on May 20, 1963 in regard to the management of the proposed new comprehensive schools, he stated:

> "*having regard to the rights of parents, who* in relation to the fundamental principles of education *are represented by the church* and in view of the church's teaching authority, I have consulted the Catholic hierarchy on the management of these schools. . . . I have not of course as yet been in a position to consult with any Vocational Education Committee on this."[27]

The development of a denominational system in accordance with the wishes of parents cannot be ascribed to the constitutional provisions which are *de jure* neutral on this matter. Viewed in the light of conditions obtaining at the time of their adoption, the constitutional provisions were extremely liberal and far-reaching enough to accommodate all philosophies and none.

Few would deny the right of parents to have their children educated in accordance with their own ethos or philosophical convictions and they have chosen to do this by their support for denominational schools of their choice. Indeed it has been held in the case of *Campbell and Cosans v. United Kingdom*[28] that parent's philosophical convictions were entitled to respect in accordance with Article 2 of the First Protocol. In addition Bunreacht na hÉireann states that parents shall not be obliged in violation of their conscience and lawful preference to send their children to schools established by the State, or to any particular type of school designated by the State. Difficulties, when they arise, generally arise in relation to administration.

There was no doubt that in the past parents or lay persons were not welcomed by the Church authorities as participants in managing primary education. The Hierarchy at a meeting held on October 9, 1934 adopted recommendations of the Central Council of the Catholic Managers Association:

(a) to maintain the rights of primary school managers;

(b) to insist that any additional monies come from central funds and not from local rates;

---

26. *ibid.* p. 320, n.37.
27. See Randles, *Post-Primary Education in Ireland, 1957–1970* (1975) App. 1, p. 333, nn. 20 and 21 (emphasis added).
28. Above, n.24.

(c) that no lay committee of any kind should be associated with the manager in school management;

(d) the site of schools must remain in the names of Trustees, one of whom should be the Bishop.

The minutes recording the adoption of these recommendations were signed by Thomas O'Doherty, Bishop of Galway, Secretary, October 15, 1934.[29]

Convention on Human Rights

Article 2 of the First Protocol to the European Convention on Human Rights requires a State to show respect for parent's religious and philosophical convictions and this includes respecting parent's wishes in relation to corporal punishment. The Article states:

> "No person shall be denied the right to education. In the exercise of any of the functions which it assumes in relation to education and to teaching, the state shall respect the right of parents to ensure such education and teaching in conformity with their own religious and philosophical convictions." *Note the specific separation of educating and teaching.*

In the *Campbell and Cosans* case[30] the Commission considered the latter part of Article 2 the "State's obligation to respect the right of parents to ensure . . . education and teaching in conformity with their own religious and philosophical convictions and stated that although *this right extended primarily to curriculum content and the manner in which it is conveyed, it also covers the organisation and financing of public education*".

In the opinion of the Commission the disciplining of children "must also be considered to form a natural and even inseparable part of the parental duties to educate and teach their children." Parent's views on corporal punishment were philosophical convictions and as such entitled to respect. The Commission concluded that measures used for the purpose of punishing and correcting faults as a matter of discipline must clearly be considered as a function assumed by the State in relation to education and teaching, thus obliging the State to respect the religious and philosophical convictions of parents. This meant that a student could not be subjected to corporal punishment against the wishes of his or her parents.

Article 44.4

Article 44.4 obliges the State, when the public good requires it to provide *other* educational facilities or institutions "with due regard, however, for the rights

---

29. Dept. of Finance S22/4/37.
30. Above, n.24.

Article 44.4

of parents, especially in the matter of religious and moral formation". The State does not have a free hand in relation to these other facilities or institutions, once again the rights of parents must be taken into account.

"especially"

It would appear that the rights of parents generally must be considered but especially in the matter of religious and moral formation.

"religious and moral formation"

The distinction between religious *education* and religious and moral *formation* was addressed by Costello P. in the *Campaign to Separate Church and State v. Minister for Education*[31] when he drew attention to the fact that parents have rights not only to provide for the religious education of their children under Article 42.1 but also rights in the matter of their religious *formation* under Article 42.4 and that Article 44.4 specifically enjoins the State when providing "educational facilities" to have regard to both of these distinct rights. He stated:

> "The difference between the ordinary meaning of these two concepts is not difficult to identify: broadly speaking, the religious education of a child is concerned with the teaching of religious doctrine, apologetics, religious history and comparative religions, whilst the religious formation of a child involves familiarising the child not just with religious doctrine but with religious practice (by attendance at religious services) and developing the child's spiritual and religious life by prayer and bible reading and I think that the Constitution should be construed so as to reflect this meaning. In the case of parents who profess the Catholic faith the religious formation of their children involves ensuring that their children attend Mass and that they pray and receive the sacraments on a regular basis."[32]

The Constitution Review Group

See section at the end of Chapter 6 above.

---

31. Unreported, High Court, Costello P., January 17, 1996.
32. *ibid.* at pp. 39–40 of the judgment.

Chapter 9

Control of Education and Religious Denominations

From the days of the ancient Irish monastic schools,[1] through the parochial schools of the middle ages down to the present day, religious have owned and controlled some schools throughout Ireland. James Johnston Auchmuty[2] states that following the dissolution of the Irish monasteries ordered by Henry VIII in 1537, for a period of two hundred and fifty years it was the dual purpose of education in Ireland to turn out English speaking and Protestant children.

The Statute 12 Elizabeth 1, An Act for the Erection of Free Schools 1570 provided:

> "there shall be from henceforth a free school within every diocese of this realm of Ireland, and the school master shall be an Englishman or of the English birth of this realm; and that the Lord Archbishop of Armagh, the Lord Archbishop of Dublin and the Lord Bishop of Meath and the Lord Bishop of Kildare, and their successors for ever, shall have the nomination, institution and appointment of the school master within their several diocese from time to time."

Schools were founded by churches and by church groups specifically for the purposes of proselytising Roman Catholic children and the titles of some of these schools and of their promoters clearly illustrates their religious nature. One such initiative was the Anglican Charity schools established and promoted by the Church of Ireland in the early eighteenth century in which the curriculum had a high catechetical content. These came under state control in 1733 because of the lack of private subscriptions to ensure their survival. Another instance was the Erasmus Smith Schools founded in 1669 to propagate the Protestant faith. These in turn inspired the Charter schools which followed. Officially called the Charter Schools of the Incorporated Society for Promoting English Protestant Schools in Ireland, they were established in 1733. They did not according to Auchmuty[3] adopt "an avowedly proselytising attitude till 1775" when none but Roman Catholic pupils were admitted until 1803.

---

1. See McGrath, *Education in Ancient and Medieval Ireland* (1979).
2. Auchmuty, *Irish Education* (1937) p. 42.
3. *ibid.* p. 57.

Stanley's Letter

Stanley's letter of 1831 (see Chapter 8 above) specifically set out to provide state financial support on a multi-denominational basis. It provided for a combined literary and a separate religious education either before or after the ordinary school hours. It was the first attempt at non denominational education in Ireland.[4]

Áine Hyland[5] point out that: "The Presbyterian Church in Ireland, through the Synod of Ulster, was the first of the main churches to oppose the system of national education". It objected, *inter alia*, to the mixed (religious) nature of the board and to the separation of religious and literary instruction. The dissatisfaction of the Anglican Church culminated in the foundation of the Church Education Society in 1839.

There is some evidence that the Catholic Church may have been appraised of the national school development in advance because in a Pastoral Letter of 1826 they stated that to secure sufficient protection for the religion of Catholic children, under a system of joint education of Protestant and Catholics they deemed it necessary that the master be a Roman Catholic in schools where the majority of the pupils were Catholics. Nonetheless the Catholic Church was less united in their attitude to national schools. Archbishop McHale of Tuam and nine other bishops were totally opposed to them while Archbishop Murray of Dublin and 16 other bishops were in favour of tolerating them. Cardinal Cullen advised Rome that with safeguards for religion in these schools they should be allowed to continue and Rome issued a Rescript on January 16, 1841, leaving it to the discretion of each bishop to permit or not permit national schools in his diocese. In view of the foregoing it seems clear that the Irish school system assumed its denominational character more than a century prior to the 1937 Constitution.

The 1936 Jesuit submission for the new Constitution[6] suggested: "... it will be the aim of the educational authorities to facilitate the provision of denominational schools for all" and the draft Article 4(e) provided: "Schools maintained or subsidised by the State shall be in principle denominational".[7] Although the authority cited in support of the submission and of the draft article was the Encyclical "Divini Illius" of Pius XI, the draft was rejected.

The Managerial System

From the earliest times religious denominations have exercised control over the primary and secondary school systems through the ownership and management

---

4. Alvey, *Irish Education, The case for Secular Reform* (1991), App. 5, p. 134.
5. Hyland and Milne, *Irish Educational Documents* (1987) Vol. 1, p. 103.
6. 1095/30 De Valera papers.
7. 1095/46 De Valera papers.

of the schools. The denominational managerial system, in particular, became virtually synomous with the primary sector.

Murnaghan J. in *Leyden v. Attorney General*[8] stated that while the original plan for the national system envisaged in Stanley's letter was the adoption of a secular type of education over the greater part of the country "the managerial system" was adopted. He stated:

> "Under this system the management of a school was entrusted to local managers, and, subject to certain standard qualifications which were prescribed by the Board (The Board of Commissioners known as the Commissioners of National Education in Ireland was created by Royal Charter 26 August 1845, A supplemental Charter was granted on 11 March 1861), the appointment of teachers rested with the managers."[9]

In *McEneaney v. Minister for Education*[10] the same judge delivering the majority decision of the Supreme Court referred to the "managerial system" devised by the Board to administer the funds provided by Parliament for Primary education and stated:

> "This system was adopted to obviate difficulties connected chiefly with religious belief. In most cases the schools were not the property of the Board but they were recognised by it as national schools. A Manager, e.g., the parish priest or rector of the Church of Ireland, was nominated by an outside authority and the nomination was sanctioned by the Board – when sanctioned the duties and functions of the manager were minutely provided for in the Rules and Regulations made by the Board."[11]

The Constitution

Politicians are reported[12] as criticising the Constitution and one is reported to have stated that: "The handing over of compulsory primary education to denominational interests, not necessarily democratically organised, did not allow for genuine educational choice." However, this may not be a valid criticism. The Constitution did not hand over compulsory education to denominational interests, the evidence points to the contrary. It may have facilitated denominational involvement or more accurately its continuance.

Séamus Ó Buachalla states that the policies pursued by the Cumann na nGaedhal Government in the 1920s were singularly important because they established a model which the education system followed with minor modifications for almost 40 years. He says:

---

8. [1926] I.R. 334.
9. *ibid.* at 354.
10. [1941] I.R. 430.
11. *ibid.* at 439.
12. *Irish Times*, August 20, 1987.

> "The relative roles of government, churches, teachers, managerial bodies, politicians and parents were established during this period with a degree of permanence which normal socio-political forces were powerless to disturb."[13]

The present Constitution recognised the status quo and Article 42.4 of the Constitution states:

> "The State shall provide *for* free primary education and shall endeavour to supplement and give reasonable aid to private and corporate educational initiative".

In *Crowley v. Ireland*[14] Kenny J. opined that the change from Article 10 of the Constitution of the Irish Free State: "All citizens of the Irish Free State (Saorstát Éireann) have the right to free elementary education" to Article 42.4 making the State "provide for" free primary education was intended to emphasise that the State's obligation was not to educate but to provide *for* it. He concluded:

> "Thus, the enormous power which control of education gives, was denied to the State: there was interposed between the State and the child the manager or the committee or board of management."[15]

The obligation to "*provide for*" relates only to primary education and therefore this conclusion is valid only in relation to it.

The independence of denominational secondary schools derives from the fact that they are private institutions, albeit ones given state aid. The same section of Article 42 specifically empowers the State to provide other educational facilities or institutions. Where this does happen, the State does control them. There are also a few model schools under direct state control. David Alvey[16] suggests that the reference to the State's role in Article 42.3.1° seems to act as a deterrent to the establishment of state-owned public schools, that while the establishment of such schools is not prohibited, there seems to be a constitutional bias against their establishment.

Boards of Management

From a legal perspective control through the composition of boards of management is relevant with regard to Article 44.2.4° and 44.2.5° of the Constitution.[17]

Article 44.2.4°

> "Legislation providing State aid for schools shall not discriminate between

---

13. Ó Buachalla, *Education Policy in twentieth century Ireland* (1988) p. 64.
14. [1980] I.R. 102.
15. *ibid.* at 126–127.
16. Alvey, *Irish Education, The Case For Secular Reform* (1991) p. 83
17. Farry, "The Green Paper, Boards of Management and the Constitution", *Decision Maker*, Issue No. 6, Autumn (1992), p. 62.

schools under the management of different religious denominations, nor be such as to affect prejudicially the right of any child to attend a school receiving public money without attending religious instruction at that school."

Article 44.2.5°

"Every religious denomination shall have the right to manage its own affairs, own, acquire and administer property, movable and immovable, and maintain institutions for religious or charitable purposes."

The State is not obliged to provide aid for schools under the management of different religious denominations, but if it does decide to do so (as it has) then it must in doing so comply with Articles 42.4, 44.2.4° and, it is suggested, with Article 44.2.5°.

Denominational primary and secondary schools within the State are private schools owned and managed by different religious denominations and Article 44.2.4° explicitly recognises the management of schools by different religious denominations. Has the State the right to prescribe the composition of boards of managements of denominational schools? Has the State the right to prescribe that the chairperson of a board of management of a denominational school should be elected rather than appointed by the patron/trustees? The 1993 Green Paper: *Education for a Changing World*, proposed the membership and composition of boards of management which the State considered appropriate for primary and secondary schools.

It is suggested that the Churches have management rights in relation to denominational schools. These rights are not dependent on the State for their existence. They are rights which exist by virtue of such schools being privately owned initiatives and also by virtue of the specific rights of denominations guaranteed by the Constitution.

Management by a Religious Denomination

Under the Constitution religious denominations are entitled to build and manage their own schools, select staff, etc. The granting of state contributions for this purpose and the conditions under which it is granted is the central issue in most of the current debate. Does the management of a school by a religious denomination come within the constitutional right to manage its own affairs contained in Article 44.2.5° of the Constitution? The Article does not confine this right to the management of its own *religious affairs* but to the management of affairs in general even though particular matters are specified. If it is accepted (as the author has) that it does, then the question arises, when is a school under the management of a religious denomination.

It must be noted that this right of every religious denomination to manage its own affairs is contained in Article 44 dealing with religion and not in Article 42 which deals with education. It should therefore be interpreted as being a safeguard for religion. However, because the denominational system of school management is also recognised in Article 44 and the protection of property of educational institutions is contained in the same Article, it is not possible to exclude an overlap between Article 42 and Article 44. It can be legitimately argued that the matters relating to education dealt with in Article 44 could have been included in Article 42 but their inclusion in Article 44 appears to be equally valid.

Can it seriously be argued that the management of a denominational school is not a matter concerned with religion? The different Articles of the Constitution, no more that their contents, cannot be read in isolation as though they were clinically encased in hermetically sealed compartments. It is the Constitution which is an entity, not its individual articles. The remarks of the late Professor Kelly[18] provided an early indication of dissatisfaction with the arrangement of Articles 40 to 44 in particular.

It is also significant that Article 44.2.6° relating to the property of religious denominations is not contained in Article 43 which deals with private property but is included in what might be termed the protection of religion under Article 44. In *Tormey v. Attorney General and Ireland*,[19] the Supreme Court has held that the Constitution must be read as a whole and that its several provisions must not be looked at in isolation "but as interlocking parts of the general Constitutional scheme".[20] The Court added that: "where two constructions of a provision are open in the light of the Constitution as a whole, despite the apparent unambiguity of the provision itself, the Court should adopt the construction which will achieve the smooth and harmonious operation of the Constitution."[21] In the *Tormey* case the Court held that there was an interrelation between Article 34.3.1° and Article 34.3.4°. Henchy J. delivering the unanimous decision of the court said that strict construction should be avoided when it would allow the imperfection or inadequacy of words used to defeat or pervert any fundamental purpose of the Constitution.

If the nominees of the trustees are in a minority on a board of management can it be claimed that the school is under the management of a religious denomination? Should the trustees have a majority of one on each school board if a school is to be under the management of a religious denomination?

One commentator has written[22] that the private property provision in the Constitution did not preclude the Oireachtas from legislating in regard to management of church run schools. This, of course, is permissible but what is at issue is the right of the State to prescribe the management composition of denominational schools, to abolish an owner/management majority on such boards of management, and the ambit and extent of the State's legislative power.

---

18. Kelly, *Fundamental Rights in the Irish Law and Constitution* (2nd ed., 1967) p. 37.
19. [1985] I.R. 289.
20. *ibid.* at 296.
21. *ibid.*
22. "Grey areas cloud Church and State roles in education", *Irish Times*, October 28, 1993.

Does "charitable purposes" in Article 44.2.5° include education? In a reference to this provision, the significance of the fact that this came after the provision dealing with discrimination between schools led the writer to suggest that "it means we should probably not read charitable to include educational, and so this provision, too, is not relevant".

This comment seemed to discount the fact that the advancement of education has been held to be a charitable purpose in Ireland long before the present Constitution, certainly for the purpose of charitable bequests and subsequent to the adoption of the Constitution the courts have endorsed this interpretation in a number of cases. The building and maintenance of schools are among the charitable purposes for which an institution may be maintained and many schools are held for the purposes of education under charitable trusts. The same commentator later explained[23] that it was quite likely that "charitable" included education. He felt, however, that on the *generalia specialibus non derogant* precept of interpretation, (that general words will not, in the absence of a definite intention to do so, undermine the effect of special words) one should pay more attention to the issues covered by the Articles, to education rather than to the religious article, when dealing with education.

In the same article it was suggested that Church interests "would be best advised to argue their case on policy grounds and not to regard the Constitution as a trump card."[24] Initially, at any rate, this was advice which church leaders did not accept because at that time, they continued to insist on board of management control as the only satisfactory means of ensuring the ethos of their schools.

The constitutional recognition of denominational schools and of the right of such denominations to manage such schools means that school owners or patrons are entitled to ensure that the denominational ethos of their schools is observed by management, principal, teachers and students. In any new educational structures introduced by legislation the owners/patron are therefore likely to insist on:

1. control over the conduct of boards of management in relation to ethos;

2. control over the selection and dismissal of teachers in relation to ethos;

3. control over the admission or expulsion of students in so far as it affects ethos.

The fact that owners/patrons rights in relation to these matters may be given statutory recognition will not inevitably mean that only co-religionists may be teachers or students in such schools.

---

23. "He who pays the Piper Calls the Tune", *Irish Press*, November 24, 1993.
24. *ibid.*

Religious Denomination

The words used in Article 44.2. 4° are not "under denominational management" but "under the management of different religious denominations." Does the use of these words in this context import formal clerical management or clerical sanction rather than participation by lay members of a particular denomination or both? Must there in any event be designation or recognition by official Church authorities? It would seem to be so, but only litigation may provide the answer. A school cannot be said to be under the management of a religious denomination merely because a majority of the nominees of different groups on the board of management are of a particular religious persuasion. To date management of a school by religious denomination has been recognised as being, management by clerics designated by church authorities, *i.e.* denominational control has been synonymous with clerical control.[25]

The word "denomination" has not been interpreted by the Irish courts but in Canada has been held to include a religious order of nuns, the Sisters of St. Joseph for the Diocese of Toronto.[26] Despite this Mr Justice Walsh in a reference to this particular provision in the Constitution[27] has stated: "it is to be noted, however, that the reference to 'religious denominations' is probably not susceptible of an interpretation that extends it to religious orders as such".[28] He considered that a religious order is a group of individuals and that it is free to change its religion as often as it likes or cease to be a religious order altogether. He observed: "The property is always the property of the individuals who make up the order"[29] and he drew attention to the fact that this provision:

> "comes under the heading of religion and not under the heading of property, so obviously it must be interpreted as being intended to safeguard religious freedom . . . Obviously, if there was not some guarantee against the arbitrary taking away of any such property, there would be a serious impediment to the freedom of religion."[30]

Some eight years previously John Kelly seems to have doubted that a religious order could be equated with 'religious denomination' and he asked if it could be said that the property of a religious order or institution is the property of a 'religious denomination'?[31] He claimed: "On a narrow construction of the phrase, the protection of Article 44.2.6° would extend only to the property, *e.g.* of the Catholic Church as such, but this is not a legal person; its 'property' is

---

25. Whyte, *Church and State in Modern Ireland* (2nd ed.) p. 17.
26. [1982] 135 D.L.R. (3rd) 177.
27. Litton (ed.), *The Constitution and Constitutional Rights, The Constitution of Ireland 1937–1987* (1988) p. 103.
28. *ibid.*
29. *ibid.*
30. *ibid.*
31. Kelly, *The Irish Constitution* (1st ed., 1980) fn. on p. 536.

normally held by its bishops or by orders or institutions sharing the Catholic faith and obedience."[32]

It is likely that the Trustees of a primary or secondary school would be regarded by the courts as the designated authority of the religious denomination involved. The Trustees of Maynooth were seen as the designated authorities of the Roman Catholic Church for the (denominational) administration of the college, certainly by O'Higgins C.J. and by Henchy J. in *McGrath and Ó Ruairc v. Trustees of Maynooth*.[33] In this case the Supreme Court held that the dismissal of the plaintiffs did not violate Article 44.2.3°, that Maynooth was a religious institution covered by Article 44.2.5° and that the college were within their constitutional rights. The argument that the prohibitions of discrimination imposed on the State in Article 44.2.3° covered or extended to institutions in receipt of State funds was rejected by Kenny J. The other judges did not address this aspect so the matter awaits final adjudication.[34]

State Funding

May the constitutional guarantees only be fully enjoyed by a denominational school which does not seek state aid? Or stated another way can the State require a denominational school to relinquish a measure of constitutional protection as a condition for obtaining state aid? Does the provision of state aid require the maintenance of a delicate balance?

Michael McDowell, S.C., has written that:

> "It is simply not competent for the State to withdraw funding from a private school because it does not conform with a management model reflecting interests stipulated by the State... or any particular balance of such interests."[35]

Professor Gwynn Morgan of U.C.C., writing during the following month[36] about the powers of the State as a consequence of funding, commented that the Church's place in education rested on the ownership of school buildings. He continued: "And even while making significant grants to schools, the State has been careful (presumably for political reasons) not to use the leverage which this money might seem to give it to effect any change in this position." Note that Gwynn Morgan referred to leverage of the State not to legal powers which was what Michael McDowell was addressing. The present author suggests that Professor Gwynn Morgan's statement (above) about political reasons inhibiting the State implies that he thinks such legislation would be constitutional. The exact extent of the State's powers is another matter.[37]

---

32. ibid.
33. [1979] I.L.R.M. 166.
34. Casey, *Constitutional Law of Ireland* (1987), p. 570.
35. "Choice and the Constitution", *Sunday Independent*, September 26, 1993.
36. See *Irish Times*, October 28, 1993.
37. See Chap. 10, below.

Professor Casey states:

> "... a challenge to the system under which denominational national schools are funded seems unlikely to succeed given the Supreme Court's decision in *Crowley v. Ireland* [1980] I.R. 102 Yet this, if correct, leads to an odd result. The State may not, by statute or administrative action, make continuing religious allegiance a ground for dismissal from the public service or from private employment, since to do so would violate Article 44.2.3° but if it hands over to religious denominations money used for paying teachers' salaries, both it and they are free from constitutional constraints."[38]

Limitations on The State

While it could be argued that in general, the minister cannot prescribe the composition of boards of management of denominational schools without infringing the right of a religious denomination to manage its own schools there is no doubt that s/he can prescribe the terms under which state aid for such schools will be made available within the constraints imposed by Article 44.2.4° that:

> "Legislation providing State aid for schools shall not discriminate between schools under the management of different religious denominations ...".

There would however, appear to be serious limitations on the State in how far it can prescribe the composition of boards of management in denominational schools. The representation prescribed by the State must be such that it does not take over the management function. In this respect it is suggested that Article 44.2.4° cannot be read in isolation that it is linked to Article 44.2.5° and must be interpreted in conjunction with it. In the writer's opinion, denominational school owners, trustees, or management cannot be required, as a condition of state funding, to forego or to act contrary to their own dogma or religious philosophy.[39]

There is a difference between state aid (which incidentally may encompass more than financial assistance) and state control, and it can be suggested that if the State can prescribe majority representation on boards this means it effectively has control. The degree of control which the Catholic Church considers necessary was publicly stated, at the turn of the century in response to attacks on the managerial system in Catholic primary schools made in the press and at meetings of the Teachers Organisation.[40] In a pastoral address[41] the

---

38. *Op. cit.* above, n.34, p. 571.
39. See Farry, "The Green Paper, the Church and the Constitution", *Studies*, Summer, Vol. 82 (1993) and Farry, "The Green Paper, Boards of Management and the Constitution", *Decision Maker*, Autumn (1992), Issue No. 6.
40. Strangely enough not referred to by T.J. O'Connell in, *100 years of progress, the Story of the INTO* (1968).
41. From the Archbishops and Bishops of Ireland meeting at Maynooth College, on June 23, 1898. See IER July/December 1898, pp. 75–79.

Hierarchy stated that it essentially included a constant supervision over the conduct of the teachers, the choice of books, and religious and moral training of the pupils, as well as over the educational efficiency of the schools. The pastoral also stated that it was quite obvious that such control could never be maintained without the power of choosing worthy and efficient teachers, and also the right of removing those whose character and conduct rendered them unfit to be entrusted with the important duty of instructing and training Catholic youth.

Rev Lambert McKenna S.J. who had been chairman of the National Program Conference on Primary Education had written in States Rights in Education: "The conferring of money by the State brings with it no right to settle, independently of parents, the nature of the education given".[42]

State Powers

The fact that primary schools are denominational does not mean that they are totally outside state control. The fact that a school is denominational relates only to its ethos where it is state funded. The provision of state financial aid is not, and should not be, unconditional. The State has a responsibility to act in the public interest, in accordance with natural and constitutional justice and to uphold the law. It also has an obligation to ensure that its delegated functions are performed in accordance with these principles, by those to whom it provides financial assistance.

In addition it has the power to insist on standards and procedures, which it has formulated being followed. In relation to primary schools it has sought to do by means of Rules and Circular Letters. The Rules for National Schools 1965 provide[43] for the withdrawal of recognition from a school where the manager refuses or fails to have any of the official rules, or decisions under them made by the Minister, complied with. In such an event no grants from State funds are payable to the manager or any teacher or other person in respect of that school. This withdrawal of recognition should be regarded as the ultimate sanction because it effects students, who may be totally innocent parties. On the other hand, as the situation presently exists the manager is not bound by the Rules as the Minister is. If a manager was so bound, the Minister or an aggrieved party could seek to enforce them directly by legal action. On occasion this remedy would be preferable to withdrawal of recognition and could be pursued without disruption of the work of the school. It may be, that all new managers or management committees should be required to formally agree in writing to accept and implement the Rules as a condition of obtaining State subsidy.

---

42. *Studies*, Vol. XVI, 1927, p. 221.
43. Rule 30.

Criticism of Present Methods

According to the Bishop of Cork and Ross, Dr Michael Murphy[44] the boards of management in the country's national schools have little or no power over policy, curriculum or staff arrangements and the extent to which they actually manage the schools is highly questionable. Curriculum and policy matters were decided by the Department of Education and the board had no function in relation to capital expenditure. Dr Murphy stated that while the board of management appointed teachers, it could only appoint persons recommended to it by selection boards set up by the patron.

Leaving aside the complaint about the lack of consultation by the State in the area of curriculum, Dr Murphy's criticism of the appointments system would be endorsed by many teachers and parents. It should, however, also be remembered that the the present arrangements are not immutable.

Staff and Ethos

The *Flynn v. Power*[45] is authority for the view that under the Unfair Dismissals Act 1977, conduct which failed to uphold the moral ethos of a school and which affects the school and its pupils can constitute a ground for fair dismissal of a teacher. It was held that the appellant's conduct amounted to a rejection of the norms of behaviour and ideals which the school were endeavouring to instil in and set for, its pupils. It was also capable of damaging the Holy Faith Sister's efforts to foster in their pupils norms of behaviour and religious tenets which the school had been established to promote. In these circumstances there were substantial grounds for dismissing the appellant. It was also held that the fact that the conduct relied on to justify the dismissal was not prohibited either expressly or by implication in the appellant's contract of employment was only part of the overall circumstance to be considered by a court under the Act of 1977 where the test is whether in all the circumstances there were substantial grounds to justify the dismissal. Costello J. referred to the judgment of the Supreme Court of Canada, in *Re Caldwell and Stuart*[46] which dealt with the reasonableness of the requirement that Roman Catholic teachers should conform to the religious tenets taught in a Roman Catholic school, and to the difference between a secular and religious school in such matters.

The constitutional implications of the use of a state subvention to support a policy of employing only practising Catholics as teachers in a Catholic school was unfortunately not raised in the *Flynn* case. Professor Casey comments:

---

44. As reported by John Walshe in the *Irish Independent*, August 5, 1987.
45. [1985] I.R. 648.
46. (1985) 15 D.L.R. (4th) 1.

"case law suggests that a constitutional challenge to this policy will be fruitless. A dismissed teacher who sued might well fail on the ground that he or she had accepted the post knowing that continuing religious profession was a term of the employment contract"[47]

The *Crizzle* Case

In the English case of *Board of Governors of Saint Matthias Church of England School v. Crizzle*[48] the Employment Appeal Tribunal held that the Board as an employer were justified under the Race Relations Act 1976 in imposing a condition that in order to be shortlisted candidates for a position as headmaster should be "suitably qualified teachers with inner city experience *who are committed communicant Christians*". The applicant, an Asian Roman Catholic, was not a communicant and in answer to one of the questions on the application form: "Are you able to produce a statement from your Parish Priest that you are a practising member of the Roman Catholic Church?", he replied no. When she was not offered the post she claimed unlawful racial discrimination under the Race Relations Act 1976. The Tribunal considered that the same tests would apply to any board of governors who restricted the head teacher to being a Jew or a Muslim, Sikh, Buddhist or any other religion, hence the importance of the present case.

In the earlier case of *Berrisford v. Woodard Schools (Midland Division) Ltd.*[49] a pregnant 19 year old school matron dismissed from a Staffordshire Church of England boarding school for seven to 18 year old girls, was held not to have been discriminated against contrary to the Sex Discrimination Act 1975. She had been dismissed when she told the headmaster that she did not plan to get married. The headmaster and the Chairman of the Board of Governors said that it would not be tolerable to retain her unmarried, while she became increasingly visibly pregnant as this was a sign of extra marital sexual relations and constituted a morally objectionable example to the pupils. A man known to have acted in a similar way would also have been dismissed. The EAT upheld the Industrial Tribunals finding that she had not been unlawfully discriminated against. Her example constituted the objectionable conduct. The real objection to her continued employment was the visible and outward sign of her conduct.

In relation to the hiring of teachers by denominational schools on the basis of their religion, Proinsias De Rossa, T.D., Minister for Social Welfare has referred to the constraints imposed on the legislature by the provisions of the 1937 Constitution and asked that the new education legislation establish clear limits on the rights and powers of patrons in this regard. He stated:

". . . my concern is that the legislation will effectively regulate those rights in

---

47. Casey, *Constitutional Law in Ireland* (2nd ed., 1992), p. 571.
48. [1993] I.C.R. 401.
49. *The Times*, March 14, 1991.

accordance with other constitutional principles e.g. freedom of conscience, freedom of expression, and the right to privacy, so that any appointment or promotion where denomination is a factor would have to be objectively justifiable to the relevant Education Board."[50]

Control and Ownership of School Premises

Article 44.2.5° also provides that: "every religious denomination shall have the right to . . . own, acquire and administer property". In 1989 the Campaign to Separate Church and State put forward a view that the ownership of schools by their patrons effectively gave a veto over educational change with which they disagreed and the suggested:

> "all national and second level school buildings should be in public ownership – preferably under decentralised, local education committees. This would facilitate democratic involvement and change in their activities."[51]

The Position Paper on Regional Education Councils[52] issued by Minister Niamh Bhreathnach, T.D., states:

> "The dispersion of school ownership can cause problems both in the efficient use of school facilities-particularly in areas where there are demands for the availability of a plurality of school types, *e.g.*, multi-denominational schools, Gaelscoileanna – and in responding to changes such as the *'rapid decline in the number of religious who are teachers and principals in schools'.*"[53]

The paper then refers to the Convention Report identifying that the establishment of intermediate educational tiers would be a useful mechanism in assisting the provision of multi-denominational education and concludes:

> "Accordingly, it would be appropriate to confer powers on the REC to own school buildings for leasing to different groups of patrons and trustees, in order to provide for the specified educational needs of the area. It is envisaged that most new school buildings, especially on green-field sites would be provided by this mechanism."[54]

Each REC would have the power to conduct periodic reviews of the trusteeship and management arrangements, to facilitate the transfer of trusteeship and management as required and to own and rent property for the purpose of their functions.

The White Paper on Education envisages that:

---

50. Text of Speech delivered to Democratic Left Conference, Listening Day on Education, Limerick, April 13, 1996. See also Letter to Editor, *Irish Independent*, April, 1996.
51. Colgan, *Minimum Requirements for Education Act(s)*, Campaign to Separate Church and State (1989), para 6.
52. Department of Education, 1994.
53. *ibid.* proposal 10.13, p. 16.
54. *ibid.*, p. 32.

> "In future education boards will own new school buildings and will lease them to different groups . . . This is in line with the practice in other member states of the European Union of providing publicly owned buildings for compulsory education. The Report on the National Education Convention noted that 'Ireland was seen as unique in requiring citizens to provide privately owned accommodation for this purpose'."[55]

State ownership of school premises would appear to be a vital element in a move toward civil control of schools. Note that the State has the option of providing State run schools but is not required to do so under the Constitution.[56]

The Constitution Review Group

In relation to Article 44.2.4° the Review Group point out that this subsection applies the principle of non-discrimination between religions in an educational context and provides constitutional authority for state funding of denominational education on the criteria specified. The Review Group states:

> "In effect, therefore, the State is permitted to engage in the practice of what might be termed the concurrent endowment of the schools of all religious denominations, provided that:
>
> (a) this is achieved by legislation;
>
> (b) there is no discrimination between the religious denominations;
>
> (c) any school receiving public monies respects the rights of each child to attend without receiving religious instruction at that school.
>
> The only legislation authorising State funding of denominational education would appear to be via the annual Appropriation Acts. However, the drafters of Article 44.2.4° probably envisaged that the legislation in question would be specific in character and establish a permanent statutory scheme whereby such aid might be disbursed. The present system of disbursing aid where, although the individual education votes are sanctioned by the Appropriation Acts, the application of these moneys to individual schools is governed by a series of non-statutory rules and circulars is unsatisfactory. It probably conforms to the letter (but not the spirit) of Article 44.2.4°. The Review Group understands that it is likely to change with the forthcoming Education Bill."

The Review Group state that Article 44.2.4° clearly has the potential in the context of an integrated curriculum to give rise to difficulties. The parents of some children not only insist on withdrawing their children from formal religious instruction but also object to the Roman Catholic ethos which permeates instruction in other subjects. The Group summarises the position as being that:

---

55. At pp. 64, 168.
56. Farry, "Education and the Constitution", *Studies*, Vol. 83, (Summer 1994), p. 170.

> "the present reality of the denominational character of the school system does not accord with Article 44.2.4°. The situation is clearly unsatisfactory. Either Article 44.2.4° should be changed or the school system must change to accommodate the requirements of Article 44.2.4°."

The Review Group did not address the right of a religious denomination to manage its own affairs as that right applies to education and schools but did not query whether Article 44.2.5° adequately preserves the autonomy of religious denominations.

The Review Group stated:

> "Article 44.2.5° is designed to preserve the autonomy of religious denominations and seems to do so satisfactorily. It is true that on a strictly literalist interpretation of this subsection it might not cover, for example, property held on trust for a religious body. The Review Group, however, agrees with Professor Casey's observations (*op. cit.*, 573) that the subsection should be recorded a purposive interpretation so that it covers 'property which, directly or indirectly, comes under the aegis of a religious denomination'. In these circumstances, no change is proposed".

Recommendation

No change is proposed.

Chapter 10

Control of Education and the State

State control of education and partisan state support for denominational education had been a feature of the Irish educational experience from the middle ages. Some Catholic prelates and nationalists had been fervent opponents of the English supported systems in Ireland but with the advent of independence both Church and politicians seemed content with the new Irish supported system. Until recently state control or indeed the absence of state control of the system has not been an issue, but the recent demand for multi-denominational and non-denominational schools has highlighted the absence of a system of state schools.

Murnaghan J. in *Leydon v. Attorney General*[1] referred to the fact that for almost 100 years state control over primary education in Ireland had been exercised by, and state aid for its development entrusted to, the Commissioners of National Education in Ireland. He added:

> "From time to time the Board issued rules and regulations, but these were not subject to the direct control of Parliament: and, save such control as the voting of money by Parliament could give, in the absence of specific statutory enactment, the legal powers of the Board depended upon its position as a common law corporation under its Charter. The legal position of the Board is, I think, clearly stated by Kenny J. in his judgment in *Newell v. Starkie*,[2] to which we have been referred."

The Department of Education

The Ministers and Secretaries Act 1924 provided for the establishment of Departments of State to administer the business of the public service in Saorstát Éireann and it states that: "each Department and the powers duties and functions thereof shall be assigned to and administered by the Minister hereinafter named as the head thereof".[3] Section 1(v) states:

> "The Department of Education which shall comprise the administration and business generally of public services in connection with education, including primary, secondary and university education, vocational and technical training,

---

1. [1926] I.R. 334.
2. [1917] 2 I.R. 73.
3. Section 1.

endowed schools, reformatories, and industrial schools and all powers, duties and functions connected with the same and shall include in particular the business powers, duties and functions specified in the Fourth Part of the Schedule to this Act, and of which Department the head shall be, and shall be styled, an t-Aire Oideachais or (in English) the Minister for Education."

In the schedule to the Act the Department of Education was assigned the task of administering the business, and public services in connection with education, including primary, secondary, and university education, vocational and technical training, endowed schools, reformation and industrial schools and all powers, duties and functions connected with the same. In particular it was assigned the business, powers, duties and functions of the branches and offices of:

1. The Commissioners of National Education in Ireland. (Primary)

2. The Intermediate Education Board for Ireland. (Intermediate)

3. The Commissioners of Education in Ireland. (Endowed schools)

4. The business and functions relegated to Technical Instruction of the Department of Agriculture and Technical Instruction. (Vocational schools)

Successive Ministers interpreted their role in the light of the Constitution and the *de facto* position of church control of denominational education. One Minister for Education stated that he regarded the position as Minister in the Department of Education as "a kind of dungaree man.", the plumber who would take the knock out of the pipes and link up everything.[4] Another said that the system was "a co-operative" and that the State did not hold all the shares.[5] Dr Patrick J. Hillery during his period as Minister stated that it was, of course, "the function and duty of a Minister for Education to be the captain of the ship and so to have the vessel in good trim and see that all hands are at work".[6] In November 1960 he said that under the system then prevailing the managers were the persons charged with the direct government of national schools, that he, as Minister, did not propose to change this system and that he therefore had no function in the setting up of parent-teacher organisations.[7] Ministers and the Department of Education have sought to exercise a degree of control by means of two books of Rules, the 1965 Rules for Primary Schools and Rules of Secondary Schools.

---

4. 159 *Dáil Reports*, 1956, *per* General Mulcahy.
5. 161 *Estimates, Dáil Reports*, 1957, *per* Jack Lynch.
6. Address to Dublin Comhairle of Fianna Fáil, February, 28, 1964.
7. See 182 *Dáil Reports*, 1960.

Rules for National Schools

The Rules for National Schools under the Department of Education were published by Dr Hillery in 1965. No authority is cited for the making of the rules but the preface recites Articles 42 and 44.2.4° of the Constitution and states:

> "In pursuance of the provisions of these Articles the State provides for free primary education for children in national schools, and gives explicit recognition to the denominational character of these schools."

The Rules deal, *inter alia*, with the patron and his duties, the manager and his duties, general conditions for recognition by the Department, building, improving and furnishing of national schools, qualifications of teachers, religious and secular instruction and inspection of schools.

McWilliam J. in his judgment in *Crowley v. Ireland*[8] stated:

> "I have been referred to the Rules for National Schools under the Department of Education given under the hand and seal of the Minister for Education on January 22, 1965, and those of the Minister for Finance 11th February 11, 1965. No party has referred me to the statutory or other authority for making these rules but, as no party has contested their validity. I will accept that they are binding. certainly, until revoked or altered, it appears to me that they should be observed by the Minister for Education."

It is likely that the basis for this statement was estoppel. Having indicated by the rules how powers will be exercised the Minister will not be allowed to go back on this representation to the detriment of a person who has relied upon them.

The absence of a statutory basis for national school rules has been adverted to as far back as 1941 when Murnaghan J. in *McEneaney v. Minister for Education*[9] stated that the present rules for national schools made by the Department of Education had no statutory foundation. He also said that it followed that those rules could be changed except in regard to the conditions of existing teachers.

The fact that the Rules for national schools do not have a statutory basis does not mean that they are without legal effect. In *Staunton v. St. Laurence's Hospital Board*[10] it was held that a clause in a Circular Letter gave rise to a contractual obligation which bound the Minister. In *Lachford & Sons Ltd. v. Minister for Industry and Commerce*[11] persons who complied with conditions published by the Minister were held entitled to claim a subsidy. However, if the Minister for Education does not comply with his/her own rules it does not mean

---

8. Unreported, High Court, McWilliam J., December 1, 1977.
9. [1941] I.R. 430.
10. Unreported, High Court, Lardner J., February 21, 1986.
11. [1950] I.R. 33.

that the Minister is acting ultra vires as would clearly be the case if the rules were of statutory origin.

Recognition by the Department

Control is exercised by the State through this mechanism in that a school which is not recognised does not receive a state subvention. This does not go quite so far as the U.K. where a school must qualify for registration and it is a criminal offence to conduct an unregistered school. Perhaps it is time that a similar system of school registration was introduced in this jurisdiction.

Post Primary Schools

This sector is, at present, composed of:

1. Privately owned and managed secondary schools
2. Vocational schools
3. Publicly owned comprehensive/community schools
4. Community Colleges.

The post-primary sector has been described by Noel Barber S.J. as a tripartite system with a clear hierarchical order, private, comprehensive/community and vocational.[12]

Private Secondary Schools

Like the private primary system the private secondary sector has no statutory origin. A privately owned and managed system was in place before the introduction of legislation. There are a number of relevant Acts which affected the system: The Intermediate Education (Ireland) Act 1878; the Educational Endowments (Ireland) Act 1885; the Intermediate Education (Ireland) Act 1900 and the Intermediate Education (Ireland) Act 1914 and the Intermediate Education (Amendment) Act 1924.

The Intermediate Education (Ireland) Act 1878

This Act established the Intermediate Education Board for Ireland to promote intermediate secular education. It introduced a system of public examinations and provided for the payment of money to the manager of a school on the basis of the results achieved by the students. This was the payment by results system which enabled the State to give indirect funding to secondary schools. The

---

12. *Comprehensive Schooling in Ireland* (1989) p. 4.

Intermediate Education Board's sole function related to examinations. It had no functions relating to management or control of schools.[13]

Educational Endowments (Ireland) Act 1885

Prior to this Act public endowment was only possible to non-Catholic schools. This Act entitled Catholic schools to a share in the Irish School endowment.

Intermediate Education (Ireland) Act 1900

A system of inspection was proposed in this Act to replace the examinations system.

Intermediate Education (Ireland) Act 1914

This Act established a register of intermediate teachers and permitted the payment of grants toward teacher salaries.

Intermediate Education (Amendment) Act 1924

This Act repealed the provision which made the payment of grants dependent on examination results. The business power, duties and functions of the Intermediate Education Board for Ireland was one of the branches of education assigned to the Department of Education in Part IV of the Ministers and Secretaries Act 1924.

The board of management in private secondary schools is composed of four Trustee nominees, two parents and two teachers. The chairperson is appointed by the Trustees and has a casting vote.

Vocational Schools and Community Colleges

Vocational schools are unique in having a firm statutory basis. The Public Libraries Act (Ireland) 1855 was introduced to give greater facilities for the establishment in Ireland of free public libraries and museums or schools of Science and Art. Land or buildings could be purchased, altered or fitted out for the purposes of the Act. The principal Act was amended by the Public Libraries (Ireland) Amendment Act 1877 when the term "Science and Art" was extended to include schools of music. Borough Councils and Town Commissioners were given liberty to apply part of the rate, which they had been authorised to levy under the 1855 Act toward the payment of salaries of teachers of a school or schools of music and the purchase of instruments, books, etc.

---

13. O'Flaherty, *Management and Control in Irish Education* (1992) pp. 9–10 and Coolahan, *Irish Education*, p. 63.

The first Bill to promote Technical Education in Ireland in 1866 was not printed. Likewise the second Bill a year later, which coincided with the formation of the City and Guilds of London Institute, was also not printed. Technical Instruction *per se* was given statutory recognition in the Technical Instruction Act 1889. The Report of the Recess Committee in 1896 led to the establishment of an Irish Department of Agriculture and Technical Instruction under the Agriculture and Technical Instruction Act 1899. The business and functions related to technical instruction of this department (vocational schools) were among those transferred in the Ministers and Secretaries Act 1924 to the Department of Education by Saorstát Éireann. The existing system was examined and the Report of the Commission on Technical Education (1927) led to the introduction of the present legislation, the Vocational Education Act 1930 under which vocational schools are established. This Act provides for the establishment of vocational education committees composed of 14 elected members to establish and maintain a suitable system of continuation education and to supply or aid the supply of technical education in its area.

Comprehensive Schools

A number of comprehensive schools were established following a press statement by Dr Patrick Hillery, T.D., the Minister for Education in 1963. They would provide a three year preparatory course for the Intermediate Certificate Examination. The buildings would be provided largely from state funds, teachers salaries would be paid directly by the State and they would be managed by a committee of management. Although built and maintained totally out of state funds, Louis O'Flaherty[14] points out that the two models of board of management which have emerged[15] are subject to a significant measure of Church control. The "Catholic model." is a three person board composed of a Chairman nominated by the Bishop, a nominee of the Minister and a nominee of the VEC. The "Protestant/Jesuit model" consists of three nominees of the Protestant Bishop or the Jesuit Provincial, a nominee of the Minister and a nominee of the VEC. There is provision that the Minister in consultation with the Bishop of the Diocese, may alter the terms of the scheme from time to time. The comprehensive school initiative was abandoned with the advent of community schools and no new comprehensive schools have been established in recent years.

Community Schools

When he introduced the Education Estimates for 1965–1966 Mr. Colley, the then Minister for Education, stated that he would seek co-operation between

---

14. *ibid.* p. 24.
15. *ibid.* p. 41.

secondary and vocational schools in each community. In November 1965, in a speech to the Cork branch of Tuairim, Mr. Colley said that uncoordinated building of secondary and vocational schools could not go on indefinitely and that since neither the secondary nor vocational authorities could be expected to call a halt, the State would have to intervene.

In January 1966, Mr Colley wrote to secondary and vocational school authorities[16] seeking co-operation and a series of meetings to discuss the findings of a survey on post primary needs carried out by the development branch of the Department of Education. The meetings achieved little. Both authorities failed to co-operate in combining school facilities and teaching. In the Autumn 1968 edition of *Studies*, the late Sean O'Connor, Secretary of the Department of Education stated that: "Single Community schools are the rational requirement in most centres outside the large urban areas."[17] The Department had adopted the community school idea and set about implementing it. The conflict between the non-denominational aspects of the vocational sector and the denominational aspects of the secondary sector meant that community schools could not fit into either system.

The Department of Education published a "working paper" on community schools in October 1970. (A copy was sent to a member of the Hierarchy on October 12, 1970, a copy was sent to the Irish Vocational Education Association three months later on January 14, 1971. Copies were sent to the ASTI and Vocational Teachers Association on April 7, 1971.) The text of the document[18] proposed: "the provision of free post primary education for all children, the elimination of barriers between secondary and vocational schools, and the elimination of overlapping and duplication in the provision of teachers, buildings and equipment". Paragraph 4 stated that community schools were seen as resulting from the amalgamation of existing secondary and vocational schools or in city areas from the development of individual single schools instead of the traditional development of separate secondary and vocational schools. The Vocational Education (Amendment) Act 1970 was introduced to facilitate VEC participation in Community schools.

The capital costs involved (site, buildings, equipment, furniture and playing facilities) would be met in full out of public funds subject to a negotiated, agreed local contribution. The current costs of running the school would be funded directly and in full by the Department.

The board of management which governs and directs the school is composed of three nominees of the religious authority concerned, three Vocational Education Committee nominees, the Principal, two parents and two teachers. The Vocational Education (Amendment) Act 1970 enables a VEC to *jointly* with a

---

16. Randles, *Post-Primary Education in Ireland* (1975), App. 2, p. 338.
17. At p. 247.
18. Published in the *Irish Times*, November 12, 1970

person maintaining a school recognised by the Minister, to establish a suitable system of continuation education, establish and maintain continuation and technical schools, and to establish and maintain courses of instruction in continuation and technical education. The VEC has representation on the board of management but the school is seen as being under the direct control of the Department of Education.

Community Colleges

Many VECs were unwilling to enter into community school projects which would result in control being vested in the Department of Education and a diminution in the number of schools under local control. Their answer was the development of community colleges under local Boards of Management established under section 21 of the Vocational Education Act 1930. These boards are comprised of three nominees of a religious authority, three VEC nominees, two parents, two staff and a person nominated by a minority religious group. In the authors opinion the reservation of a place on the basis of religion may well be unconstitutional under Article 44.2.3°.

Rules for Secondary Schools

These Rules were made by the Minister for Education pursuant and by virtue of the Intermediate Education (Ireland) Acts 1878 to 1924, and of every other power enabling him so to do.

The 1878 Act established the Intermediate Education Board for Ireland with functions of instituting and carrying on a system of public examinations of students, providing for the payment to managers of schools complying with the prescribed conditions, of fees "dependent on the results of public examinations" of students, and generally applying the funds placed at the disposal of the Board. It also had functions of defining the subjects and nature of examinations. The Intermediate Education (Amendment) Act, 1924 repealed the words "dependent on the results of the public examination of students" in paragraph 3 of section 5 and this enabled provision for the payment to managers of schools complying with the prescribed conditions.

The Rules give the Minister power:

1. to institute and carry on a system of public examinations;

2. to provide for the payment of prizes and the award of certificates to students;

3. to provide for payment to managers of schools complying with prescribed conditions;

4. generally to apply the funds for the purpose of the Act.

It should be pointed out that the existence of a statutory authority or basis does not necessarily mean that rules made under or by virtue of such authority must of necessity be unchangeable or inflexible.

State Right to Regulate

According to a report on the National Education Convention[19] the Attorney General had indicated that if the State choose to draw up detailed legislation covering education it would in all likelihood be entitled to prescribe not only the content of education in terms of subject syllabuses, but also the manner of its delivery in terms of school hours per day, days per year, required subjects, methods of assessing efficiency of education by inspection of teaching and the assessment of pupils as well as any other matter the Minister might deem necessary to regulate.

Clearly in the light of the Supreme Court decision in *Re Article 26 and the School Attendance Bill, 1942*[20] the State does not have the power to prescribe the manner in which a child is educated at home or in a private school (see Chapter 7, above). It is precisely because of this judgment that the *School Attendance/Truancy Report*, is careful to state:

> "Where children are to be educated *in school*, the State, in carrying out its constitutional duty, must also be in a position to decide such matters as the period during which a child must attend school, the length of the school day, the subject matter to be taught and the manner of the teaching. Children and parents must abide by the school regime, subject only to parent's rights to withdraw their children from religious instruction."[21]

---

19. See *Irish Times*, October 19, 1993.
20. [1943] I.R. 334.
21. Department of Education, April, 1994, p. 5 (emphasis added).

Chapter 11

Interference with Education

The right of the State to interfere or regulate education under Article 42 is specifically confined in the Article itself. By virtue of Article 42.3.1° the State is prevented from obliging parents "in violation of their conscience and lawful preference to send their children to schools established by the State, or to any particular type of school designated by the State." The State cannot dictate the school which a child must attend or prescribe that s/he attend a state school or a school designated by the State. Whereas the rights specified in Article 40 are "subject to public order and morality" there is no such general limitation or justification for State interference contained in Article 42. Mr Justice Brian Walsh referring to the absence of these constraints has stated:

> "It is to be noted that the overriding consideration of public order and public morality is not referred to in Article 41, which deals with the family, or Article 42 which deals with Education."[1]

Article 42.3.2° does, however, justify the State requiring that children receive a certain minimum education, on the ground that it is the guardian of *the common good* and under Article 42.4 when the *public good* requires it the State is obliged to provide other educational facilities or institutions.

Landers v. Attorney General

In *Landers v. Attorney General*[2] it was claimed that legislation frustrated the decision of parents that a young boy should commence a professional singing career (which was a decision concerning his education) in a manner not required to ensure that he received a minimal education and was therefore in defiance of Article 42 of the Constitution.

The family of eight year old Michael Landers decided that he should accept paid engagements to sing professionally. Some engagements were performed in licensed premises. Summonses were served and convictions obtained against his father Thomas and his manager, for breaches of section 2(b) and (c) of the Prevention of Cruelty to Children Act 1904. The plaintiff issued High Court

---

1. Litton (ed.), *The Constitution and Constitutional Rights, The Constitution of Ireland 1937–1987* (1988).
2. (1975) 109 I.L.T.R. 1.

proceedings alleging that the said subsections were repugnant to the Constitution and were not carried forward by Article 50, and no longer formed part of the law of the State.

The High Court held that the sections of the Act were not repugnant to the Constitution and were therefore carried forward by virtue of Article 50. Finlay J. concluded that the proper definition of education as provided for in Article 42 did not include the public singing career of a child between the age of seven and 10 years. He stated:

> "If the subsections challenged in this case in any way inhibited the training or practice of Michael Landers in his musical accomplishment then a question of his education and the rights guaranteed to the family and to his parents in regard to his education might arise. The precise restriction, however, which is imposed by the 1904 Act and which is in these proceedings challenged seems to me to touch not at all upon the education of Michael Landers as a musician or as a singer nor upon any part of his education but only upon his professional public appearance at his present age. For these reasons I do not find Article 42 of the Constitution in any way applicable to these proceedings."[3]

Inhibiting Education

The comment of Finlay J. (as he then was) in the *Landers* case about inhibiting the training of the plaintiff was echoed by Professor Osborough when he stated:

> "The purposive character of the latter's [The Chief Justice's] definition of 'education', however, could in certain circumstances, have constitutional *sequelae*. It is hard to avoid the conclusion that any impediment threatening adversely to affect the maximisation of a child's intellectual talents by means of teaching and training, even if unconnected with educational arrangements at school, is liable to proscription on the initiative of parents choosing to rely on their constitutional rights. It would seem, for example, that the labour dispute ensuing on the appointment of Mr. McCarthy to the permanent principalship at the Drimoleague school [in the *Crowley* case], could be regarded as such an extraneous impediment."[4]

Professor Osborough then pointed out that the Ó Dálaigh definition of education in *Ryan v. Attorney General* (see Chapter 5, above) appeared to have been forgotten, or, ignored:

> "at least by those advising the litigants in the Drimoleague case. There, significantly, the claim presented was not one in which it was maintained that the rights of parents had been interfered with (Article 42.1); rather was it sought to establish that the right of the children to free primary education had been breached.(Article 42.4)."[5]

---

3. *ibid.* at 5.
4. "Education in the Irish Law and Constitution" (1978) XIII Ir. Jur. 171 (*N.S.*).
5. *ibid.*

The Conspiracy in *Crowley v. Ireland*

In the *Crowley* case[6] the plaintiff claimed that the teachers' trade union, the INTO, and the members of its executive committee conspired to deprive the infant plaintiff of her constitutional right to free primary education. The INTO had issued a circular to teachers in schools adjoining Drimoleague parish instructing them not to enrol Drimoleague pupils. The High Court held that because the purpose of refusing to enrol the Drimoleague children was to coerce the manager of the three Drimoleague schools to accede to the teachers' demands, the refusal constituted an unlawful act which was actionable at the suit of the children who had been deprived of their constitutional rights.

In the High Court hearing of the *Crowley* case McMahon J. stated:

> "The claim of the plaintiffs against the INTO is for damages alleged to have been suffered by the plaintiffs by reason of a conspiracy on the part of the INTO to deprive the plaintiffs of their constitutional rights. (Counsel), for the plaintiffs, made it clear that they did not in this action challenge the right of members of the INTO to withdraw their labour from the Drimoleague schools, and that they limited their claim to a contention that the directive (stating that children from the Drimoleague schools affected by the withdrawal of the teacher's services should not be enroled in other neighbouring schools) was an unlawful interference with the constitutional rights of the plaintiffs to free primary education."

McMahon J. then dealt with the plaintiffs reliance upon the decision in *Meskell v. C.I.E.*[7] and the reference by Walsh J. in *Murphy v. Stewart*[8] to the possible abuse of constitutional rights which might require the intervention of the courts and he continued:

> "I think it is doubtful whether the refusal of members of the INTO to enrol children from the Drimoleague schools can be treated as being a partial withdrawal of labour and the exercise of a constitutional right. If it is not the exercise of a constitutional right, there is no answer to the children's claim, because, as Mr. Justice Walsh pointed out in *Meskell v. Corás Iompair Éireann* it is no answer to a claim based on infringement of a constitutional right to say that the defendant was exercising a common law right . . .".[9]

The Primary Purpose

Mr. Justice McMahon then explained that the character of an act depends on the circumstances in which it is done and the exercise of a constitutional right for the purpose of infringing the constitutional rights of others was an abuse of

---

6. [1980] I.R. 102.
7. [1973] I.R. 121.
8. [1973] I.R. 97.
9. Above, n.6, at 109.

114   *Interference with Education*

that right which, in his opinion, could be restrained by the courts: He continued:

> "The teachers who refused to enrol the Drimoleague school children in adjoining schools *did not act primarily for the purpose of exercising a right to work or not to work, or to choose the conditions under which they would work*. In my view *their purpose was to deprive the Drimoleague children of primary education* in order to exert pressure on Fr. Crowley; what was done amounted to the use of unlawful means to deprive the Drimoleague children of their constitutional right. Therefore, it is actionable at the suit of the children who can show that they have been deprived of their constitutional right by the action of the teachers."[10]

The primary purpose for which the teachers acted was central to the decision against them. "Pursuit of genuine self interest, including trade union objectives, was established as a justification for that form of civil conspiracy where no more than the act of combination was illegal" writes Rideout[11] who cites Lord Cave in *Sorrell v. Smith*[12] as stating that:

> "If the real purpose of the combination is not to injure another, but to forward or defend the trade of those who enter into it, then no wrong is committed and no action will lie, although damage to another ensues".

Other Conspiracies

In *Crofter Hand Woven Harris Tweed Co. Ltd. v. Veitch*[13] the respondents, officers of the Transport and General Workers Union, acting in combination with each other instructed dockers at Stornoway, the main port of the island of Lewis to refuse to handle yarn imported from the mainland consigned to the appellants and also to refuse to handle cloth made by the appellants. The dockers without any breach of contract acted in accordance with these instructions and the appellants sought to stop the embargo. It was held that the *predominant purpose* of the combination was the legitimate promotion of the interests of the persons combining and since the means employed were neither criminal nor tortious in themselves, the combination was not unlawful.

In the English case of *Meade v. Harringay LBC*[14] the Court of Appeal held that an LEA which decided to shut its schools in sympathy with striking school caretakers was in breach of its statutory duty under section 8 of the Education Act 1944. The collusion between the LEA and the trade unions amounted to a *conspiracy to perform an unlawful act* and should be restrained. An order of mandamus (see Chapter 12 below) was granted.

Thirty odd years after the *Harris* case McMahon J. applied the predominant

---

10. *ibid.* at 110 (emphasis added).
11. Rideout with Dyson, *Rideout's Principles of Labour Law* (4th ed., 1983), p. 469.
12. [1925] A.C. 700.
13. [1942] A.C. 435.
14. [1979] 2 All E.R. 1016.

purpose test in *Crowley*, and, as indicated above, found that the primary purpose of the teachers action was to deprive the children in order to exert pressure on Fr. Crowley. At that hearing the evidence had not identified any of the infant plaintiffs as having been refused enrolment in neighbouring schools and the question of entitlement to damages stood reserved. Later in the Supreme Court Kenny J. endorsed McMahon J.'s finding and remarked that it was significant that INTO and the members of its central executive committee had not appealed against this finding and concluded: "Therefore INTO have been held to have caused an unlawful interference with the constitutional rights of the infant plaintiffs. . . ."

The question of damages for this unlawful interference with the constitutional right to free primary education fell to be decided by Miss Justice Carroll in *Hayes v. Ireland* in 1986[15] and by Barron J. in *Conway v. INTO*.[16]

In 1991 The House of Lords in *Lonrho v. Fayed*[17] held that the tort of conspiracy to injure can be established in two ways.

1. by showing that the intention to injure the plaintiff was the predominant purpose even though the means used was lawful, or

2. by showing an intention to injure the plaintiff and that unlawful means were used.

When unlawful means are used it is no defence to show that the primary or predominant purpose was to further or protect some legitimate interest of the defendant. It is sufficient to make the action tortious that the means used are unlawful.

---

15. *Hayes v. Ireland* [1987] I.L.R.M. 651.
16. Unreported, High Court, Barron J., December 7, 1988.
17. [1991] 3 All E.R. 303.

Chapter 12

Remedies

The late Chief Justice Ó Dálaigh in *The State (Quinn) v. Ryan*[1] stated that it was not the intention of the Constitution in guaranteeing the fundamental rights of the citizen that these rights should be set at nought or circumvented. The intention was that rights of substance were being assured to the individual and that the courts were the custodians of these rights. He added that:

> "As a necessary corollary it follows that no one can with impunity set these rights at nought or circumvent them and that the Court's powers in this regard are as ample as the defence of the Constitution requires."[2]

Special Category of Claim

Although it has been stated[3] that it is only in the absence of a common law or statutory cause of action that there is a necessity to sue directly for a breach of a constitutional right, the concept that there is a special category of claim for damages for unlawful interference with a constitutional right was accepted by the Supreme Court in *Meskell v. C.I.E.*[4] In this case Walsh J. opined:

> "In my view, upon the facts proved in this case the plaintiff is entitled to a declaration that his dismissal was a denial and a violation of and an unlawful interference with his constitutional rights, and that the agreement between the trade unions concerned and the defendants to procure or cause that dismissal was an actionable conspiracy because the means employed constitute a breach or infringement of the plaintiff's constitutional rights. In my view, the plaintiff is entitled to such damages as may upon inquiry be proved to have been sustained by him."[5]

---

1. [1965] I.R. 70.
2. *ibid.* at 122.
3. See Carroll J. in *Murphy v. Ireland*, unreported, High Court, Carroll J., February 21, 1996. In the English case of *Re S. (a minor), The Times*, March 30, 1993 it was held that there is no such tort as interference with parental rights and that an action for damages based upon allegations of infringement of such alleged rights will be struck out.
4. [1973] I.R. 121.
5. *ibid.* at 136.

General Damages

The first claim to reach the courts arising out of the judgment in *Crowley v. Ireland*[6] was *Hayes v. Ireland*.[7] The plaintiff had been a student at one of the Drimoleague schools affected by the teacher strike in April 1976 and was refused enrollment at neighbouring schools as a result of the INTO directive to their members. He claimed damages for the unlawful interference with his right to free primary education pursuant to Article 42.4. No special damages were claimed so the claim lay solely in general damages. Carroll J. stated: "I am satisfied that there should be an element of mental distress allowed as was allowed by McWilliam J. in *Cosgrave v. Ireland*[8] where he held the plaintiff was entitled to recover such damages as had been proved to have been sustained by him and also general damages for foreseeable mental distress, anxiety and inconvenience."[9] A sum of £4,000 general damages was awarded to the plaintiff.

In the *Cosgrave* case both special and general damages were awarded to the plaintiff whose statutory rights under the Guardianship of Infants Act, 1964 had been disregarded by the Department of Foreign Affairs in issuing passports for his children without his consent. Carroll J. deduced in *Hayes v. Ireland* that:

> "A plaintiff who establishes unlawful interference with a constitutional right must be in as strong a position as a plaintiff whose statutory rights have been infringed, and is entitled to recover damages for injury suffered by him."[10]

Miss Justice Carroll referred to the fact that in the Supreme Court majority judgment, Kenny J. agreed with the trial judge's finding that there was an unlawful interference with the constitutional rights of the infant plaintiffs to free primary education and she concluded:

> ". . . in my opinion the entitlement to damages does arise as a result of the unlawful interference by the teachers with a constitutional right. This is not the case of a lawful exercise of a constitutional right which comes into conflict with the constitutional right of another. The action of the INTO in issuing the directive and the action of the teachers in obeying it were unlawful. A plaintiff who establishes unlawful interference with a constitutional right . . . is entitled to recover damages for injury suffered by him."

This claim is in a category of its own being a claim for damages for unlawful interference with a constitutional right, a concept which was accepted by the Supreme Court in *Meskell v. C.I.E.*[11]

---

6. [1980] I.R. 102.
7. [1987] I.L.R.M. 651.
8. [1982] I.L.R.M. 48 at 55.
9. Above, n.7 at 658.
10. Above, n.7 at 655.
11. *op. cit.*, above, n.4. Hogan and Morgan point out in *Administrative Law in Ireland* (1st ed., 1986), p.383 that in *Kearney v. Ireland*, unreported, High Court, Costello J., March 13, 1986

Miss Justice Carroll held that the plaintiff was entitled to recover in full such damages as he could prove had been sustained by him. They were not to be reduced by any considerations relating to the teachers' position. She was satisfied that the plaintiff did suffer a detriment by reason of the loss of two years of school. But only one year could be held to be the responsibility of the defendants. The directive was only in existence from August 1976 to June 1977 and the plaintiff could have gone back to school in September 1977. So the damages claimed by the plaintiff could only relate to the academic year 1976/77.

No special damages were claimed so the claim lay solely in general damages. Carroll J. concluded:

> "I am satisfied there should be no element of mental distress allowed. It seems to me that this is not a case which would attract high general damages, neither is it one where future general damages should be awarded...In my opinion the appropriate figure for general damages to date is £4,000."

Michael Forde points out that the law regarding damages for breach of constitutional rights is only developing and that a number of important matters remain to be resolved.[12]

Exemplary Damages

The plaintiff in *Conway v. INTO*[13] was also a student adversely affected by the Drimoleague episode, but in addition to claiming general damages for the distress, upset, general inconvenience and detrimental effect on her educational progress, her character formation, her career prospects and her earning capacity she also sought exemplary damages by reason of the particular wrong suffered. Barron J. accepted that any interruption in schooling was damaging and that the extent of the damage depended upon the age at which it occurred, the length of time it continued, and the ability of the child affected. He considered that the defendants were responsible for the fact that the plaintiff:

> ". . . arrived at secondary school with less grounding in Irish and English than she would otherwise have had. As a result she was obliged to concentrate on those subjects which must have affected her overall performance in other subjects. As a matter of probability this must have affected her approach to the choice of a university course. As a matter of further probability this would have prevented her from achieving somewhat better results. . . ."[14]

---

where it was held that non-delivery of letters in prison was not a tort but an unjustified infringement of a constitutional right, Costello J. seems to suggest that the *Meskell* principle may be invoked only where ordinary tort law does not adequately defend or vindicate the constitutional rights of the citizen.

12. Forde, *Constitutional Law of Ireland* (1987), p. 788.
13. [1991] 2 I.R. 305. The defendants appealed unsuccessfully against the assessment of damages contending, *inter alia*, that exemplary damages should not have been awarded at all.
14. *ibid.* at 310.

In his summation he stated:

> "The principal started a special fourth class in February, 1977 during the dispute and Miss Conway attended this. The said break in her education lasted from April, 1976 to mid-February 1977".[15]

He did advert to the fact that it was only in August 1976 when the directive not to enrol was issued that the interference with the plaintiff's constitutional rights was unlawful. He was convinced that had she resumed schooling in September 1976 she would quickly have made up the loss of a terms work. He concluded that it was the further loss added to the effect of the lost term which caused her the loss for which she sought damages. The loss of schooling following the directive put her situation beyond recovery, there being no suggestion that better teaching after her schooling re-commenced, would have made up the loss.

Mr. Justice Barron also stated that it seemed to him that the reasoning of Hamilton P. in *Kennedy and Arnold v. Ireland*[16] applied to the instant case. There was *a totally conscious and deliberate action* on the part of the defendants to gain their own ends without any thought to those who would suffer as a result. In his view exemplary damages should be measured in an amount to meet the wrongdoing rather than to benefit the wronged. For that reason he would measure exemplary damages at £1,500, being a total of £100,000 spread equally among 70 claimants. He awarded the plaintiff damages under two other headings £7,500 for general loss and £2,500 for loss of career prospects.

The defendants appealed against the assessment of damages, contending, *inter alia*, that exemplary damages should not have been awarded at all. The Supreme Court dismissed the appeal holding that *exemplary damages are properly awardable in the case of a breach of a constitutional right even where the defendants are neither servants nor agents of the government or the executive.*

Reasons for Exemplary Damages

The object of awarding such damages is to punish the wrongdoer for his outrageous conduct, to deter him and others from any such conduct in the future and to mark the court's (or jury's) detestation and disapproval of that conduct. *Rookes v. Barnard*[17] was not followed. Finlay C.J. gave the following reasons:

(a) The right which was breached was one *expressly* vested in a child by the Constitution;

---

15. *ibid.*
16. [1987] I.R. 587.
17. [1964] A.C. 1129.

(b) The right which was breached was one which, having regard to the education and training of a child was of supreme and fundamental importance;

(c) It must be presumed that the defendants were aware of that importance;

(d) The breach of the constitutional right involved was an *intended*, as distinct from an inadvertent, consequence of the defendant's conduct.

Other Remedies

No remedy is provided in the Constitution in the event of the State failing to make provision for the benefit of citizens but according to Walsh J. in *Byrne v. Ireland*:

> "In several parts of the Constitution duties to make certain provisions for the benefit of citizens are imposed on the State in terms which bestow rights upon the citizens and unless some contrary provision appears in the Constitution, the Constitution must be deemed to have created a remedy for the enforcement of these rights. It follows that where the right is one guaranteed by the State, it is against the State that the remedy must be sought if there has been a failure to discharge the constitutional obligation imposed."[18]

The fact that the State has delegated the implementation of the right or protection on some other organ or servant does not absolve the State, (upon whom the primary obligation has been imposed) from responsibility to carry out the duty imposed upon it by the Constitution.

Article 10 of the Constitution of Saorstát Éireann provided that all citizens of the Irish Free State: "have the right to free elementary education" In the view of Walsh J. this was clearly enforceable against Saorstát Éireann if no provision had been made to implement that Article of its Constitution. He stated:

> "There are several instances in the Constitution of Ireland also where the State undertakes obligations towards the citizens. It is not the case that these are justiciable only when some law is being passed which directly infringes these rights or when some law is passed to implement them. They are justiciable when there has been a failure on the part of the State to discharge the obligations or to perform the duties laid upon the State by the Constitution."[19]

The State was also vicariously liable for the non-performance by its various organs of their duties.

In the *Crowley* case the Supreme Court held that the State had not been in breach of its constitutional obligation. This finding relative to the liability of the State has been criticised, perhaps too harshly. It may not be quite fair to state that the finding indicated a waning of judicial activism or that the work of

---

18. [1972] I.R. 241 at 264.
19. *ibid.* at 280.

Other Remedies

constitutional expansionism had ended or slowed down. A new constitutional right had been upheld. The question of liability was an entirely different matter.[20]

The right was implied from the duty. Would it then be reasonable to go from an implied right to a liability? The matter of liability had to rest on the duty, specifically on the wording imposing the duty. Given the precedents and the duty imposed, it was somewhat easier to find the existence of the right than that the State were liable because of the wording of the Article. One of the matters yet to be resolved by the courts is: "whether there are special defences open to the State which are not available to defendants in tort cases, such as executive necessity."[21]

Mandamus

Mandamus is an order of the High Court directing a person or body to carry out their legal duty by doing some specified act. In the *O'Donoghue* case[22] an order of mandamus was sought, *inter alia*, to compel the first two respondents to provide for free primary education for the applicant but was not granted by O'Hanlon J. He expected that the institutions of the State would respond by taking appropriate action to vindicate the constitutional rights of the applicant. He did, however, reserve liberty to the applicant to apply to the court again in the future, should it become necessary to do so, for further relief by way of mandamus or otherwise. Michael Forde points out[23] that there is no reported instance, where the courts have ordered the government to do things because they are required by the constitution or issued mandatory injunctions against the government compelling it to act in a manner consistent with the constitution.

Although the event is unreported, McWilliam J. in *Crowley v. Ireland*[24] did grant a mandatory injunction against the first two defendants requiring them, to provide transport for the plaintiffs, to a convenient school from the commencement of the next school term until the hearing of the action or further order of the court. The plaintiffs had also sought an injunction requiring the committee, members and INTO to withdraw a direction not to enrol children from the Drimoleague school and an injunction restraining them from interfering, preventing or hindering the provision of free primary education for the plaintiffs. At the time of application they were only withdrawing their labour and no order was granted against them. In the English case of *Meade v. Harringay LBC*[25] an order of mandamus was granted to parents making a Local

---

20. See Osborough, "A waning of Judicial Activism" (1976–80), D.U.L.J. 101–3 and also (1978) XIII Ir. Jur. 180 (*N.S.*).
21. Forde, *Constitutional Law of Ireland* (1987), p. 789.
22. Unreported, High Court, O'Hanlon J., May 27, 1993.
23. Above, n.21, p. 722 and p. 790.
24. Unreported, High Court, McWilliam J., December 1, 1977.
25. [1979] 2 All E.R. 1016.

Education Authority perform its statutory duty under section 8 of the Education Act 1944 to provide education. Lord Denning M.R. in the Court of Appeal pointedly referred to the duty of the Council to keep the schools open at all proper times for the education of children.

Injunction

The fact that an injunction may be granted to prevent an infringement of a constitutional right is illustrated by the case of *Parsons v. Kavanagh*[26] where the plaintiff was granted an injunction to prevent competition from an alleged carrier, on the basis of an unlawful interference with the plaintiff's constitutional right to earn a livelihood. O'Hanlon J. in the High Court stated:

> "Having regard, however, to the provisions of the Constitution, the right to earn one's livelihood by any lawful means carries with it the entitlement to be protected against any unlawful activity on the part of another person or persons which materially impairs or infringes that right; and in the present case the plaintiff has made out a case for the granting of an injunction against the defendant."[27]

Injunction Criteria

The Supreme Court approved *Parsons v. Kavanagh* in *Lovett v. Gogan*[28] and held that:

> "Where criminal offences are being committed contrary to statute which have the effect of infringing an individual's constitutional right to earn a livelihood by lawful means such an individual is entitled to seek redress against those persons who have infringed that right.
>
> The remedy in such circumstances includes the granting of an injunction where the plaintiff can establish that it is the only way of protecting him from the threatened invasion of his constitutional rights. *Meskell v. Corás Iompair Éireann* [1973] I.R. 121 applied.
>
> In determining whether to grant an injunction to protect the invasion of an individual's constitutional rights the matter should not be considered in the light of the criteria governing the discretion of the court to grant the equitable remedy of an injunction and the doctrine that a plaintiff seeking such relief must come to court with clean hands. Instead the text to be applied by the court is whether the plaintiff has a constitutional right and if that right is being threatened".[29]

---

26. [1990] I.L.R.M. 560.
27. *ibid.* at 561. *Murtagh Properites Ltd v. Cleary* [1972] I.R. 330 and *dicta* in *Attorney General v. Paperlink Ltd* [1984] I.L.R.M. 373 approved.
28. [1995] 1 I.L.R.M. 12.
29. *ibid.* at 13.

A Declaratory Order

A declaration by a court resolves doubts as to the existence of an individual's rights, and wrongs alleged against such rights. Michael Forde[30] states that a mere declaration of an individual's rights or obligations is also a remedy because, as a general rule, others will respect the rights and carry out the obligations as declared by the court. Additional remedies are frequently sought in addition to a declaration.

One of the remedies sought in the *O'Donoghue*[31] case was an order of the court declaring that in failing to provide for free primary education for the applicant and in discriminating against him as compared with other children, the respondents had deprived him of his constitutional rights under Articles 40 and 42 of the Constitution. An order was granted declaring that in failing to provide for free primary education for the applicant and in discriminating against him as compared with other children the respondents had deprived him of constitutional rights arising under Article 42 of the Constitution, with particular reference to Article 42.3.2° and Article 42.3.4° thereof. The court did not find it necessary to deal with the claim under Article 40 of the Constitution and it took the view that it was normally sufficient to grant declaratory relief in the expectation that the institutions of State would respond by taking appropriate action on foot of the declaration.

Criminalisation

In the course of his judgment in *Meskell v. CIE*[32] Walsh J. stated:

> "To infringe another's constitutional rights or to coerce him into abandoning them or waiving them . . . is unlawful as constituting a violation of the fundamental law of the State . . . a right guaranteed by the Constitution or granted by the Constitution can be protected by action or enforced by action even though such action may not fit into any of the ordinary forms of action in either common law or equity and . . . the constitutional right carries within it, its own right to a remedy or for the enforcement of it."[33]

Hamilton P. in *Attorney General (S.P.U.C.) v. Open Door Counselling*[34] concluded that the power of the courts in regard to the enforcement and protection of personal rights does not depend on legislation and he continued:

> "Though ordinarily it is no function of the courts to extend the criminal law, it may well be that where there is a breach of, or interference with, a fundamental

---

30. Above, n.21 at p. 780.
31. Above, n.22.
32. Above, n.4.
33. *ibid.* at 134.
34. [1987] I.L.R.M. 477.

personal or human right, they may be under a constitutional obligation so to do, in order to respect, and as far as practicable, to defend and vindicate that right."[35]

He then referred to *Shaw v. Director of Public Prosecutions*[36] and the residual power of the courts to guard the safety, order and moral welfare of the State and to the apparently conflicting statement of the former Chief Justice in *Norris v. Attorney General*,[37] that the sole function of the court was to interpret the Constitution and the law the sole and exclusive power of altering the laws of Ireland is vested in the Oireachtas. Michael Forde points out[38] that in no comparable jurisdiction has contravention of constitutional rights been held to be a criminal offence *per se*, and that such a development would require to be consistent with the principle of legality, in particular *nullum crimen sine lege*.

Assessment Of Damages

In relation to the measure of damages in tort, where the wrongdoer has acted *mala fide, i.e.* in bad faith. If the courts feel that a defendant has been actuated by some ill-will toward the plaintiff, that his motive was deliberately to injure the plaintiff, they will conclude that he was actuated by malice. Lord McNaughten in *Quinn v. Leatham*[39] stated that a violation of a legal right committed knowingly is a cause of action.

In *Hickey & Co. Ltd. v. Roches Stores (Dublin) Ltd*[40] Finlay P. in the High Court dealing with the assessment of damages stated as a principle that in assessing damages for loss incurred by an injured party either in tort or by reason of breach of contract, the court, if satisfied that a loss has occurred, under a particular heading, should not by reason of difficulty in proof of the amount of that loss, as distinct from failure to adduce available evidence of it, be deterred from assessing compensation for it and should in this context be both alert and ingenious in assessing a general sum for damages even though it may involve some element of speculation. In *Hawkins v. Rogers*[41] where the assessment of damages was difficult because it depended on the probability of a horse winning prize money in races, and the enhanced value of the animal if he had done so, the loss depended on a contingency, the second branch of it on a double contingency. The court accepted that *Chaplin v. Hicks*[42] was authority for the view that this did not disentitle the plaintiff to damages, but only made their assessment more difficult.

---

35. *ibid.* at 492 (emphasis added).
36. [1962] A.C. 220.
37. [1984] I.R. 36.
38. Above, n.21, p. 791.
39. [1901] A.C. 495 at 510.
40. Unreported, High Court, Finlay P., July 14, 1976.
41. [1951] I.R. 48.
42. [1911] 2 K.B. 786.

Assessment of Exemplary Damages

As to the assessment of exemplary damages see the remarks of Barron J. in the High Court and of Finlay C.J. in the Supreme Court in *Conway v. INTO*[43] discussed above.

The Obligation on the State

Although no particular Article of the Constitution was cited in the pleadings of the *Crowley* case one of the arguments relied on by the plaintiffs was that under Article 40.3.1° the State was bound to defend and vindicate the personal rights of the citizen, which included the right to free primary education. This contention was rejected by the Supreme Court, Kenny J. holding:

> "The obligation imposed on the State by both sub-sections of section 3 of Article 40 is as far as practicable *by its laws* to defend and vindicate the personal rights of the citizen. It is not a general obligation to defend and vindicate the personal rights of the citizen. It is a duty to do so by its laws. . . . No suggestion has been made by the plaintiffs' counsel of a failure by the State by its laws to defend their rights . . .".[44]

In relation to the *Crowley* case Professor Casey states that the majority of the judges in the Supreme Court saw the claim as based on Article 40, *i.e* that the childrens right to free primary education had to be defended and vindicated under Article 40.3.1°. He then observes "nor is it clear why Article 40.3 was invoked. The constitutional right to free primary education could have been treated as springing directly from Article 42.4, *i.e.* as a right correlative to the duty imposed by that provision."[45] It is not clear why Article 40.3.1° was invoked since obviously in doing so the existence of the personal right was asserted. However, if it had been certain that there was such a right at the time, a claim under Article 42.4 might have been taken. This was the provision on which the court did uphold the right. Professor Casey continues:

> ". . . to concentrate attention on Article 42.4 is advantageous in emphasising the State's constitutional obligation here. For, as the judgments in *Byrne v. Ireland*[46] show, failing action by other organs of State it falls to the courts to secure the performance of such obligations."[47]

---

43. [1991] 2 I.R. 305.
44. Above, n.6 at 130.
45. Casey, *Constitutional Law in Ireland* (1st ed., 1987), pp. 518–519.
46. [1972] I.R. 241.
47. Above, n.45, p. 519.

Statute of Limitations

In *McDonnell v. Ireland* [48] and in *Murphy v. Ireland* [49] Miss Justice Carroll held that section 11(2) of the Statute of Limitations applied to a breach of constitutional right in the nature of a tort. Mr Murphy had been convicted on a number of counts connected with importing firearms in the M.V. Claudia in 1973 and the Department of Local Government had implimented the forfeiture of his position under section 34 of the Offences Against The State Act later held to be unconstitutional in *Cox v. Ireland*.[50]

Section 11(2) of the Statute of Limitations Act 1957 provides that an action founded in tort (other than one claiming damages in respect of personal injuries or for slander) shall not be brought after the expiration of six years from the date on which the cause of action accrued. Miss Justice Carroll held that the word "tort" was not defined in the Act and that breach of statutory duty had always been considered to be included within the meaning of the word "tort". In the McDonnell case she held that the word "tort" was sufficiently wide to include breach of a constitutional right.

---

48. Unreported, High Court, Carroll J., January 19, 1996.
49. Unreported, High Court, Carroll J., February 21, 1996.
50. [1992] 2 I.R. 503.

Chapter 13

Religion and Education

Article 44.2.2°

Under Article 44.2.2° of the Constitution: "The State guarantees not to endow any religion." This provision is relevant to education in so far as it can be claimed that payment of chaplains and religious teachers by the State in effect constitutes the endowment of a religion. It is also relevant in relation to the "integrated curriculum" which forms an integral part of the traditional Catholic case for denominational education, *i.e.* that religion is just not a separate subject but permeates every subject which is taught within a school.

"endow"

The meaning of "endow" in this context has not been decided by the courts although it clearly means the transfer of property or money out of state finances. Whether such provision is on a once off basis or a continuing basis may not be relevant if it generates revenue. Michael Forde states that "endow" undoubtedly embraces direct payments into a church's coffers but "in what circumstances does it cover indirect subventions to religion is not clear".[1]

Professor Michael Nolan who surveyed the funding of the teaching of denominational theology throughout the European Community points out that faculties of theology at Oxford, Cambridge and 22 other British Universities are eligible for funding by the University Funding Council.[2] He also states that had Parliament intended by the Government of Ireland Acts of 1920 or 1914 to prohibit all payments for any religious purposes, it had words to hand. Section 7 of the Irish Universities Act of 1908 provides that: "no sum shall be applied for the provision or maintenance of any church, chapel or other place of religious worship or observance or for the provision of any theological teaching or study." He concludes that it seems reasonable to relate the Westminster prohibition of the endowing of religion by an Irish government to the disendowment of the Church of Ireland.

The purpose or purposes for which the transfer, payment or subvention by

---

1. Forde, *Constitutional Law of Ireland* (1987), p. 535.
2. Nolan, "Church, State and Theology in the European Community", *Studies,* Summer (1993), Vol. 82, No. 326.

the State is made, is a crucial issue. If it has been made to assist in the provision of education, even in schools under denominational management or control it may not constitute endowment of religion. Article 42.4 permits the State to supplement and give reasonable aid to private educational initiative and Article 44.2.4° provides that legislation providing state aid for schools shall not discriminate between schools under the management of different religious denominations.

In *Edwards v. Hall*[3] it was held that the commonly understood meaning of endowment of a school or hospital or chapel was not the building, or provision of a site, but "the providing of a fixed revenue for the support of those by whom the institutions are conducted." On the other hand in an Australian case of *Fielding v. Harrison*[4] Higgins J. held that: "the person who endows does not keep up a perpetual series of payments, but he provides property or makes over some income or fruits of some property which he . . . owns or buys or causes to be bought."[5]

Chaplains

The Campaign to Separate Church and State have long contended that payments by the State to chaplains in Community schools could be in breach of this Article because it might constitute an indirect endowment of religion. The organisation has gathered information about the number of Chaplains employed by various government departments who are paid out of State funds. In 1990 the *Irish Times*[6] revealed that the Minister for Health, had informed Deputy Pat McCartan Workers Party that 290 chaplains received stipends for services as chaplains. The annualised amount was £821,318 of which £586,078 was paid to R.C chaplains £200,025 to Church of Ireland chaplains £24,196 to Presbyterian and £11,019 to Methodist chaplains. With respect to voluntary hospitals £261,152 was paid by hospitals in respect of Roman Catholic chaplaincy services.

Mr. Justice Costello in the High Court, however, has held in the *Campaign to Separate Church and State v. Minister for Education*[7] that the State payment of Chaplains attached to community schools does not infringe the Constitution because the purpose of the payment is to fulfil the State's obligation to respect parental rights and to facilitate their exercise. He rejected the U.S authorities which were concerned with the "establishment" of religion and the Northern Ireland authorities concerned with endowment in section 5 of the Government of Ireland Act 1920. The latter on the ground that the provisions in the Irish Constitution dealing with education in Article 42 were absent from the 1920

---

3. 25 L.J. Ch. 82.
4. [1908] 7 C.L.R. 393.
5. *ibid.* at 457.
6. *Irish Times*, October 27, 1990.
7. Unreported, High Court, Costello P., January 17, 1996.

Act and were highly relevant in considering the construction of the prohibition in the 1937 Constitution.

Having held, on examining Article 44 of the Constitution, that the payment of state salaries to teachers of religion in community schools (even if such teachers are ministers of religion or members of religious orders) does not constitute an endowment of religion he continued by examining Article 42. He stated:

> "I have underlined the words "religious and moral formation" to draw attention to the fact that this Article recognises that parents have rights not only to provide for the religious education of their children (sub-paragraph (1)) but also rights in the matter of their religious formation (sub-paragraph (4))"....[8]

His Lordship then examined the difference between the concepts of education and formation and continued:

> "... one of the important reasons why chaplains as well as teachers of religion are appointed to the staff of Community Schools is for the purpose of assisting the religious formation of the children attending the school (assistance which, *inter alia*, is given by the celebration of Mass in the school). In effect, the State by paying the salaries of chaplains is having regard to the rights of parents *vis-à-vis* the religious formation of their children and enabling them to exercise their constitutionally recognised rights. If this is the purpose and effect of the payment how can it be said that it is unconstitutional?"[9]

Primary Education

In 1990[10] John Walshe, then Education Correspondent of the *Irish Times*, anticipated that the Primary Education Review Body Report due out the next day would refer to the absence of any statutory base for the primary school system, would recommend the continuance of the management structure and would also accept that the schools are state-aided under local diocesan patronage with the State giving explicit recognition to their denominational character. Mr. Sean McCarthy representative of the Teachers Union of Ireland in a minority report issued by his union referred to the financing of primary schools and stated that since the Second World War, the State had provided $1,000 million in current prices for primary school building.

Hundreds of schools had closed and information as to the amount of public funds that had been refunded to the Exchequer from disposal and sale of such schools was not publicly accessible. He proposed that new regulations could define a situation whereby new schools could be built entirely from state money. Sites would be bought by the State and buildings could be vested in new local

---

8. *ibid.* at p. 39 of the judgment.
9. *ibid.* at pp. 40–41 of the judgment.
10. See *Irish Times*, December 6, 1990.

education authorities which would provide for primary and post-primary schools in their areas. He continued:

> "At a time when taxpayers and others are being asked to make sacrifices to bring the finances of the State under control, it is not acceptable that a black hole in the economy should be allowed to exist in relation to the lack of accountability with regard to large amounts of public funds in the educational sector."[11]

School Closures

The idea that huge sums of money are due to the State because of school closures is rebutted by the fact that only £86,291 was recouped by the Department from the release of its interest in closed schools between 1990 and 1995. It should be noted that while the Department pays 90% of the building cost the remaining 10% and the site are supplied by the trustees. A lease commits the trustees to keep the property open as a school for a certain time. If it closes as a school prior to the period of the lease the Department is entitled to claim repayment of a sum equivalent to the unexpired portion of the lease. In 1989 the Campaign to Separate Church and State proposed that statutory provision must be made to ensure that the State recouped "the present value" of its investment.[12]

In May 1994[13] the Minister Niamh Bhreathnach, T.D., announced the beginning of talks with the CPSMA to establish formal procedures for the closing of schools. The 1995 White Paper on Education[14] states that in future, education boards will own new school buildings and will lease them to different groups, thus bringing this problem to an end.

UN Report

In 1988 a Report by a Special UN Rapporteur on *Religious Intolerance and Discrimination in Ireland*[15] compiled by Mr. Angelo Vidal d'Almeida Ribero, a special rapporteur to the commission, contained a number of allegations that the State was infringing the constitutional rights contained in Article 44.2.2° and Article 44.2.3° of the Constitution and the reply of the Irish authorities to those allegations. The State guarantee not to endow any religion was not specifically dealt with although infringement of Article 44.2.2° was a ground of complaint.

---

11. Report of the Primary Education Review Body, December 1990, Minority Report, p. 120 *et seq.*
12. Colgan, *Minimum Requirements for Education Act(s)*, Campaign to Separate Church and State (1989), para. 6.
13. See *Irish Times*, May 12, 1994 and *Sunday Times*, May 15, 1994.
14. *Charting Our Education Future*, Department of Education, April 12, 1995, p. 64, Launch Copy.
15. E/CN. 4/1989/44.

Religious Instruction

Article 42.3.2° of the Constitution provides:

> "The State shall, however, as guardian of the common good, require in view of actual conditions, that the children receive a certain minimum education, *moral, intellectual and social*." whereas the duty of parents under Article 42.1 is to provide "for the *religious* and moral, intellectual, physical and social education of their children." (Emphasis added.)

Religious education is not among the components which the State can require a child to receive. If the State cannot require that a child receive it, has the state a legitimate right to provide it? If the State does provide it, is the State endowing religion by doing so? Mr. Justice Brian Walsh has stated:

> ". . . there seems to be no objection to the state providing religious education, if the parents wish it for their children, and to the State providing the type of religious education requested by the parents."[16]

His use of the words "there seems to be no objection" is a carefully guarded statement. He justifies the State providing religious education on the basis that as taxpayers, parents should be free to require that some of their tax be devoted to the teaching of what they wish their children to learn. A generalisation, which in the opinion of the author, may not be universally true. He is emphatic that state provision of religious education in such circumstance is not a contravention of the provision of Article 44 not to endow any religion and he points out: "The teaching of religion, or of any particular religion, as a subject in education is not to be confused with the endowment of a religion."[17] Few would disagree with this statement but the question at issue is whether the payment by the State of persons to teach a particular religion constitutes "endowing that religion" within Article 44. of the Constitution. Mr. Justice Walsh continues:

> "The United States constitutional jurisprudence, in relation to the constitutional bar upon the 'establishment' of any religion, has perhaps gone unnecessarily far in that, in effect, it has been construed as meaning that it is against the teaching of religion, or any particular manifestation of religion that might be regarded as the teaching of it."[18]

Drafting the Constitution

Professor Basil Chubb points out[19] that De Valera claimed that Article 44 gave him more anxiety than anything else in the Constitution. The present writer

---

16. Litton (ed.), *The Constitution and Constitutional Rights, The Constitution of Ireland 1937-1987* (1987), p. 99.
17. *ibid.*
18. *ibid.*
19. Chubb, *The Politics of The Irish Constitution* (1991), p. 27.

feels that the section on the endowment of religion was not the source of that anxiety because this merely restated the beginning of section 16 of Treaty Agreement of December 6, 1921;

> "Neither the Parliament of the Irish Free State nor the Parliament of Northern Ireland shall make any law so as either directly or indirectly to endow any religion."

Restated in Article 8 of the Constitution of The Free State of Ireland, of 1922 as:

> "no law may be made either directly or indirectly to endow any religion."

When this was being drafted, and indeed, when the 1937 Constitution was in the course of preparation Dr. Alfred O'Rahilly had submitted a draft Constitution, Draft "C" which proposed an Article 59(1): "there is no established or State-endowed Church." Both the 1922 and the 1937 Constitutions went further than O'Rahilly but complied with the Treaty agreement. There was little significant change between the two Constitutions despite the fact that:

> "What de Valera wanted to bring to an end, of course, was the Constitution of 1922. What he wanted to rewrite, as he thought it should have been written in the first place, was the Anglo-Irish Treaty of 1921. What he wanted to destroy was the Irish Free State."[20]

There is a significant difference between not endowing a Church and not endowing "any religion." The Treaty agreement may have aimed at preventing the establishment of any church but in fact went further. H. Calvert on the other hand, states that the omission of a prohibition of "establishment" may be referred to as a desire to confer special recognition on the Roman Catholic Church.[21]

As pointed out by Costello P. in *Campaign to Separate Church and State Ltd. v. Minister for Education*,[22] Article 8 of the 1922 Constitution introduced a prohibition against the endowment of religion but not against its establishment and this was re-enacted in Article 44.2.2° of the 1937 Constitution with the omission of the words "directly or indirectly".

With regard to the present constitution, it appears that the recognition of the special position of the Holy Catholic Apostolic and Roman Church contained in the now deleted Article 44.1.2° was as far as de Valera was prepared to go to prove his bona fides to the Catholic hierarchy. According to Revd Enda McDonagh professor of moral theology at St. Patrick's College Maynooth:

> "The religious freedom provision of Article 44 and its original recognition of

---

20. Fanning, "Mr de Valera Drafts a Constitution", *De Valera's Constitution and Ours* (1988), p. 34.
21. Calvert, *The Constitution of Northern Ireland*, p. 256.
22. Above, n.7.

all the Churches in Ireland by the names they call themselves, including recognition of the 'special place' of the Roman Catholic Church, was a move by de Valera in defence of the earlier Irish politico-religious tradition *in the face of pressure to establish the Catholic Church*. The later removal of this section by an overwhelming majority restored the healthier nineteenth-century tradition."[23]

Under Article 44.2.2° of the Constitution: "The State guarantees not to endow any religion." The Treaty Agreement, Section 5 of the Government of Ireland Act, 1920 and Article 8 of the 1922 Constitution provide that "no *law* may be made" and indeed no law has been made to endow religion either directly or indirectly.

Northern Ireland

In *County Council of Derry v. McGlade*[24] Mr. Justice Wilson stated that the Northern Ireland Legislature did not have the power by virtue of section 5 of the Government of Ireland Act 1920, to provide either paid Roman Catholic or paid Protestant religious instruction in schools maintained by public money. The religious instruction of the Roman Catholic children would:

> "have to be provided voluntarily in the future as it was in the past by some private arrangement or contrivance for it never was a legal right. This seems to be the political result of the drawn battle of the creeds for supremacy which ended in equality outside the reach of any assistance from public money."[25]

He added that if the Northern Parliament enacted that a Roman Catholic should be provided and paid out of public money to teach the children their Roman Catholic Religion, "it would be be argued that this was an endowment *pro tanto* of that religion. . . ."[26] At the same time the State has a legitimate interest in promoting the development of better citizens for the welfare of all. Surely anything which helps this objective should be encouraged.

McGrath and O'Ruairc v. Trustees of Maynooth College

The first case in the Republic in which the prohibition on endowment of religion contained in Article 44 has been referred to is that of *McGrath and O'Ruairc v. Trustees of Maynooth College*[27] and then only *obiter* by Kenny J. at p. 11 of his judgment where he referred to the dilemma posed by counsel for the plaintiffs that:

---

23. McDonagh, *Philosophical-Theological Reflections on The Constitution, The Constitution of Ireland 1937–1987* (1988) p. 202.
24. [1929] N.I. 47.
25. *ibid.* at 56.
26. See Osborough, "Education in the Irish Law and Constitution" (1978) XIII Ir. Jur. 153 (*N.S.*).
27. Unreported, Supreme Court, November 1, 1979.

> "The subventions paid to Maynooth cannot be paid to it as a seminary for this would be an endowment of a religion which is prohibited by Art.44 s.2 sub-s.2 of the Constitution. Therefore Maynooth is primarily a college of a University and not a seminary or the subventions were paid to it illegally".

The answer according to Kenny J. was, that the words "a college of a university" in section 1(1)(b) of the Higher Education Authority Act 1971 were wide enough to include a recognised college of a university. He stated: "The words of the Act of 1971 are not 'a constituent college' but 'a college'. Maynooth is a recognised college of a university but that does not prevent it being primarily a seminary."[28] He pointed out that much of the plaintiffs argument was based on a fallacy that a seminary was an institution in which students for the priesthood *only* were educated but that this was not so. He said: "A proper education for a student for the priesthood should include some contact with the profane world in which he will have to exercise. . . ."[29]

Only Kenny J. dealt with the problem of 'endowment' in the Maynooth case and Michael Forde concludes: "Because, however, the matter was not considered in any depth, and indeed was not particularly relevant to the issue in that case, it remains very much an open question."[30]

Integrated Curriculum and Endowment of Religion

It has been stated that the very fusing of secular and religious instruction deprives the curriculum of its secular nature and that arguably the State is providing a religious body with funding for a religious purpose. Without going too deeply into this aspect the following observations come to mind. Despite a recent tendency to the contrary, in the USA state aid for children attending parochial schools has been considered as aid for education not religion[31] and the "predominant object" test applied in older judgments like *Bradford v. Roberts*[32] aid to a Catholic hospital, and *Quick Bear v. Leupp*[33] aid to a Catholic school, tended to support this conclusion. State capitation grants are paid in respect of students and arguably it is the students who are being aided not the institution.

Article 44.2.3°

Article 44.2.3° provides:

> "The State shall not impose any disabilities or make any discrimination on the ground of religious profession, belief or status".

---

28. *ibid.* at p. 11 of the judgment.
29. *ibid.*
30. Forde, *Constitutional Law of Ireland* (1987), p. 536.
31. *Everson v. Board Of Education* 330 U.S. (1947).
32. 1175 U.S. 291 (1899).
33. 210 U.S. 50 (1908).

In the *McGrath and O'Ruairc v. Trustees of Maynooth College* case[34] the Supreme court pointed out that the prohibition in Article 44.2.3° against discrimination on the grounds of religious profession, belief or status applied to the State, not to other persons or bodies and the fact that Maynooth college received a subvention from the State did not alter this. Henchy J. stated:

> "Far from eschewing the internal disabilities and discriminations which flow from the tenets of a particular religion, the State must on occasion recognise and buttress them . . . they are part of the textured and essence of the particular religion; so *the State* in order to comply with the spirit and purpose inherent in this constitutional guarantee, *may justifiably lend its weight to what may be thought to be disabilities and discriminations deriving from within a particular religion.*"[35]

In *Molloy v. Minister for Education*[36] a salary scheme which confined increments for teaching service abroad, to lay teachers was held to be a discrimination based on religious status and unconstitutional.

"Religious profession"

"Religious profession" is the particular religious faith which is professsed by the person in question.

"Religious Status"

"Religious status" in both the Irish and English texts of the Constitution, related clearly to the position or rank of a person in terms of religion in relation to others either of the same religion or of another religion or to those of no religion at all. See *McGrath and O'Ruairc v. Trustees of Maynooth*, above.[37]

State Aid

Article 44.2.4° provides:

> "Legislation providing State aid for schools shall not discriminate between schools under the management of different religious denominations, nor be such as to affect prejudicially the right of any child to attend a school receiving public money without attending religious instruction at that school."

This Article recognises the provision of State aid for schools under the management of different religious denominations, *i.e.* the denominational system. The history of Irish education shows that the evolution of the denominational

---

34. Above, n.27.
35. *ibid.* at p. 34 of the judgment (emphasis added).
36. [1975] I.R. 88.
37. Above, n.27.
38. Lane (ed.), *Education, Religion and the Constitution* (1902) p. 110 *per* Whyte.

system was due to Church agitation to obtain the management control of schools in order to control the ethos within them by means which included integrated curricula. Separate secular and religious education was rejected by the Churches in the nineteenth century, none of which wanted a denominational system for the sake of managing itself, but for its potential in the work of catechises and the control over the ethos which it gave.

At once this subsection constitutes a restraint on the legislative competence of the State and it is also a further acknowledgment of the supremacy of parental choice relative to religious instruction of children. It prudently keeps the State outside the denominational system and neutral in its approach.

Every year the Appropriations Act provides for the grant from the Central Fund of a specified amount of money for education under various headings, *i.e.* Office of the Minister, Primary Education, Post Primary Education and Special Schools. Only the major headings are contained in the Appropriations Acts, therefore it is these which are given statutory effect, the sub-headings are not.

Gerry Whyte claims[38] that it is arguable that state aid for schools can only be provided for by way of legislation and that any other system of disbursement, such as by way of Ministerial Circular, is unconstitutional. He cites two reasons in support of this argument, the absence of the degree of parliamentary scrutiny required for legislation, and the fact that the President is denied the right she has in relation to legislation to refer the matter to the Supreme Court under Article 26 for an opinion on its constitutionality.

The State is also prohibited from legislating compulsory attendance at religious instruction as a condition of admission to a school receiving public money. The author is not aware of any legislation which purports to do this and does not consider that an integrated curriculum imposed by a school management would necessarily infringe this provision.

Michael McDowell S.C. argues:

> "The constitutional ban on endowment of religion does not extend to State aid for private denominational education. Furthermore, any child at a school receiving public money is not obliged to receive religious instruction against parental wishes."

He points out that the State is not merely authorised, but is actually "required" to endeavour to give "reasonable aid" to private education. He then concluded "Accordingly, the rights of parents to send their children to private schools rather than to State schools carry with them a constitutional expectation that such private schooling will receive State aid."[39]

Article 44.2.6°

Article 44.2.6° provides:

---

39. "Choice and the Constitution", *Sunday Independent*, September 26, 1993.

> "The property of a religious denomination or any educational institution shall not be diverted save for necessary works of public utility and on payment of compensation."

Having commented that the reference here to religious denominations is probably not susceptible of an interpretration that extends it to religious orders Walsh J. has stated:

> "This provision, it should be noted, comes under the heading of religion and not under the heading of property, so obviously it must be interpreted as being intended to safeguard religious freedom."[40]

"public utility"

According to the late Prof. J.M. Kelly[41] "a clear view of what is meant by "works of public utility" is afforded by the old Article 8, which forbade the diversion of the property envisaged "except for the purpose of roads, railways, lighting, water or drainage works or other works of public utility" This suggests to Professor Kelly that "public utility" "could not be construed so as to privilege some grander function, in pursuit of which a Government might wish to take over an existing religious or educational establishment." Walsh J.[42] considered that the purposes for which property may be 'diverted' must come within the judicial interpretation of the phrase 'necessary works of public utility'.

In *Crichton v. Land Commission and Gault*[43] in 1947 the Land Commission compulsorily acquired land, the Land Registry map of which (the boundaries on the Folio being deemed conclusive) showed a Church of Ireland Schoolhouse, in the parish of Drumreilly as being on the Folio. A certificate by the Lay Commissioners of the Land Commission certified that the lands were required for the purposes of the Land Acts and on the appointed day the Land Commission took possession of the schoolhouse. Subsequently the Land Commission stated that the school house was not required for the purposes of the Land Acts. The plaintiffs claimed that the Land Commission had no statutory or other authority to acquire the schoolhouse and relied on their statement that it was not required for the purposes of the Land Acts, and on Article 44.6 of the Constitution.

It was held by Sheehy J. that the plot and schoolhouse had not been vested in the Land Commission as it had no power to acquire them except for their statutory purposes, under the Land Acts. The Land Commission had no power at all to acquire the property of a religious denomination or educational institution. He stated:

---

40. Above, n.16, p. 103.
41. Kelly, *The Irish Constitution* (1st ed., 1980), p. 536.
42. Above, n.16, p. 103.
43. [1950] 84 I.L.T.R. 87.

"This school house was held by a religious body for educational and religious purposes. The Land Commission did not require it for their purposes under the Land Acts, therefore the attempted acquisition by the Land Commission was unconstitutional and void."[44]

In a reference to this judgment J.M. Kelly states "Judge Sheehy's reference to Article 44 is (as reported) logically incomplete as well as unnecessary for the purpose of the case"[45] and later in his book, *The Irish Constitution*, states "apart from being a case decided in a lower court (the Circuit court), its status as a constitutional case seems spurious."[46]

While it seems that the establishment of state schools or multi-denominational schools does not constitute "necessary works of *public utility*" it may be remarked that the Article would not support the State diverting school property owned by a religious denomination for such purposes.

"payment of compensation"

Walsh J. comments: "It must be assumed that the compensation will also be just compensation".[47]

Article 44.2.1°

Article 44.2.1° provides:

"Freedom of conscience and the free profession and practice of religion are, *subject to public order and morality,* guaranteed to every citizen." (Emphasis added.)

The limitation imposed on this freedom means that the State can curtail religious practices of a particular individual or religion on the grounds of public order and also on grounds of morality.

The Constitution Review Group

The Review Group states that broadly speaking the provisions of Article 44 are satisfactory and have worked well. The guarantees of free practice of religion and the prohibitions of non-endowment and non-discrimination are far reaching and comprehensive.

The Review Group recommended no change in Article 44.1 and then considered whether, having regard to the uncertainties associated with the word "endowment", a different form of wording should be employed in Article 44.2.2°.

---

44. *ibid.* at 88.
45. Kelly, *Fundamental Rights in the Irish Law and Constitution* (1961), p. 187.
46. Above, n.41, p. 536.
47. Above, n.16, p. 103.

Recommendation

No change is proposed.

The Group then addressed the question as to whether institutions (such as schools and hospitals) which retain a religious ethos should be eligible to receive public funding and suggested the insertion of a new clause in Article 44 which would seek to strike a fair balance between competing rights and interests and the Report states:

> "In effect, what is proposed is that publicly-funded institutions which retain a religious ethos should not be debarred from public funding, provided there is no discrimination on grounds of religious practice or belief save to the extent that the institution could show in any given case that this was necessary to maintain its own religious ethos. This could mean that a school with the religious ethos of a minority denomination might legitimately give preference in its admission policies to children of that denomination where it could demonstrate that this was necessary to maintain the religious ethos of the school. On the other hand, such a school might find it difficult to justify religious exclusivity in the case of the employment of, say, a language or mathematics teacher."

Recommendation

A majority of the Review Group considers that Article 44 should be amended to provide that institutions which retain a religious ethos should not be debarred from public funding, provided that they do not discriminate on grounds of religious practice or belief, save where this can be shown, in any given case, to be necessary in order to maintain their own religious ethos.

As to whether Article 44.2.4° required amendment the Review Group considered three key phrases of this Article as follows:

"legislation providing State aid for schools . . ."

The Report states:

> "As already noted, Article 44.2.4° appears to envisage that any state funding of denominational education must be sanctioned by Act of the Oireachtas. Article 44.2.4° cannot mean that the State may elect to fund schools on an administrative basis, still less that, if it does so, it would not be bound by the injunction not to discriminate between the schools under the control of religious bodies, because such an interpretation would strip this subsection of all purpose and effect. The Review Group is, of course, aware that the annual Appropriation Acts are the only such legislation which has been enacted to date provided for State aid to schools."

Recommendation

No change is proposed.

"... *shall not discriminate between schools under the management of different religious denominations* ..."

The Report states:
> "This part of Article 44.2.4° is also satisfactory by providing for a guarantee of equality in relation to the funding of denominational schools. It is important to stress that the object of this part of Article 44.2.4° is to ensure that there is no discrimination on *religious grounds*. The Review Group considers that this is a special subsection of the Constitution dealing with a particular issue and there is no need to extrapolate this principle any further."

Recommendation

No change is proposed.

"... *nor be such as to affect prejudicially the right of any child to attend a school receiving public money without attending religious instruction at that school*"

The Report states:
> "... the opening words of Article 44.2.4° sanction (under certain conditions) State funding for denominational education. Yet it seems implicit in Article 44.2.4° that a school in receipt of public moneys cannot insist on a policy such as admitting only co-religionists as pupils, and the practice of an integrated curriculum would appear to be at variance with this guarantee."

Recommendation

No change is proposed.
    In relation to Article 44.2.6° the Review Group considered that the word "diverted" is a euphemism and is neither a suitable word nor a good translation of the Irish "a bhaint díobh".

Recommendation

The Report states:
> "Delete the word 'diverted' in Article 44.2.6° and replace it by the word 'compulsorily acquired'. There is no need for a change in the Irish language version."

The Group state that the words "necessary work of public utility" (which has not received authoritative judicial interpretation) gives rise to potential difficulties of interpretation but opined that it was best not to attempt a definition but rather to leave their interpretation to the courts.

Recommendation

No change is required.

Chapter 14

The White Paper and the Constitution

Constitutional Interpretation

Two approaches to constitutional interpretation are outlined in the White Paper on Education, *Charting Our Education Future*. The first is the hierarchical approach, *i.e.* to place conflicting constitutional rights in order of importance and give each right a priority relative to the other rights involved. A second approach is the doctrine of harmonious interpretation which involves interpreting any particular Article in a manner which is in harmony with the other provisions and with the Constitution as a whole.

The White Paper refers to the fact that there are precedents which suggest that a hierarchical approach will only be adopted by the courts when a harmonisation of constitutional rights is impossible. One such precedent is the case of *Murray v. Ireland*[1] where Costello J held:

> "In construing the Constitution, the courts should adopt a purposive approach to interpretation which would examine the text of the Constitution as a whole and identify its purpose and objectives in protecting human rights, in order to achieve a *harmonious interpretation* and to avoid a strict construction which would allow the imperfection of words to defeat or pervert any of the Constitution's fundamental purposes."[2]

Harmonious Interpretation

Where a number of constitutional rights arise or appear to conflict the courts are obliged to seek to apply a harmonious interpretation of both rights. The notion of a hierarchy of constitutional rights may only be resorted to where a harmonious interpretation is impossible. Finlay C.J. in *Attorney General v. X.*[3] commented:

> "I accept that where there exists an interaction of constitutional rights *the first objective of the courts* in interpreting the constitution and resolving any problem thus arising *should be to seek to harmonise such interacting rights*. There are

---

1. [1985] I.R. 532.
2. *ibid.*
3. [1992] 1 I.R. 1.

instances however, I am satisfied, as the authorities appear to establish, that there is a necessity to apply a priority of rights."[4]

Express Limitation of Constitutional Rights

It is implicit in the White Paper that new education legislation will involve a careful balancing but also the limitation of some constitutional rights: "So that the exercise of rights by one of the partners in education does not unreasonably delimit the exercise of their rights by any other."[5]

Many constitutional rights are expressly limited in the Constitution itself by phrases like "subject to public order and morality" (Article 40.6 and Article 44.2.1°) "the exigencies of the common good" (Article 43.2.2°) and "save for necessary works of public utility" (Article 44.2.6°). These qualifying words clearly permit the State to legislate in relation to these areas and to impose limitations on the rights referred to.

In relation to the educational provisions of the Constitution Article 42.3.2° imposes an obligation on the State "as guardian of the common good "to require that children receive a certain minimum education" and this clearly permits the State to legislate in relation to this particular matter.

Article 40.3 provides:

> "The State guarantees in its laws to respect, and, *as far as practicable*, by its *laws* to defend and vindicate the personal rights of the citizen."

and Article 40.3.2° provides:

> "The State shall in particular, by its laws protect *as best it may* from unjust attack and in the case of injustice done, vindicate the life, person, good name, and property rights of every citizen." (Emphasis added.)

The personal rights of the citizen are on the one hand entitled to be protected by the State and on the other hand limited. The degree of protection and the obligation on the State are both expressly limited. The obligation on the State is expressly limited by the phrases: "as far as practicable", "as best it may", and "unjust attack".

"as far as practicable"

The Irish version is: "sa mhéid gur féidir é" which means "as far as possible" but this difference has been discounted by McCarthy J. in the *Attorney General v. X.*[6] case where he held that there was no material discordance between the English and Irish version. He pointed out that: "Although Article 25.5.4° of the

---

4. *ibid.* at 57 (emphasis added).
5. At p. 207.
6. [1992] 1 I.R. 1.

Constitution provided that its Irish text should prevail over the English in cases of conflict, this conflict may arise only due to the translation of the original English text."[7] "Sa mhéid gur féidir é" is also the Irish version of "so far as it is practicable" in Article 16.2.3° in relation to Dáil Éireann elections and in *O'Donovan v. Attorney General*[8] it was held that in forming constituencies the legislature had not maintained the ratio of T.D.s to population the same throughout the country "so far as it is practicable".

In *Cox v. Ireland*[9] the provisions of section 34 of the Offences Against the State Act 1939 potentially constituted an attack, firstly on the unenumerated constitutional right to earn a living and secondly, on certain property rights, such as the right to a pension, gratuity or other emolument already earned, or the right to the advantages of a subsisting contract of employment. The case arose when the plaintiff, a County Longford vocational teacher, was convicted in the Special Criminal Court of a scheduled offence involving possession of firearms. As a consequence of section 34 he was deemed to have forfeited his office, was disqualified from pension, and also disqualified from holding any like office for a period of seven years.

The Supreme Court held that the State was entitled by its laws to impose onerous and far reaching penalties and forfeitures in respect of offences threatening public peace and order and the authority of the State. In pursuing these objectives, however, there is an obligation on the State *as far as practicable* by its laws to protect the constitutional rights of the citizen. The question for the court had therefore to be, as to whether section 34 of the Offences Against the State Act, 1939 when read in conjunction with other relevant provisions of the Act, constituted a failure of *such* protection *not warranted by the objectives* of the Act. The provisions of section 34 of the Act of 1939 *failed as far as practicable* to protect the constitutional rights of the citizen and were, accordingly, *impermissibly wide and indiscriminate*, and invalid, having regard to the provisions of the constitution. The court balanced the curtailment of the constitutional personal rights of the citizen with the objective in the legislation and this type of exercise has been termed *proportionality*. It is suggested that the court was obliged to consider the proportionality aspect because of the qualified words "as far as practicable" contained in Article 40.

"as best it may"

In *Moynihan v. Greensmyth*[10] O'Higgins C.J delivering the judgment of the Supreme Court stated in relation to "as best it may":

---

7. *ibid.* at 4.
8. [1961] I.R. 114.
9. [1992] 2 I.R. 503.
10. [1977] I.R. 55.

"It is noted that the guarantee of protection given by Article 40 s.3., subs. 2 of the Constitution is qualified by the words "as best it may". This implies circumstances in which the State may have to *balance* its protection of the right as against other obligations arising from regard for the common good."[11]

"Unjust attack"

A further qualification of the obligation on the State in Article 40.3.2° is that it only applies to protection against unjust attack and that vindication is only necessary where injustice has been done. In *Daly v. The Revenue Commissioners*[12] Mr. Justice Costello observed that in order to claim that his constitutionally protected right to private property in Article 40.3.2° had been infringed and that the State had failed to protect it, the plaintiff had to show that those rights had been subject to "an unjust attack". He could do this by showing that the law which restricted the exercise of his rights or which infringed them failed to pass a *proportionality test*. Even where the Constitution itself expressly provides for limitation of a constitutional right, legislation introduced to do so must be proportionate.

The right to free primary education as decided in the Crowley case was not a personal right under Article 40 but a right under Article 42.4 correlative to the duty on the State to provide it. This could have significant implications for the application of the doctrine of proportionality.

Limitation of Constitutional Rights Generally

The concept that all constitutional rights may be limited has been developed by the courts from the interpretation of constitutional rights in accordance with the principles contained in the Preamble to the Constitution and by the approval of the principles laid down by Costello J. in *Murray v. Ireland.*[13] The Preamble states:

> ". . . We, the people of Éire. . . . And seeking to promote the common good, with due observance of Prudence Justice and Charity, so that the dignity and freedom of the individual may be assured. . . . Do hereby adopt, enact and give to ourselves this Constitution."

Finlay C.J. in *Attorney General v. X.*[14] [1992] 1 I.R. 1 stated:

> "According to the Preamble, the people gave themselve the Constitution to promote the common good, with due observance of prudence, justice and charity so that the dignity and freedom of the individual might be assured. The judges

---

11. *ibid.* at 71.
12. [1995] 3 I.R. 1.
13. [1985] I.R. 532.
14. Above, n.6.

must, therefore, as best they can from their training and their experience interpret these rights in accordance with their ideas of prudence justice and charity."[15]

The centrality of the Preamble and the nexus of its importance in constitutional interpretation had been signalled some 16 years earlier by O'Higgins C.J. in *The State (Healy) v. Donoghue*[16] where he opined that in his view:

> "... this preamble makes it clear that rights given by the Constitution must be considered in accordance with concepts of prudence, justice and charity, which may gradually change or develop as society changes and develops and which fall to be interpreted from time to time in accordance with prevailing ideas. The premable envisages a Constitution which can absorb or be adapted to such changes."[17]

Finlay C.J. in the *X.* case on appeal to the Supreme Court accepted this principle along with that relating to change expressed by Walsh J. in *McGee v. Attorney General*[18] as being correct and appropriate principles which he must follow.

Perhaps the most importance case of all in relation to limitation of constitutional rights is that of *Murray v. Ireland*[19] where Costello J. in the High Court held that the restriction on the plaintiff's right to beget children was a reasonable consequence of the State's power to imprison and was constitutionally permissible. The rights of the family and its integrity as a unit group could be validly restricted by the State in the exercise of the powers lawfully conferred on it, in spite of the fact that there is no reference in Article 41 of the Constitution to any restrictive power to delimit the exercise of these rights. He stated:

> "The State, as guardian of the common good, is empowered by the Constitution to restrict rights in certain circumstances ... the power of the State to delimit the exercise of constitutionally protected rights is expressly given in some Articles and not referred to at all in others, but this cannot mean that, where absent, the power does not exist. For example, .no reference is made in Article 41 to any restrictive power but it is clear that the exercise by the Family of its imprescriptible and inalienable right to integrity as a unit group can be severely and validly restricted by the State when, for example, its laws permit a father to be banned from a family home or allows for the imprisonment of both parents of young children."[20]

Although the Supreme Court[21] upheld the judgment of Costello J. it held that the right to beget children was a right under Article 40 rather than Article 41. As such it was liable to limitation as are all other rights under the same

---

15. *ibid.* at 52.
16. [1976] I.R. 325.
17. *ibid.* at 347.
18. [1974] I.R. 284.
19. Above, n.13.
20. *ibid.* at 533–538.
21. [1991] I.L.R.M. 465.

Article. However, Finlay C.J. (Hamilton P., O'Flaherty and Keane JJ. concurring) went on to say:

> "of the rights which I have outlined it is possible to say that only a right of communication, and that without privacy and a right by communication to take some part in the education of children of the marriage would ordinarily survive a sentence of imprisonment as a convicted prisoner. . . . I therefore am in complete agreement with the principles set out by Costello J. in his judgment which I have summarised in the numbered clauses 1-5 inclusive in this judgment."[22]

The Murray case was followed some years later in 1990 by the Supreme Court in *Fajujonu v. Minister for Justice*[23] where despite the constitutional rights of the family it was held that the Minister for Justice, pursuant to the powers contained in the Aliens Act 1935, could force the family to leave the State, if after due and proper consideration, he was satisfied that the interests of the common good and the protection of the State and its society justified an interference with what was clearly a constitutional right.

The Court also acknowledged that the children born within the State to alien parents, were citizens and as such had a constitutional right to the company, care and parentage of their parents within a family unit.

In the High Court Barrington J. stated that since the rights of the family were guaranteed by the Constitution in the context of the welfare of the Nation and the State and having regard to the common good, the laws enacted by the Oireachtas for control of the movements of aliens within the State were permissible limitations in the interest of the common good upon the family and personal rights asserted by the plaintiffs.

Thus the power of the State, as guardian of the common good to limit the exercise of constitutional rights in accordance with prudence, justice and charity, even in the absence of an express power to do so, has been asserted.

The Preamble

Recourse to the Preamble[24] as a judicial aid to interpretation has been a continuing feature of Irish case law over the years. In 1960 Lavery J. delivering the judgment of the Supreme Court in *Attorney General v. S.I.T.*[25] said:

> "The preamble to the Constitution should also be considered as has been done in several of the Constitutional cases . . . the words of the preamble . . . may held in determining the meaning of and effect to be given to particular provi-

---

22. *ibid.* at 472.
23. [1990] 2 I.R. 151.
24. For an examination of the Preamble see Hogan and Whyte, *Kelly: The Irish Constitution* (3rd ed., 1994), pp. 1-9.
25. [1960] I.L.T.R. 161.

sions. The words of the preamble appropriate to the purpose in hand are that the people in enacting the Constitution are: 'seeking to promote the common good' ..."[26]

In *McGee v. Attorney General*[27] Walsh J. referred to the Preamble and to the notion that judges must interpret constitutional rights in accordance with their ideas of prudence, justice and charity and stated that no interpretation was intended to be final for all time. It is given in the light of prevailing ideas and concepts. The observations of Walsh J. in *McGee* and also those of O'Higgins C.J. in *The State (Healy) v. O'Donoghue*[28] were adopted by McCarthy J. in *Norris v. Attorney General*.[29]

The Constitutional Review Group state that the identification of rights by reference to these concepts is unsatisfactory because they are capable of different interpretations.[30]

School Governance and Property Rights

Significantly a section of the White Paper on Education in Chapter 18[31] links school governance and property rights and states that: "The right of ownership of private property carries with it the right to decide how it is used." This is undoubtedly true but subject to the limitation in Article 43, that it is one "which the State may delimit by law ... with a view to reconciling their exercise with the exigencies of the common good."

The White Paper then concludes: "A requirement that schools have management boards, the composition of which is regulated by statute, need not amount to an improper or unconstitutional infringement of that right," *i.e.* the right of ownership of private property. Clearly in the light of these statements the State sees the right of a religious denomination to manage its own schools as a property right. If such indeed is the case the State may clearly be within its rights to restrict such right in the interests of the common good. Although ownership of premises and management of activity within it, coincide in the case of most existing denominational schools, it is not necessary that they should do so, and managing a school predominantly involves managing an activity.

Property rights may normally be protected by Article 40 or Article 43, but in the case of religious denominations the right to administer property, maintain institutions for religious or charitable purposes and to manage their own affairs is specifically protected in Article 44.2.5° and is separate from the rights to own,

---

26. *ibid.* at 175.
27. Above, n.15.
28. [1976] I.R. 325.
29. [1984] I.R. 36.
30. Report of the Constitution Review Group (May, 1996).
31. See Launch Copy, pp. 211–212.

acquire and administer property. Both rights appear to be religious rather than property rights. Management of a denominational school could, thus, conceivably come within the limitations in Article 44.2.1° and be subject to public order and morality. Article 44.2.6° does provide specifically that the property of a religious denomination may be diverted but this clearly relates to real property and specifies that the only permissible diversion must be for necessary works of public utility.

Without exploring the difficulties of whether the establishment of state schools or multi-denominational schools constitutes "necessary works of public utility"[32] it may be remarked that the Article does envisage circumstances where the State could divert school property owned by a religious denomination. There are no such circumstances specified in relation to the right of a religious denomination to manage its own affairs. However, in the light of the Preamble cases instanced above and in particular *Murray v. Ireland*[33] it seems that the State can enact legislation which (to promote the common good) limits the constitutional right of a religious denomination to manage its own (educational) affairs under Article 44.2.5°. Such legislation would be subject to the application of the doctrine of proportionality.

An argument advanced against the assertion that the State has authority to legislate the composition of denominational school governance is a philosophical one based on the anti-Statist underpinning of Article 42.[34]

Constitutional Proportionality

Constitutional proportionality is a principle or criteria used by the courts to reconcile the existence of a constitutional right and the limitation of that same right by means of legislation.

Hogan and Morgan[35] contend that the notion of equal treatment before the law:[36] "draws with it the idea that, if there are any differences in treatment, that there are only jusitifiable if they bear some sensible proportion to differences in circumstances."[37] They also suggest that where substantive constitutional rights are concerned, some notion of proportionality is always involved.[38]

The principle of proportionality also exists in administrative law and according to Barron J. in *Hand v. Dublin Corporation*[39] if the principle exists in Irish law it applies to administrative action only and not to legislation. Hogan

---

32. See Chap. 13 above.
33. Above, n.13.
34. Whyte, "The White Paper on Education: A Lawyer's Response", *Studies in Education*, Vol. 11, No. 2 (1995).
35. Hogan and Morgan, *Administrative Law in Ireland* (1991).
36. See Equality and Article 40.1 at chap. 15, below.
37. Above, n.35, p. 541.
38. *ibid.*
39. [1989] I.R. 26.

Constitutional Proportionality

and Moran suggest that the distinction depends upon "a fairly unimportant point of semantics".[40]

Constitutional proportionality basically means that any legislation enacted which impinges on a constitutional right must have a sufficiently important objective, must impair the constitutional right or rights which it purports to regulate or limit as little as possible and be in proportion to the objective which the legislation seeks to achieve. In *Heaney v. Ireland*[41] Mr. Justice Costello explained:

> "In considering whether a restriction on the exercise of a right is permitted by the Constitution the courts in this country and elsewhere have found it helpful to apply the *test of proportionality*, a test *which contains the notion of minimal restraint on the exercise of protected rights and the exigencies of the common good in a democratic society.*"[42]

Criteria for Proportionality

Costello J. pointed out that the test of proportionality was:

> ". . . frequently adopted by the European Court of Human Rights (see, for example *Sunday Times v. U.K.* (1979) 2 E.H.R.R. 245) and has recently been formulated by the Supreme Court in Canada in the following terms. The objective of the impugned provision must be of sufficient importance to warrant overriding a constitutionally protected right. The means chosen must pass a proportionality test. They must:
>
> (a) be rationally connected to the objective and not be arbitrary, unfair or based on irrational considerations,
>
> (b) Impair the right as little as possible, and
>
> (c) be such that their effect on rights are proportionate to the objective. (*Chaulk v. R.* (1990) 3 SCR 1303, 1335-1336."[43]

Professor James Casey[44] cites Dickson C.J. in *R. v Edwards Books and Arts Ltd*[45] on the tests applied by the Canadian courts in relation to proportionality. These tests are:

1. the legislative objective which the limitation is designed to promote must be of sufficient importance to warrant overriding a constitutional right;

2. the means chosen to attain those objectives must be proportional or appropriate to the ends and must:

---

40. Above, n.35, p. 544.
41. [1994] 2 I.L.R.M. 420.
42. *ibid.* at 431 (emphasis added).
43. *ibid.* at 431–432.
44. Casey, *Constitutional Law in Ireland* (2nd ed., 1992) p. 313.
45. [1986] 35 D.L.R. (4th) 1.

(a) be carefully designed or rationally connected to the objective;

(b) must impair the right as little as possible; and

(c) their effects must not so severely trench on individual or group rights that the legislative objective, is outweighed by the abridgement of rights.

Application of Proportionality

One of the rights which come within the guarantee of a fair trial in Article 38(1) is the immunity of an accused by which he is not required either to give evidence or to adduce evidence on his own behalf and cannot be questioned against his will. In *Heaney v. Ireland* [46] the applicant refused to give an account of his movements as required under section 52(1) of the Offences Against the State Act 1939 but it was held that the restriction on the right to silence imposed by the section could not be regarded as excessive and was proportionate to the objective which it was designed to achieve. Accordingly it did not infringe Article 38. Incidentally the right to silence was held to be protected under Article 38 and was not an unenumerated personal right within the meaning of Article 40.3.1°.

Proportionality was also central to the decision of the Supreme Court in *Re the Matrimonial Home Bill 1993*[47] where it held that the provisions of the Bill did not constitute a reasonably proportionate intervention by the State with the rights of the family. The Bill amounted to a failure by the State to protect the authority of the family guaranteed by Article 41 and was repugnant to that Article of the Constitution.

In 1995 it was held in *Daly v. Revenue Commissioners*[48] that section 26 of the Finance Act 1990 which amended section 18 of the Finance Act 1987 failed the proportionality test because the effects on the taxpayers property rights was not proportionate to the objective to be achieved and section 26(1) was declared to be unconstitutional and invalid. It was held to be manifestly unfair to established taxpayers. It caused them hardship in that:

(a) the collection of withholding tax reduced their ability to pay the income tax which it had been collected to discharge, and

(b) it required double payment of tax.

This unfairness was not mitigated by the interim refund provisions.

Under Article 40.3.1° proportionality applies to personal constitutional rights because of the words "as far as practicable" while under Article 40.3.2° the particular rights of every citizen to life, person, good name, and property

---

46. Above, n.41.
47. [1994] I.L.R.M. 241.
48. Above, n.12.

rights are subject to proportionality because they are to be protected by the State "as best it may". With regard to the application of proportionality to the property rights of every citizen, the exigencies of the common good may justify legislation which imposes restrictions on the exercise of this constitutional right.

If it is accepted that no constitutional right is absolute or that the constitutional right of a religious denomination to control and manage schools which they own is derived from property rights, then it follows that such rights may be limited by the State on the basis of proportionality.

The Constitution Review Group

The Review Group considered whether the Preamble was a provision of the Constitution and open to amendment as provided in Article 46. The fact that it had been cited in cases and involved in judicial decisions seemed to confirm that it was part of the Constitution and subject to amendment as provided in Article 46. The Review Group also decided: "it seems that it does have legal effect." Most members of the Group felt that the language in the Preamble is overly Roman Catholic and nationalist in tone, gender biased and objectionable to many people. The preferred option of a majority of the Review Group was to amend it.

Recommendation

A majority of the Review Group favours the replacement of the present Preamble by the basic formula of enactment of the Constitution by the people of Ireland. If, however, a more extensive, revised Preamble is preferred, guidelines are suggested.

Chapter 15

New Education Legislation

The White Paper on Education, *Charting Our Education Future*, refers to the complexity of legislation in social areas and to the fact that legislation in education is especially complex.[1] It correctly points out that a number of specific constitutional provisions which impact on education have not been subject to the level of detailed interpretation by the Courts as would allow a clear view of their importance and of how they should be interpreted. It sees legislation as being a particularly important element underpinning the new framework. The first matter dealt with is the approach to legislation and constitutional interpretation because any proposed new legislation "must reflect a careful balancing" of many rights.[2]

The White Paper states that legislation must have regard to the following matters:

(a) constitutional rights and duties of parents and the State (dealt with in earlier sections of this book);

(b) property rights and rights of religious denominations to manage their own affairs, (also dealt with in earlier sections of this book);

(c) the legal principles of estoppel, legitimate expectation and proportionality as well as;

(d) equality principles and the interests of the common good.

Estoppel and Legitimate Expectation

The type of estoppel referred to in the White Paper on Education is promissory estoppel and it is noteworthy that estoppel by representation is included in the definition which states:

> "Estoppel arises where a person makes a promise or a representation as to intention to another, on which that other person acts. The representor is bound by that representation or promise."[3]

---

1. Chap. 18 on the Legislative and Constitutional Framework for Educational Development, p. 206.
2. *ibid.* p. 207.
3. *ibid.* p. 208.

Estoppel by conduct, which includes estoppel by representation was defined by Lord Denman Ch. J. in *Pickard v. Sears*[4] as being:

> "... where one by his words or conduct wilfully causes another to believe the existence of a certain state of things, and induces him to act on that belief, so as to alter his own previous position, the former is concluded from averring against the latter a different state of things as existing at the same time;"[5]

Legitimate expectation is defined as a principle which allows a person to claim that, in view of the existence of a regular practice by a public authority, s/he is entitled to expect that it will continue. The White Paper states that the principle is still in its early development stage and that this presents difficulties in assessing its likely impact on legislation.[6]

The principle of legitimate expectation was first applied in this country in *Webb v. Ireland*[7] where Finlay C.J. described it as:

> "but an aspect of the well recognised concept of promissory estoppel whereby a promise or representation as to intention may in certain circumstances be held binding on the representor or promissor."[8]

In a reference to this description in *Association of General Practitioners v. Minister for Health*[9] O'Hanlon J. stated: "Estoppel has traditionally been regarded as providing a shield and not a sword" and he went on to hold that legitimate expectation cannot create any new cause of action where none existed before, so that where a promise is made which is not supported by any consideration, the promisee cannot bring an action. (*Combe v. Combe*[10] considered.)

Earlier in *Duggan v. An Taoiseach*[11] it was held: "If a person can establish that he has a legitimate expectation of receiving a benefit or privilege the courts will protect that expectation by judicial review as a matter of public law."[12]

Legitimate expectation of consultation in employment law had been recognised and applied by the English House of Lords in *CSSU v. Minister for the Civil Service*[13] in 1985 and in the Irish case of *Duggan v. An Taoiseach*[14] four

---

4. (1837) 6 Ad. & El 469.
5. *ibid.* at 541. For a fuller and more accurate definition of estoppel by representation see that of Evershed M.R. in *Hopgood v. Brown* [1955] 1 All E.R. 550 at 559.
6. See Delany, "Recent Developments Relating to the Doctrine of Legitimate Expectations" (1993), 11 *I.L.T.* 192. Note that in *Hempenstall v. Minister for the Environment* [1993] I.L.R.M. 318, Costello J. stated at 327: "The law relating to the doctrine of legitimate expectations is an evolving one, whose parameters have not yet been defined and whose exact scope has not yet been established".
7. [1988] I.R. 353.
8. *ibid.* at 384.
9. [1995] 2 I.L.R.M. 481.
10. [1951] 2 K.B. 215.
11. [1989] I.L.R.M. 710.
12. *ibid.* at 711.
13. [1985] A.C. 374.
14. Above, n.11.

years later. Lord Fraser of Tullybelton in the *CSSU* case explained that:

> "even where a person claiming some benefit or privilege has no legal right to it, as a matter of private law, he may have a legitimate expectation of receiving the benefit or privilege, and, if so, the courts will protect his expectation by judicial review as a matter of public law. . . . *Legitimate or reasonable expecation may arise either from an express promise given on behalf of a public authority or from the existence of a regular practice* which the claimant can, reasonably expect to continue. . . ."[15]

There must be sufficient past practice to support a legitimate expectation. In *R. v. Secretary of State for Education, ex parte London Borough of Southwark*[16] when the Secretary of State decided to approve the according of grant maintained status to Friars Primary School the LEA applied for Judicial Review claiming that there had been a breach of their legitimate expectation of consultation. They had been informed on the December 23, 1993, of the Secretary's intention and only had three working days to respond. It was held that there was insufficient past practice in respect of consultation at that point in the decision making process to warrant the recognition of a legitimate expectation of consultation.

In order for an applicant to obtain relief this expectation must be legitimate. In *Wiley v. Revenue Commissioners*[17] while the appellant had an expectation, it was not a legitimate expectation. O'Flaherty J. cited *Attorney General (New South Wales) v. Quinn*[18] where Brennan J. stated:

> "Judicial Review provides no remedies to protect interests falling short of enforceable rights which are apt to be affected by the lawful exercise of executive or administrative power. . . ."

In *Abrahamson v. Law Society of Ireland*[19] the applicants claim failed because a regulation on which they claimed that a legitimate expectation would inure for their benefit had been declared invalid.

---

15. Above, n.10 at 401. In some cases the Irish courts have queried whether an "unqualified assurance" has been given. See *Devitt v Minister for Education* [1989] I.L.R.M. 639 and *Webb v. Ireland* [1988] I.R. 353. While in *Dempsey v. Minister for Justice* [1994] I.L.R.M. 401 Morris J. stated there must be either a "direct assurance" or the expectation must be based on conduct, which is well established and regular.

    In 1995 the Supreme Court held that there was no legitimate expectation arising on the facts in *Re "La Lavia"* [1996] 1 I.L.R.M. 194 there was nothing in the nature of a promise held out to the plaintiffs in such a manner as would bind the State. Denham J. referred to the absence of a "verbal assurance" as was given in the *Webb* case and to a second aspect of legitimate expectation arising from the well established practice of giving rewards.
16. [1994] Crown Office Digest 298.
17. [1993] I.L.R.M. 482.
18. [1990] 170 C.L.R. 1 at 35.
19. Unreported, High Court, McCracken J., July 15, 1996.

Relevance of Legal Principles

There is little doubt that the present funding arrangements governing state subvention of denominational schools has existed for some time and has become a regular practice. Aim 3 of the Introduction to the Green Paper on Education[20] proposes: "all schools receiving State support would have a representative Board of Management." This was followed by the Position Paper on the Governance of Schools,[21] section 4.1(i) of which sets out that:

> "the receipt of State funding by a school would be conditional on putting in place a Board of Management consistent with the approach and criteria outlined in this paper."

Would a denominational school authority be entitled to claim that the existing scheme cannot be unilaterally altered by the State, that the State is bound by its previous representations and practice under the doctrines of estoppel and legitimate expectation? In effect could they claim that they are entitled to continued state funding nonetheless? The managers and proprietors of Irish denominational schools have received state funding for many years on the basis of compliance with Department requirements and the indications are that there is an established practice in relation to funding.[22]

In accordance with the the definition of Finlay C.J. in *Webb v. Ireland*[23] legitimate expectation was treated as a variation of estoppel, the two concepts as variations of the same doctrine, but in *Hempenstall v. Minister for the Environment*[24] Costello J. stated that no estoppel could arise to prevent the discharge by the Minister of a statutory discretion and indicated that a claim based on the doctrine of legitimate expectation could not have succeeded had the facts been as claimed. The same judge in *Tara Prospecting Ltd v. Minister for Energy*[25] seems to distinguish between legitimate expectation as a form of procedural protection and legitimate expectation as a substantive right. It appears that in some circumstances an equitable right arising from estoppel may prove substantive, but not in cases involving the exercise of a discretionary statutory power. In the course of his judgment Costello J. summarised the legal principles as follows:

> "(1) There is a duty on a minister who is exercising a discretionary power which may affect *rights* or *interests* to adopt fair procedures in the exercise of the power. Where a member of the public has a *legitimate expectation* arising

---

20. Department of Education, April, 1992.
21. Department of Education, July, 1994.
22. If state funding of denomination schools was held to be an endowment of religion and therefore unconstitutional any expectation of continued funding by the State would not be a legitimate expectation.
23. Above, n.7.
24. [1993] I.L.R.M. 318.
25. [1993] I.L.R.M. 771. Note that at the time of writing the decision in *Tara Prospecting Ltd v. Minister for the Environment* is under appeal.

from the minister's words and or conduct that (a) he will be given a hearing before a decision adverse to his interests will be taken or (b) that he will obtain a benefit from the exercise of the power then the minister also has the duty to act fairly towards him and this may involve a duty to give him a fair hearing before a decision adverse to his interests is taken. There would then arise a correlative right to a fair hearing which, if denied, will justify the court in quashing the decision.

(2) The existence of a legitimate expectation that a *benefit* will be conferred does not in itself give rise to any legal or equitable right to the *benefit itself* which can be enforced by an order of *mandamus* or otherwise. However, in cases involving public authorities, other than cases involving the exercise of statutory discretionary powers, an equitable right to the benefit may arise from the application of the principles of promissory estoppel to which effect will be given by appropriate court order.

(3) In cases involving the exercise of a discretionary statutory power the only legitimate expectation relating to the conferrring of a benefit that can be *inferred* from words or conduct is a conditional one, namely, that a benefit will be conferred provided that at the time the minister considers that it is a proper exercise of the statutory power in the light of current policy to grant it. Such a conditional expectation cannot give rise to an enforceable right to the benefit should it later be refused by the minister in the public interest.

(4) In cases involving the exercise of a discretionary statutory power in which an explicit *assurance* has been given which gives rise to an expectation that a benefit will be conferred no enforceable equitable or legal right to the benefit can arise. No promissory estoppel can arise because the minister cannot estop either himself or his successors from exercising a discretionary power in the manner prescribed by parliament at the time that it is being exercised."[26]

Has the Oireachtas the power (despite the doctrines of estoppel and legitimate expectation) by statute to prescribe new conditions for eligibility for state funding which require a specified management board for each school? The short answer is yes, the Minister does have such power. A denominational school authority cannot rely on estoppel or legitimate expectation to prevent the State legislating school governance in the public interest. In such circumstances the rights of the individual would be subservient to the rights of the State. However it seems likely that the State would have to continue funding at present levels to school authorities which do not adopt a statutory board of management model. This could possibly lead to a two tiered system of funding.

---

26. *ibid.* at 788-789 (emphasis added).

Minister Fettering His/Her Discretion

Spencer, Bower and Turner, state:

> "An estoppel cannot be raised to prevent the exercise of a statutory discretion or to prevent or excuse the performance of a statutory duty, for it is well establised that it is impossible in law to suggest any principle which will preclude a party from alleging the invalidity of that which a statute has, on grounds of general public policy, enacted shall be invalid."[27]

In *R. v. London Borough of Bexley, ex parte Jones*[28] which arose out of the failure of the Local Education Authority to pay a discretionary student grant, it was held that the exercise of a discretionary power must not be fettered through the adoption of a binding policy to which no exceptions are permitted.

In *Devitt v. Minister for Education*[29] Lardner J. stated that while the Minister for Education was entitled to adopt general rules and procedures in relation to the exercise of his statutory discretion:

> "... he is not, in my view, entitled by any such rules or procedures to limit the scope of the discretion entrusted to him or to disable himself from the full exercise of it. Nor in my judgment may such a practice or conduct be relied upon by the applicant as estopping the Minister from the full exercise of the discretion vested in her by the Act. See the observations of Henchy J. in *Re Greendale Building Co. Ltd.* [1977] I.R. 256 at 264."[30]

More recently in *Gilheaney v. The Revenue Commissioners*[31] Costello J. referred to the *Devitt* case stating:

> "It is well established that the doctrine (of legitimate expectation) cannot be invoked to limit the exercise of a discretionary power.... Examples of the application of this doctrine are to be found in this country in *Devitt v. Minister for Education* [1989] I.L.R.M. 639 and in England in *In re Findlay* [1985] A.C. 318 in which Lord Scarman (at page 338) pointed out that the unfettered discretion conferred by a statute upon a Minister cannot be restricted so as to hamper or even prevent changes in policy."[32]

The Power of the State to Legislate

The State, acting for the common good, has the power to enact any legislation which is constitutionally valid. Once it has enacted such legislation "it is

---

27. Spencer Bower and Turner, *The Law Relating to Estoppel by Representation* (2nd. ed., 1966) p. 133.
28. [1994] Crown Office Digest 393.
29. [1989] I.L.R.M. 639.
30. *ibid.* at 649.
31. Unreported, High Court, Costello J., October 4, 1995.
32. *ibid.* at p. 31 of the judgment. See also *Hempenstall v. Minister for the Environment* [1993] I.L.R.M. 318.

incompatible with parliamentary democracy for the courts, under the guise of estoppel or waiver or any other doctrine, to set aside the will of parliament constitutionally embodied in a statute." *per* Henchy J., Supreme Court (with Griffin and Kenny JJ. in agreement) in *Re Greendale Building Co. Ltd.*[33]

Government Contracts and Executive Power

Not alone may a government not be prevented from enacting legislation by estoppel or legitimate expectation but in addition a Government cannot fetter its own future executive action, even by contract. This conclusion arises from the decision in *Rederiaktie Bolaget Amphitrite v. The King*.[34] In this case the plaintiff claimed damages for the breach of the guarantee by the British Government that their ship the "Amphitrite" would be allowed free passage from Britain during the first world war. It was held that the Government's undertaking was not enforceable in a court of law, it not being within the competence of the Crown to make a contract which would have the effect of limiting its power of executive action in future. Rowlatt J. stated:

> ". . . it is not competent for the Government to fetter its future executive action, which must necessarily be determined by the needs of the community when the question arises. It cannot by contract hamper its freedom of action in matters which concern the welfare of the State."[35]

According to Spencer Bower and Turner, public policy is very much a consideration in such a decision as it is in relation to observance of a statute. They state:

> "if the public, or a class or section of the community, are interested, as well as himself, in the general observance of the conditions prescribed by the statute it has always been held on the ground of public policy that there can be no waiver, even by express contract or consent of the right to such observance by any individual party; *Griffitt v. Evans* (1882) 46 L.T., *Harris v. Harris* [1952] 1 All E.R."[36]

It therefore seems clear that neither estoppel or legitimate expecation can be invoked against a statute enacted in the public interest. When such a statute is in place estoppel cannot be used to negate its operation.[37]

In relation to previous assurances (if any) of continued funding or continuation of management structures, which may have been given to denominational groups, such assurances might not amount to contracts and even if they did, it

---

33. [1977] I.R. 256 at 264,
34. [1921] 3 K.B. 500.
35. *ibid.* at 503.
36. Above, n.27, p. 135.
37. See *Beesley v. Halwood Estates Ltd.* [1960] 2 All E.R. 314 at 324.

is not within the competence of a Government to make a contract which would have the effect of limiting its power of executive action in future.[38]

Legislation and School Governance

Chapter 18 of the White Paper on Education asserts that: ". . . the authority of the State to enact legislation relating to school governance seems beyond doubt, subject to any provisions being proportionate and objectively necessary in the interests of the common good."[39] Earlier the White Paper on Education submits:

> "The State, by virtue of its role *as promoter and guardian of the common good*, could reasonably be expected to ensure that the rights and interests of all the partners in the education system are reflected in the basic element of that system, the individual school, in a way which gives due weight to each and to ensure that schools operate to the highest levels of effectiveness and efficiency. In addition, in view of the State's role in providing most of the funding for schools, there must be confidence on the part of the State agencies providing that funding that there are appropriate structures in place in schools to ensure that public funds are used in the manner intended."[40]

The failure of the State to develop an alternative system of non-denominational or multi-denominational schools has provoked disquiet in some circles about denominational control of the system which they claim is based on the ownership of property and on the rights of religious denominations. The Campaign to Separate Church and State claim that the vast majority of national schools are under the control of clerics or their nominees and that: "Successive social surveys show that between one quarter and one half of Irish adults don't like this situation."[41]

State Control through Legislation

State control of schools owned and managed by denominational groups by means of legislation, is complicated by the constitutional rights of such groups which have been outlined previously. See Chapters 9 and 10 above.

Agreement on School Governance

It now seems that the application of the concept of proportionality to legislation regulating the management composition, or procedures of denominational schools will not be challenged by Church interests but the President could decide to refer any such Bill to the Supreme Court under Article 26 to test its constitutional validity.

---

38. *Rederiaktie Bolaget Amphitrite v. The King*, above, n.23.
39. At p. 211.
40. *ibid.*
41. Colgan, *Minimum Requirements for Education Act(s)* (1989), para. 2.

Chapter 10 of the White Paper on Education dealing with the Governance of schools reveals that: "General agreement has now been reached on a governance model for primary schools, subject to agreement being reached on a model deed of trust, which will provide a legal basis for guaranteeing the specific ethos of each school." Later on[42] it is stated that the degree of accord and progress at primary level will provide a basis for discussion to secure agreed structures for the management of second level schools. Nonetheless the White Paper also indicates that the principle of proportionality will be used by the State in its approach to legislation and constitutional interpretation. The *Irish Independent* of October 12, 1996 reported that Dr Thornhill, Secretary of the Department of Education, had stated in Cork that: "agreement on new structures for boards of management in primary schools is expected shortly . . . in time to allow the new boards to take effect early in 1997."

Limits on State Intervention

Even if the principle of proportionality did apply, in the author's opinion the following limitations on state intervention cannot be circumvented.

1. The State cannot require that the management of a denominational school act contrary to their own religious beliefs or philosophy. To do so would be going too far.[43]

2. The State cannot take over or assign the management function to others. The State cannot appoint persons to the boards of management or remove persons from them. Only the denominational authority may do so. This also has significance in relation to the composition of boards of management and the appointment of a chairperson who has a casting vote.

    As previously stated by the author Article 44.2.4° should not be read in isolation, it is linked to Article 44.2.5° and should be interpreted in conjunction with it.[44]

3. The State cannot impose such conditions as would turn a denominational school into a non-denominational one.

The existence and the implied constitutional right of denominational schools to State subvention is well established. This would require leaving the ethos and control of the ethos firmly in the hands of the denomination involved.[45]

---

42. At p. 147.
43. Farry, "The Green Paper, The Church and The Constitution", *Studies*, Vol 82, Summer (1993), p. 160. Two years later it was accepted that an institution ought not be required to do any act contrary to its philosophy and code of ethics in the case of *Re a Ward of Court* [1995] 2 I.L.R.M. 1 (the "Right to Die" case).
44. Farry, "The Green Paper, Boards of Management and The Constitution, Irish Education", *Decision Maker*, No. 4, Autumn (1992).
45. Above, n.32.

Indications in the White Paper

Although legal issues identified in the White Paper have not been expounded in detail, the indications are that a carefully crafted minimalist intervention to democratise boards of management is proposed. Readers will be able to judge for themselves to what extent the new education legislation complies with the proportionality criteria outlined above. It is however, worth remembering that the constitutional protection of denominational control will still exist regardless of agreement on school governance.

Equality and Article 40.1

Finally, in relation to equality principles the relevant constitutional provision is Article 40 which provides:

> "1. All citizens shall, as human persons, be held equal before the law. This shall not be held to mean that the State shall not in its enactments have due regard to differences of capacity, physical and moral, and of social function."

"citizens"

Although the Article specifically refers to "citizens" the principle of equality before the law, has been applied in personal liberty cases to non-citizens without discrimination.[46]

In the case of *Northampton County Council v. ABF & MBF*[47] in 1981 Hamilton J. (as he then was) held that non-citizenship had no effect on the interpretation of Article 41 or the entitlement to the protection afforded by it. Subsequently in 1985 in the case of *The State (Bouzagou) v. Station Sergeant, Fitzgibbon St.*[48] Barrington J. in the High Court held that a non-citizen is entitled to rely upon Article 41 and also Article 42 of the Constitution stating:

> "I am prepared to accept that the rights recognised by Articles 41 and 42 of the Constitution are not confined to citizens and that in a proper case, the prosecutor would be entitled to rely upon these Articles."[49]

"as human persons"

The guarantee in this Article, as presently interpreted by the courts, does not extend to artificial legal entities, it only extends to human persons. In *Quinn's Supermarket v. Attorney General*[50] the plaintiffs challenged the validity of an

---

46. See *The State (Trimbole) v. Governor of Mountjoy Prison* [1985] I.R. 550. As for the natural law theory that fundamental rights can be invoked by non-citizens: see Hogan and Whyte, *Kelly: The Irish Constitution* (3rd ed., 1994), p. 679.
47. [1982] I.L.R.M. 164.
48. [1985] I.R. 426.
49. *ibid.* at 433.
50. [1972] I.R. 1.

Order specifying hours of trading for victuallers shops on the grounds that it discriminated between shops which sold fresh meat and those which sold meat killed and prepared by the Jewish ritual method. The Supreme Court held that the guarantee in Article 40.1 of the Constitution was not relevant to the plaintiff as no question of *human equality or inequality* arose.

Walsh J. delivering a majority decision stated that Article 40.1 was a guarantee *of equality as human persons* and (as the Irish text made clear) *was a guarantee related to their dignity as human beings*. He then continued:

> "... it need scarcely be pointed out that *under no possible construction of the Constitutional guarantee could a body corporate or any entity but a human being be considered to be a human person for the purposes of this provision.*"

In the earlier case of *The State (Nicolaou) v. An Bord Úchtála*[51] Walsh J. delivering the judgment of the Supreme Court stated:

> "In the opinion of the court section 1 of Article 40 is not to be read as a guarantee or undertaking that all citizens shall be treated by the law as equal for all purposes, but rather as an acknowledgment of the human equality of all citizens and that such equality will be recognised in the laws of the State."[52]

"the State shall not in its enactments"

The Irish version of enactments is "ina chud achtachán". Hogan and Whyte[53] state that the wording of the second sentence in Article 40.1 makes it clear that the precept of equality in the first sentence is intended to apply to the process of enacting law and not merely to the process of applying law already enacted.

In *East Donegal Co-operative Livestock Mart Ltd v. Attorney General*[54] the Supreme Court held:

> "That the power of the national parliament under Article 40.s.1 of the Constitution to have due regard in its enactments to differences of capacity and social function, *did not extend to a delegation of that power to a Minister of State* so as to enable him to exempt a particular individual from the operation of the (Livestock Marts) Act of 1967 in the circumstances...".[55]

Some ten years later Henchy J. in the Supreme Court (O'Higgins C.J, Griffin, Kenny and Parke JJ. concurring) in *Dillane v. Ireland*[56] treated Rule 67 of the District Court Rules: "as part of the enactments of the State". The District Court Rules 1948 (1947 No. 431) were made by the District Court Rules Committee with the concurrence of the Minister for Justice. The Committee

---

51. [1966] I.R. 567.
52. *ibid.* at 639.
53. *Kelly: The Irish Constitution* (3rd ed., 1994) p. 712.
54. [1970] I.R. 317.
55. *ibid.* at 318 (Emphasis added).
56. [1980] I.L.R.M. 167.

Equality and Article 40.1

and the Minister were designated the rule making authority by section 90 of The Courts of Justice Act 1924 and were given the authority to make such rules under section 91 of the same Act. Rule 67 prohibits a Justice from awarding costs against: "a member of the Garda Síochána acting in discharge of his duties as a police officer."

When criminal proceedings against the plaintiff were withdrawn by the prosecuting Garda the District Court had no power to award costs against the Garda. The plaintiff claimed that Rule 67 was in breach of the guarantee of equality before the law in Article 40.1 of the Constitution and also that it failed to respect, and amounted to an unjust attack, on his property rights in Article 40.3. The High Court dismissed the plaintiff's claim and he appealed to the Supreme Court.

It was held that Rule 67 did not contravene Article 40.1 since *the discrimination in favour of the Garda was justified* on the ground that there was a *difference of social function* within the meaning of the second sentence of Article 40.1 between on the one hand a garda who prosecuted, acting in discharge of his duties as a police officer and on the other hand, a common informer who was either a mere member of the public or a garda not acting in discharge of his duties as a police officer.

The court also held that eligibility for costs was not a property right of the plaintiff under Article 40.3 since the District Court had no inherent power to award costs but even assuming it was such a right, *harmonious interpretation* indicated that since the denial of costs to the plaintiff was warranted under Article 40.1 it could not amount to an "unjust" attack on property rights within the meaning of Article 40.3.

Invidious Discrimination

In *O'Brien v. Keogh*[57] Ó Dálaigh C.J. stated:

> "Article 40 does not require identical treatment of all persons without recognition of differences in relevant circumstances, see [1966] I.R. p. 639. It only forbids *invidious discrimination*."[58]

This reference by Ó Dálaigh C.J. is to *The State (Nicolaou) v. An Bord Úchtála*[59] where it was submitted that the Adoption Act 1952 violated Article 40 by discriminating unfairly aginst the natural father on the grounds of his sex or paternity, and that it treated illegitimate children unfairly in that it allowed them to be deprived of the society and support of a willing parent. The Supreme Court responded by referring to Article 40.1 and stating:

---

57. [1972] I.R. 144.
58. *ibid.* at 156. This definition was cited by Walsh J. in *de Burca and Anderson v. Attorney General* [1976] I.R. 38 at 68 where he commented: "It import to Aristotelian concept that justice demands that we treat equals equally and unequals unequally."
59. [1966] I.R. 567.

> "The section itself in its provision, 'this shall be held to mean that the State shall not in its enactments have due regard to differences of capacity, physical and moral, and of social function', is a recognition that inequality may or must result from some special abilities or from some deficiency or from some special need and it is clear that the Article does not either envisage or guarantee equal measure of all things to all citizens. To do so regardless of the factors mentioned would be inequality."[60]

Kenny J. in *Murphy v. Attorney General*[61] referred to the dictionary meaning of invidious as (of comparisons or distinctions) unfairly or offensively discriminatory and stated that this meaning could be used to describe the inequality prohibited by Article 40.1.

Personal Rights

Indeed Kenny J. in *Ryan v. Attorney General*[62] commented on the fact that none of the personal rights of the citizen are unlimited and that their exercise may be regulated by the Oireachtas when the common good requires it.

Equality and Legislation

The acknowledgment in the White Paper on Education that future education legislation must have regard to equality principles follows from the provisions of Article 40.1 above. In *Dillane v. Attorney General*[63] Henchy J. delivering the judgment of the Supreme Court laid down guidelines in order for legislation to comply with this constitutional provision as follows:

> "When the State, whether directly by statute or mediately through the exercise of a delegated power of subordinate legislation, makes a discrimination in favour of, or against, a person or a category of persons, on the express or implied ground of a difference of social function, the courts will not condemn such discrimination as being in breach of Article 40.1 if it is not arbitrary, or capricious, or otherwise not reasonably capable, when objectively viewed in the light of the social function involved, of supporting the selection or classification complained of."[64]

Some four years later in *O.B. v. S.*[65] it was claimed tht the word "issue" used in the Succession Act 1965 did not include illegitimate children and discrimi-

---

60. *ibid.* at 639.
61. [1982] I.R. 241. Note also that the Supreme Court in *O'B. v. S.* [1984] I.R. 316 at 317 held that the discrimination involved was not an invidious discrimination in the sense of being *unjust, unreasonable or arbitrary* and was not invalid having regard to the provisions of the Constitution.
62. [1965] I.R. 294.
63. [1980] I.L.R.M. 167.
64. *ibid.* at 169.
65. [1984] I.R. 316.

nated in favour of legitimate "issue" thus contravening the provisions of Article 40.1. The Supreme Court referred to the Ó Dálaigh judgment in *O'Brien v. Keogh*[66] and to that of Walsh J. in *de Burca v. Attorney General*[67] and stated:

> ". . . the object and the nature of the legislation concerned must be taken into account, and distinctions or discriminations which the legislation creates must not be unjust, unreasonable or arbitrary and must, of course, be relevant to the legislation in question."[68]

"The common good"

The Irish version of the words "common good" in the Preamble to the Constitution is "mhaiteas phoiblí" and in Article 42.3.2° is "leasa an phobail". The Irish version of "public good" in Article 42.4 is also "leasa an phobail". Apparently there is no significant difference between the terms "common good" and "public good". As to a Minister being required to take account of the "common good see *Fajujonu v. Minister for Justice*.[69] Chapter 14 above where Walsh J. stated that the Minister would have to be satisfied for stated reasons, that the interests of the common good of the people of Ireland were so predominant and so overwhelming in the circumstances.

See "public good", Chapter 4, above.

---

66. Above, n.54.
67. [1976] I.R. 38.
68. *ibid.* at 335. The court held that the discrimination involved could not be justified as being due to any difference of capacity or of social function but nevertheless was justified by Art. 41.1 and Art. 41.3
69. [1990] 2 I.R. 151.

Appendix

Papal Encyclicals and the Constitution

Catholic doctrine and belief had a significant impact on the drafting and formulation of various Articles in the Constitution quite apart from the inputs of the Jesuit order and John Charles McQuaid. A number of commentators including Professor John Kelly, Professor Basil Chubb, and Dr Dermot Keogh have highlighted this influence. According to Basil Chubb:

> "The clearest and most unequivocal enunciation of Catholic principles in Bunreacht na hÉireann is to be found in Articles 41 and 42 which deal with the family and education. Kelly considered them wholly inspired by Christian (or, more specifically, by Catholic) orthodoxy, in particular by well known encyclicals of modern Popes; and he mentions two in particular, both of Pius XI, namely Divini Illius Magistri (English Title: On the Christian Education of Youth, 1929) and Casti Connubii (English Title: On Christian Marriage, 1930.)"[1]

The Encyclical Letter of Pius XI on Christian Education of Youth "Divini Illius Magistri" of December 31, 1929[2] had a significant impact on the Catholic Bishops response to the Vocational Education Act 1930 and indeed also at a later date on the formulation of the 1937 Constitution. Just how significant that influence was, is clearly illustrated by a comparison of the following extracts from the encyclical "Divini Illius" with Article 42.

The Encylical stated:

> "The *first natural* and necessary element in this environment, as regards education is the family, and this precisely because so ordained by the Creator Himself."[3]

> "*The family* therefore holds directly from the Creator the mission and hence *the right to educate the offspring, a right inalienable* because inseparably joined to the strict obligation, a right anterior to any right whatever of civil society and the State, and therefore *inviolable* on the part of any power on earth."[4]

---

1. Chubb, *The Constitution and Constitutional Change in Ireland* (1978), p. 46. See also Kelly, *Fundamental Rights in the Irish Law and Constitution* (1988), p. 33.
2. "Divini Illius Magistri", Cod. 1. C.c. 1113, *Seven Great Encyclicals* (Paulist Press, New York, 1939, 1963).
3. *ibid.* p. 57 (emphasis added).
4. *ibid.* p. 45 (emphasis added).

"It must be borne in mind also that the obligation of the family to bring up children, includes not only *religious and moral education, but physical and civil education as well.*"[5]

Article 42.1 of the Constitution provides:

"The State acknowledges that the primary and natural educator of the child is the Family and guarantees to respect the inalienable right and duty of parents to provide, according to their means, for the religious and moral, intellectual, physical and social education of their children."

. . . .

"It also belongs to *the State* to protect the rights of the child itself *when the parents are found wanting either physically or morally* in this respect, whether by default, incapacity, or misconduct, since as has been shown, their right to educate is not an absolute and despotic one . . . subject . . . to the vigilance and administrative care of the State in view of the *common good . . . always in conformity with the natural rights of the child . . .*".[6]

Article 42.5 provides:

"In exceptional cases where the parents for physical or moral reasons fail in their duty towards their children, the State as guardian of the common good, by appropriate means shall endeavour to supply the place of the parents, but always with due regard for the natural and imprescriptible rights of the child"

. . . .

". . . unjust and unlawful is any monopoly, educational or scholastic, which, physically or morally, *forces families to make use of government schools, contrary to the dictates of their Christian conscience, or contrary even to their legitimate preferences.*"[7]

Article 42 3.1° provides:

"The State shall not oblige parents in violation of their conscience and lawful preference to send their children to schools established by the State, or to any particular type of school designated by the State."

. . . .

"It pertains to the State, in view of the common good, *to promote* in various ways the *education* and *instruction* of youth.

It should begin by encouraging and *assisting*, of its own accord, the initiative and activity of the Church and the family . . . it should, moreover *supplement their work whenever this falls short of what is necessary, even by means of its own schools and institutions.*[8]

---

5. *ibid.* p. 47 (emphasis added).
6. *ibid.* p. 49 (emphasis added)
7. *ibid.* (emphasis added).
8. *ibid.* (emphasis added).

> "... in a nation where there are different religious beliefs ... it becomes the duty of the State ... *to leave free scope* to the initiative of the Church and the family, while giving them such assistance as justice demands."[9]

Article 42.4 provides:

> "... The State shall provide for free primary education and shall endeavour to supplement and give reasonable aid to private and corporate educational initiative, and, when the public good requires it, provide other educational facilities or institutions with due regard, however, for the rights of parents, especially in the matter of religious and moral formation."

According to Rev E. Cahill S.J. the qualification: "with due regard, however, for the rights of parents, especially in the matter of religious and moral formation." was inserted as a safeguard against the liberalist principles of laicism and secularism in education and the Masonic ideal of Ecole Unique which was upheld at that time by many governments in Europe and America.[10]

> "... the State can exact, and *take measures to secure* that *all its citizens* have the necessary knowledge of their civic and political duties, *and a certain degree of physical, intellectual and moral culture*, which, considering the *conditions of our times*, is really necessary for the *common good*."[11]

Article 42.3.2° provides:

> "The State shall however as guardian of the common good, require in view of actual conditions that the children receive a certain minimum education, moral, intellectual and social."

> "... It is the duty of the State to protect in its legislation, the prior rights, already described, of the family as regards the Christian education of its offspring, and consequently also to respect the supernatural rights of the Church in this same realm of Christian education."[12]

While the Standing Comittee of the Church of Ireland has been criticised for having made no representations when the 1937 Constitution was being drawn up.[13] De Valera's record of talks with church leaders in April 1937[14] clearly shows that he consulted with Church of Ireland, Presbyterian and Methodist leaders as well as Catholic churchmen. On 10, 12, 14 and 16 April 1937 he met Dr Irwin of the Moderator of the Presbyterians. On April 12 he called on Dr Gregg, Church of Ireland Archbishop of Dublin and on April 26 Mr Moynihan

---

9. *ibid.* p. 61 (emphasis added).
10. See De Valera papers Ref. P.100 1095 Cahill File, also, *Kelly: The Irish Constitution*, p. 6.
11. "Divini Illius", above, n.2, p. 49 (emphasis added).
12. *ibid.* p. 48.
13. *Irish Times*, April 26, 1994.

saw Archbishop Gregg, and Dr Robinson (Papal Nuncio) and got a letter from Gregg to D'Arcy. Robinson went to see D'Arcy on April 27. On April 13 he saw Rev. W.H. Massey, head of the Methodist Church in Ireland.

Mr. J. Barry Deane, Honorary Secretary of the Church of Ireland has stated that there was no record in the Journals or in the minutes that the Standing Committee had said or done anything at the time the Constitution was being drafted and enacted. The item was not included on its agenda.

---

14. See Farrell (ed.), *De Valera's Constitution and Ours* (1988) and Dr Dermot Keogh, *Church, State and Society*, pp. 112–113.

INDEX

Adoption, 71
Agriculture and Technical Instruction, Dept. of, 107
　establishment of, 107
Akensen, 76
aliens
　control of within the State, 146
Alvey, David, 89
Anglican Church, 87
application under Article 40.4.2°, 44
Art, School of, 106
association, freedom of, 4, 5
　and unions, right to form, 4. *See also* Trade Unions
Association of Secondary Teachers of Ireland (ASTI), 108
Auchmuty, James Johnston, 86

Barber, Noel S.J., 105
Bhreathnach (Niamh), Minister for Education 79, 99
Binchy, Prof. William, 4
bodily integrity, right to, 5
Brennan, Fr Martin, 82

Cahill, E S.J., 56, 69
Calvert, H., 132
Campaign to Separate Church and State, 99, 128, 130, 159
Casey, Prof. James, 20, 51, 95, 97, 98, 101, 125, 149
Catholic Managers Association, 57
Central Council
　Recommendations, 83
chaplains
　payment by State, 127, 128
　community schools, 128, 129
charitable purposes, 92
　trusts, 92, 101
child care assistant support, 54

children
　assess standard of education, 82
　born within State to alien parents, 146
　deprivation of education, 113, 115, 117
　disciplining of, 63, 64
　education at home, 110
　education at private school, 110
　minimum education, 111
　religious and moral formation, 79, 96
　rights of, 21, 71, 72, 100, 111, 115, 117, 119
Chubb, Prof. Basil, 131, 169
Church of England, 98
Church of Ireland
　Anglican charity schools, 86
　chaplains, 128
　de Valera, and, 169, 170
　disendowment, 127
　Erasmus Smith schools, 86
Church Education Society
　foundation, 87
citizen, 8
City and Guilds of London Institute, 107
Coleridge, Lord, 58
Colley, George, Minister for Education, 107, 108
Commissioners of Education in Ireland, 29, 103
Commissioners of National Education in Ireland, 29, 76, 77, 102, 103
　board of, 76, 88, 102
　charter, 88
　rules and regulations, 88
community colleges, 106, 107
　boards of management, 109
　constitutionality, 109

comprehensive schools, 83, 107
  management, 107
  funding, 107
  examination, 107
  board models, 107
community schools
  board of management, 108, 109
  building of, 108
  chaplains, 128, 129
  control of, 109
  courses, 109
  Department of Education Working Paper 1970, 108
  funding, 108
  religious formation, 69
  system of education, 109
Connell, Desmond, Archbishop of Dublin, 4
conscience, freedom of, 99
conspiracy, 113, 114
  to injure, tort of, 115
    actionable, 116
Constitution of Ireland
  Austrian, 56
  Belgian, 56
  construction of, 91
  harmonious interpretation, 141, 142, 163
  hierarchical interpretation, 141
  interpretation of, 4, 16, 19, 20, 21, 92, 101, 141, 146, 152, 160
  judges interpretation, 3
  Polish, 56
  proportional interpretation, 148, 149, 150, 151, 160, 161
  Report of Committee on the, 1967, 41, 42, 52
Constitutional Committee 1934, 9, 20
Constitutional Review Group, Report of, 1996, 3 4, 7, 12, 21, 42, 54, 73, 74, 85, 100, 138, 147, 151
  amendments, 151
  conclusions, 8
  recommendations, 7, 8, 21, 37, 55, 74, 101, 139, 140, 151

constitutional rights
  breach of, exemplary damages for, 119
    limitation of action for, 126
  enumerated, 1
  express limitation of, 142, 143, 144, 145, 146
  fundamental rights
  injunction against, 122
  nature of a tort, 126
  proportionality, doctrine of, 143, 144, 147, 148, 149, 150, 151
  remedy for infringement, 122
  unenumerated, 1
  unlawful interference, damages for 116, 117. *See also* personal rights
Cope Foundation, 53
Cork Polio and Aftercare Association, 53
corporal punishment, 65, 84
court
  guard safety ,order and moral welfare of the State, 124
  interpretation of the Constitution, 16, 124
  powers of, 116, 117, 118, 119, 120
  role of, 6, 19
  separation of powers and, 20
Cullen, Cardinal, 87
Cumann na nGaedhal
  model system of education, 88
curriculum
  for schools for the severely and profoundly handicapped, 41
  integrated, 134, 136
  "Towards Independence" of Department of Education, 41
custody of an illegitimate child by the child's unmarried mother, right of, 6

de Rossa, Proinsias Minister for Social Welfare, 98
de Valera, Eamon, 9, 13, 56, 61, 63, 83, 131, 169, 170
  papers, 16, 18, 20

Index

damages
  anxiety, 117
  detrimental effect to educational progress, 118
  failure of the State, 120
  inconvenience, 117, 118
  interruption of schooling, 118
  learning capacity, 118
  mental distress, 117, 118
  unlawful interference with constitutional right, 117
declaratory order, 123
definitions. *See* Words and Phrases
denominational education, 87
  Catholic, 127
denominational schools, 78, 79, 83, 90
  funding of, 94, 95, 96
  national, 95
  primary, 90
  recognition of, 92
  religious management of, 90, 91, 92, 94, 95, 103
  secondary, 90
Deering, Thomas, 57
Dillon, James, T.D., 57
disassociation, right of, 4, 5
Drimoleague, 112, 113, 114, 117, 118, 121. *See also Crowley v. Ireland*

Eastern Health Board, 36
education
  boards, 100, 105
  curriculum and policy, 97
  Department of, 9, 20, 54, 63, 66, 81, 102, 103, 106, 107,
  Minister for, 103
    binding rules on, 96, 103, 104
    powers, 12
  proposed legislation, 98, 100
  school recognition, 105
E H B. *See* Eastern Health Board
English Cabinet, 11
enumerated right, 4
equality guarantee, 161, 162, 164
European Commission on Human Rights, 42, 63
European Convention on Human Rights, 8, 36, 61, 73, 82, 83, 84
European Court of Human Rights, 61, 149
estoppel, 152, 155, 156, 158
  conduct, by, 153
  legitimate expectation, 153, 154, 155, 156, 157
  promissory, 152
  representation, by, 152
examination
  Intermediate Certificate, 107
expression, freedom of, 99

family
  definition of, 60, 61
  protection of, 70, 71, 73
  rights and duties, 1, 5, 56, 57, 58, 59, 60, 70, 71, 73, 145, 146, 150
  violation of authority, 5
  violation of right to physical education of children, 5
Farrell, Brian, 19
Forde, Dr Michael, 35, 118, 121, 123, 124, 127, 134
Foreign Affairs, Department of, 117
  issuing of passports, 117
fundamental rights, 1, 4, 5, 8, 116

good name, right to, 5
Green Paper 1993: *Education for a Changing World*, 90
Green paper 1992: *Education*, 155
Grogan, Vincent, S.C., 24, 49, 51

Habeas Corpus. *See* application under Article 40.4.1°, 40.4.2°
Health Board, powers of, 64
Health, Minister for, 128
Henry VIII, 86
Hillary, Dr Patrick, Minister for Education, 83, 103, 104, 107
Hogan, Gerard, 30
Hogg, Professor, 41
Holy Faith Sisters, 97

Home Education, 67, 77, 78, 79, 80, 82
Hyland, Áine, 87

Incorporated Society for Promoting English Protestant Schools in Ireland
   charter schools, 86
Industrial School, 63
Intermediate Education Board for Ireland, 103
   Department of Education, and, 106
   establishment, 105
   examinations, 106
   inspection, 106
International Covenant on Civil and Political Rights, 8
INTO
   see Irish National Teachers Organisation
Irish Catholic Bishops, 11, 12
Irish Congress of Trade Unions, 79
Irish Free State, 14, 15
Irish National Teachers Organisation, 7, 10, 13, 17, 18, 19, 25, 95
Irish School Endowment, 106
Irish Vocational Education Association, 108
Jesuits, 11, 56, 63, 169
   1936 submission for the 1937 Constitution, 65, 87
Judicial Review, 19, 20

Keogh, Dr Dermot, 65, 169
Kelly, Prof. J.M., 16, 17, 49, 50, 53, 81, 91, 93, 137, 138, 169

Law Reform Commission, 30
Legal Aid, justice and fair procedures, right to, 6
legislation, 152, 153
   effected by estoppel, 152, 155, 158
      legitimate expectation, 153, 154, 155, 156, 157, 158
   fettering Executive action in the future, 158, 159
   non-statutory Rules and Circulars, 100, 103, 104, 105,

legislation—*contd.*
   school governance, 157, 159
   State, power to enact, 157, 159
   state control, 159
   statutory, 105, 106, 107, 108, 109 discretion, 157
Libraries, Public, 106
life, right to, 5
   and freedom from torture and slavery, 8
litigate, right to, 5
livelihood, right to earn, 5, 122
   remedy for infringing, 122
Local Government, Department of, 126
Lord Lieutenant of Ireland, 76

MacCarthy, Seán P, 30, 129, 130
MacNeill, Professor, 11
McCartan, Pat T.D., 128
McDonagh, Enda Rev., 132
McDowell, Michael S.C., 34
McHale, Rev. Archbishop of Tuam, 87
McKenna, Lambert Rev. S.J., 10, 12, 57, 96
McQuaid, John Charles, Archbishop of Dublin, 11, 56, 63, 169
Management, Boards of, 89, 92, 95, 97, 98, 99, 103, 106, 155, 156
   appointing teachers, 97
   Church rights, 90, 91, 92
   democratisation of, 161
   legal basis of, 104
   property, 99
   state intervention, 90, 91, 95
   Trustees, 91
mandamus, order of, 114, 121, 122
marry, right to, 6
Maynooth College, 133, 134
   religious institution, 94
   trustees of, 94
Methodist
   chaplains, 128
   De Valera, and, 169, 170
model school, 89
   direct State control, 89
Morgan, Prof. David Gwynn, 94

Index

Murphy, Dr Michael, Bishop of Cork and Ross, 97
Murray, Archbishop of Dublin, 87
museums, public, 106
Music, School of, 106

national education, system of, 87
National Education Convention, report on, 79, 81, 100, 110
National Institute of Higher Education, 36
National Programme Conference on Primary Education, 10, 96
national schools, 77
    boards of managment, 97
    Department of Education recognition, 104
    inspection, 104
    instruction in, 104
    manager, 104
    patron and duties, 104
    premises, 104
    rules for, 27, 28, 104
    rules for, 1832, 29
    rules for, 1833, 29
    rules for, 1932, 29
    rules for, 1965, 7, 30, 31, 66, 96, 103, 104, 105
    teachers qualifications, 104
natural law, 1, 2, 3, 4, 57
N.I.H.E. *See* National Institute of Higher Education
Nolan, Prof. Michael, 127
non-denominational education, funding of, 87
Northern Ireland
    endowment, 128
    legislation, 133
    payment of religious teachers, 133

Ó Buachalla, Séamus, 88
O'Connell, T.J., 10, 18
O'Doherty, Thomas, Bishop of Galway, 84
O'Donovan, Patricia, 79
O'Flaherty, Louis, 107

O'Hanlon, Mr Justice Rory, 53, 54
O'Rahilly, Dr Alfred, 23, 34, 35, 132
Osborough, Prof. Niall, 26, 30, 39, 51, 81, 112,

Papal Encyclicals, Appendix
    "Casti Connubii" 1930, Appendix
    "Divini Illius Magistrii" 1929, 56, 87, Appendix
Papal Nunico
    de Valera, and, 170
parent-teacher organisations, 103
Parent, fathers right as a, 62
Parents
    custody and control of the children, 57, 62, 63
    definition of, 62
    education of their children, 57
    nature of education , choose, 64
    representation of, 82
    religious instruction of their children, 57
    restitution of rights, 63
    rights of, 56, 57, 58, 59, 60, 61, 63, 64, 65, 66, 68, 69, 70, 72, 73, 75, 77, 78, 79, 81, 82, 83, 84, 85, 129
    state obligation, 128
    surrender of rights of, 63, 64
person, right to protection, 5
personal liberty
    trial, right to a fair, 150
personal rights, 1, 4, 5, 6, 8
    protection and enforcement of, 123
post-primary schools
    admission tests to, 79, 80
    assisted places scheme, 80. *See also* community colleges; community schools; comprehensive schools; secondary schools, vocational schools
Pope Alexander III, 12
Pope Pius XI, 56
Presbyterian
    chaplains, 128
    Church in Ireland, 87

Presbyterian—*contd.*
   de Valera, and, 169
   Synod of Ulster, 87
President of Ireland
   limitations of powers, 136
   referral of Bill, 159
primary education, 7, 76, 89, 129
   right to free, 11, 12, 16, 21, 25, 26, 27, 113
   courts acknowledgement of, 17
   conspiracy to deprive, 113
   deprivation of, 14
   management of, 83
   provisions of, 7
   State's acknowledgement of, 18
   State control of, 102
   state funding, 129, 130
Primary Education Review Body Report, 1990, 30, 129
primary school
   control of syllabi, 81
   denominational management of, 88
   governance model, 76, 160
   private, 75, 76
   Roman Catholic Church, 95
   Rules and Circular letters, 96, 103, 104
   state control, 96
   trustees, 94
Privacy
   right to, 2, 99
   right to marital, 5
   right to and homosexual rights, 2
private schools, 75, 78, 80, 90, 105
   control of syllabi, 81
   funding, 79
   legislation for, 105
   secondary, 105, 106
   teacher selection, , 80
profound retardation and multiple impairment, 41
Pro-Life Campaign, 4
property
   protection of, 91
   rights, 5, 147, 148
   management, 99, 104
   religious denomination, and, 147, 148
   school premises, control and ownership, 99, 100
   state ownership, 100
prudence, justice and charity, 3, 4, 146, 147
public examinations, 105

Recess Committee, Report, 1896, 107
Regional Education Councils
   convention report, 99
   position paper, 99
religion
   Church of Ireland, disendowment of, 127
   endowment of, 132, 134
   non-endowment of, 133
   prohibition on endowment, 133
   state endowment of, 127, 128
religions
   proselytising, 86
   salaries of chaplains, 69
   school ownership by, 86
religious denominations, 75, 76, 93
   autonomy of, 101
   control of, 92, 93
   designated authority, 94
   manage own affairs, right to, 101
   property of, 93
   property rights of, 147, 148
   statutory recognition, 92
religious education
   payment for by State, 131
   teaching of, 131
   United States approach, 128, 131
religious instruction, 81, 97
remedies
   citizens, 120
      criminal offence, 124
      constitutional, 123, 124

Index

remedies—*contd.*
  damages
    assessment, 119, 124, 125
    exemplary, 118, 119, 120, 121, 124
    general, 117
    special, 117
  declaratory order, 123
  injunctions, 121, 122
  judicial review, 153, 154
  mandamus, 121, 122
  state failure to discharge obligations, 120
Report of the Committee on the Constitution 1967, 41, 42, 52
Ribero, Angelo Vidal d'Almerida, 130
Roman Catholic Church, 87, 93, 94, 95, 96, 98, 102
  bishops, 57
  chaplains, 128
  comprehensive school model, 107
  ethos, 100
  hierarchy, 108, 132
  Pastoral Address Maynooth College 1898, 95, 96
  Pastoral Letter 1826, 87
  Pastoral letter, 1990, 77
  policy, 57
  schools, 106

Saorstát Éireann, 107. *See also* Irish Free State
  departments of state, 102.
schools
  closures, 130
  compulsory attendance, 11, 37
  governance, position paper on the, 155
  moral ethos, 97
  registration, 105
  Roman Catholic, 97
  syllabus, 73, 81, 82
    monitoring of, 82
  systems of management, 87, 88
  trustees and closures, 130
School Attendance/Truancy Report, 1994, 66, 110
Science, School of, 106

secondary education, right to free, 21
secondary schools
  board of management, 106
  building of, 108
  examinations, 105, 109
  funding, 105, 109
  governance model, 160
  independence of denomination, 89
  inspection, 106
  Minister for Education, powers of, 109
  model, 76, 77
    rules of, 1911-1912, 77
  private, 75, 76, 105, 106
  rules of, 1965, 103, 104, 109
  statutory basis, 105, 110
  trustees, 94, 106
silence, right to, 150
Sisters of St. Joseph for the Diocese of Toronto, 93
social equity, 79
St. Thomas
  Summa Contra Gentilis, 57
  Summa Theologica, 57
Staines, Michael, 61, 62
Stanley, E.G., 76, 87
State
  accountability, 8
  aid, 135, 139
    different religious denominations, 135, 140
    legislation for, 136
    private schooling, 136
  authority, 104
  chaplains, payment of, 127, 131
  Christian and democratic nature of, 1, 2, 6
  control of education, 75, 78, 94, 95, 102, 105
  defence of Executive necessity, 121
  discrimination, religious profession belief or status, 135
  duty of, 71, 81, 84
    non-performance of, 120, 121

State—*contd.*
   funding, 87, 90, 127, 156
      in United States, 134
      of students, 134
      withdrawal of, 94, 95, 96, 100
   grants, 79, 96
   guarantee, not to endow any religion, 130
   limitation of, 82, 95, 160
   obligation on, 125
   obligation to provide for education, 23, 24, 25
   ownership of property, 96
   powers, 81, 82, 96
   regulation, 111
   religious teachers, payment of, 127, 131
   remedy against, 120
   role of, 66, 67, 68, 99, 100, 103
   separation of powers, 8
   subsidy, 24, 26
   support, 102
   vicarious liability of, 120
students
   admission or expulsion, 92
   religious and moral training, 96, 97
Sutherland, Peter, S.C., 19
syllabus, 110

teachers, 106
   appointment, 97
   Church of England, 98
   contract of employment, 97, 98
   conduct of, 96, 98
   discrimination on religious status, 135
   funding, 106
   intermediate, register of, 106
   payment of religious, 127, 129
   payment of salaries, 95, 107
   Roman Catholic, 97, 98
   selection and dismissal, 92, 96, 97, 98
Teachers Union of Ireland, 30, 129
   Primary Schools, Educational Review Body, Minority Report, 129, 130

Technical Education Report of Commission on, 1927, 107
Technical Instruction of the Department of Agriculture and Technical Instruction, 103
Titley, Brian E, 10, 57
tort
   malice, damages for, 124
Trade Unions, 4, 5
travel, right to, 2, 6
   free movement within the State, 6
   outside the State, 2
TUI. *See* Teachers Union of Ireland

Unis, N., 10
United Nations
   Convention and Resolution of the General Assembly, 45
   Religious Intolerance and Discrimination in Ireland, Report on, 130
University Funding Council of England, 127

V.E.C. *See* Vocational Education Committee
Vocational Education Committee, 32
Vocational Schools, 106
   building of, 108
   committees, 107
   statutory basis, 106, 107
Vocational Teachers Association, 108
vocational hospitals
   chaplains, 128

Walsh, Mr Justice Brian, 52, 53
Walshe, John, 129
White Paper: *Charting our Education Future*, 130, 152, 160
   legislation, 152
   limitation Constitutional rights, 142, 147, 152, 159
Whyte, Gerard, 26, 30, 48, 49, 50, 51, 52, 61, 136

Index

words and phrases
- acknowledges, 59
- actual conditions, 33
- as best it may, 143, 144
- as far as practicable, 142, 143
- a certain minimum, 49, 54
- certain minimum education, moral, intellectual and social, 81
- breach of a constitutional right, 127
- breach of statutory duty, 126
- charitable, 92
- Christian and democratic nature of the State, 1
- citizens, 161
- college, 134
- the common good, 165
- conscience, 64
- constituent college, 134
- denomination, 93
- diverted, 140
- due regard, 37, 68, 69, 78
- due regard for rights of parents, 68
- education, 38, 39, 40, 41, 42, 112
- educational facilities, 84
- education and formation, 129
- endeavour, 34
- endow, 127
- endowment, 134
- especially, 78, 84
- every religious denomination shall have the right to manage its own affairs, 75
- family, 60, 61, 73
- human persons, as, 161
- inalienable, 59, 60, 74
- issue, 164, 165
- integrated curriculum, 127
- intellectual, 74
- invidious discrimination, 163, 164
- in view of actual conditions, 52, 54, 55, 82
- legislation providing State aid for schools, 139
- the managerial system, 88
- moral intellectual and social, 53
- natural, 74
- and natural, 59, 74
- natural law, 1, 2, 3
- necessary works of public utility, 137, 138, 140
- other, 69
- other educational facilities or institutions 68, 75, 76
- parents, 62, 74
- in particular, 5
- payment of compensation, 138
- personal rights, 5, 164
- primary, 59
- private and corporate educational initiatives, 34
- provide for, 89
- provide other educational facilities or institutions, 34
- prudence justice and charity, 3
- public good, 34
- public utility, 137
- reasonable aid to private and corporate educational initiatives, 75, 76
- religions, 74
- religious and moral formation, 69, 84
- religious denominations, 93
- religious intellectual and social, 74
- religious profession, 135
- religious status, 135
- shall not discriminate between schools under the management of different religious discrimination, 140
- seminary, 134
- shall, 34
- social, 74
- the State shall, 48
- the State shall not in its enactments, 162
- the State shall provide for free primary education, 15
- subject to public order and morality, 111, 138
- tort, 126
- under the management of religious denominations, 93
- unjust attack, 144